KARNA

Book 2

KARNA

THE SON OF SURYA

Kevin Missal

SIMON & SCHUSTER

London · New York · Sydney · Toronto · New Delhi

First published in India by Simon & Schuster India, 2024

This edition published in 2024

1 3 5 7 9 10 8 6 4 2

Simon & Schuster India
818, Indraprakash Building,
21, Barakhamba Road,
New Delhi 110001

www.simonandschuster.co.in

Paperback ISBN: 978-81-974895-3-2
eBook ISBN: 978-81-974895-1-8

Typeset in India by SÜRYA, New Delhi

Printed and bound in India by Replika Press Pvt. Ltd.

FSC
www.fsc.org
MIX
Paper | Supporting responsible forestry
FSC® C016779

To my family.
We don't give them enough credit for tolerating us.

Note to the Reader

Don't read this book if you love Karna.

Sometimes love makes us lose objectivity. Sometimes love makes us have pre-conceived notions.

That's why.

Karna: The Son of Surya could be read as a standalone book as well as the sequel to *Karna: The King of Anga*, but remember one thing: this is not the Karna you've always known and loved.

This is a very different Karna. The kind that is hidden between the pages of the Mahabharata. This series, and this book especially, is meant to delve into the curiosity to understand what happens in his everyday life.

I was always fascinated by what was happening with the figures from the Mahabharata in between the big events that transpired. I didn't want to write what was already out there in the public domain, but something that explored his life, his familial relationships, his insecurities, his fears, his successes.

So if you want to find Karna as he's portrayed on television, movies and books before—don't pick up this book.

But if you want to read a different version of him, one that explores his psyche and his relationships—then this is the book for you.

Thank you. And hope you enjoy this one.

PART ONE

1

Adhirath, the father to Angaraja Karna, *knew* his death was close.

He had already lost so much in his life. He had lost his kingdom, his son for a while, his wife and his pride by becoming a charioteer.

But no.

It wasn't because of that.

It was because he had an obsidian blade held right next to his pupils, as he lay on the floor, spread out like a butterfly, with his chest being pushed by a giant of a man.

"What do you want?"

The assassins didn't speak. Didn't even utter a single word. They watched him like hawks. And they weren't the usual kind. No. They were possibly from a different world. They had large, inked tattoos circled around their bodies, in the shape of a python, while their necks were adorned by a large ceremonial necklace made of human bones. They had eyes like a leopard, and their bodies were larger than that of an ordinary man.

Adhirath realised that when one is so close to their death, one doesn't notice the intricacies of their killer, instead recalls the regrets of their life.

He wished he could be there with his sons. One became an ascetic. Shon. Another became the ruler of his kingdom, along with his wife. After Radha, his wife, died, he had begun to live with Karna, to be close to him, and he would go on hunts occasionally. He would bring a hare back, or probably a rabbit sometimes. A party would follow him, with cooks and chaperones.

But today, these assassins, these fiends had happened to murder everyone around him.

The lush forest of darkened woods, seemed crimson in colour, drenched in the karma of his past life.

"Who..." he coughed, "are...you?"

Another assassin appeared, looking similar, with darker skin. He knelt down, and with the blood that swallowed the earth he wiped Adhirath's face.

At that moment, he saw his entire life flash before his eyes. He saw when he and Radha found Karna in a basket. He saw how his pride vapourised when he begged at Dhrithashastra's feet to save him. He saw the years he hadn't been around his son, only to meet him and reprimand him again. And he saw his son rule like a hero, in a kingdom where many had disrespected him.

And he smiled.

For he was about to meet his wife. For he had truly achieved, what very few fathers could.

He was able to see his son became a *man*.

The assassin chortled, and breathed next to Adhirath's face, and said...

"We...are...a...message."

2

Today, she was not a mother. Today, she was a queen.

Shanaya never knew being a queen would be like another *job*.

It sounds fancy, and you go to the occasional party where you get noticed. But other than that, running a monarchial kingdom like Anga, was more about the boring stuff. From sorting out administrative structures, to finding out about enemy spies, and keeping sure the allies are happy by handing out gifts and inviting them over for feasts. After a while, it does get awfully exhausting, and with no husband in sight, she felt all alone.

Karna, by far, wasn't a bad partner, of course. But when he had handed her the kingdom, he had informed her he will be absent, for his fealty rested with Suyodhan. He wouldn't be a part of Anga, but only the face of it.

And at that time, Shanaya had taken it up in good spirits, but now, it was getting tougher. Especially now that she was pregnant with her third child, almost seven fortnights in already.

On every sunup, she holds an assembly, during which she has a small court hearing in her throne room, where the people of the state, the ministers, and the soldiers, would listen to the captors and Shanaya would give a sentence that would be appropriate and accepted by the people of the state as well.

And she was good at it. Pretty good.

But not today.

Today, she was afraid. She had seen the list of people who were coming for the court hearing, and one of the prosecuted was someone she knew.

I miss Vasu.

Shanaya was a simple Greek girl from the island of Essos, before her father had whisked her off to this place. Marriage with Karna was not supposed to be about love, but they ended up falling in love. And while it was true that he had other wives, in other parts of the country, they were more martial and trade alliances than anything else.

For him, she was the only one. And nothing would ever change that. *Hopefully.*

A young albino boy appeared on the stand, white as a steel cloud on a hazy morning; he had red eyes, and chapped lips. He was wearing an ornate dress, and his hands were tied in the front, he had a stern face and clenched mouth.

Shanaya nervously sat on the throne, shifting, and turning. The royal guard noticed her uneasiness and inquired about it, which she dismissed. She had not seen the albino in months.

"My lady," called the minister of law, who had a belly far bigger than her, a double chin that would embarrass even frogs with his slimy eyes, "we present you Vrishaketu. A vicious beast of a boy, a troublemaker of the highest order."

Vrishaketu remained stoic and stern.

"I am sure you must have heard of his antics, but we found him, and dragged him here from the deserts, where he had been hiding with his pack, like bandits. He had been scrounging the earth, for all I care, and we as the people of Anga, we are very glad, that a horrible, dishonourable..."

"I get it, Ugra," spoke Shanaya with a whip. "Continue with the charges."

The minister of law gleefully chuckled. "As you are aware, King Yudhistr of Indraprastha," he rolled his eyes, as if it was just something he had to say, "held a Asvamedha Yagna, at the behest of his priest, who had recommended it. The horse, as you know, with a pack of his men, travelled to different places, and the ones who dared to stop it, were met with the greatest of challenges thrown in by King Yudhistr's brothers and allies."

"Thereafter, they had lands to themselves, and so much blood was shed. They dared not to insult Anga, with such a pretentious ceremonial thingy. They stayed away, thanks to you, my lady, as well as the Great Lord of Sun Suryaputr Karna..."

"Ugra, continue. No need to impress us. You already do that by being the butt of many jokes in the ministry." She snapped.

Ugra got embarrassed, while everyone chuckled, but only Vrishaketu remained stoic.

"Anyway, Vrishaketu, who is a citizen of this land, had happened to side with and become an ally of Yudhistr, without our government's knowledge. Even though he knew very well it would not be entertained, and we shall never agree to becoming allies of Yudhistr, he continued to run campaigns for him, in secret." Ugra spat. "And worst of all, he won a campaign. The King Anushalva of the Chandravamsha Dynasty, a great ally and a patron of moonlit arts, he was broken down and killed by this very man!" He pointed to the meek albino, who had a shrewd smile on his face now. "Not only did he side with our enemies, he killed our ally and the other allies of our land have begun to worry. They think Anga can't control its citizens. My lady, do a favour to Anga, and sentence him to a punishment of the worst kind, so he's served..." he moved closer to Vrishaketu, smelling him, "what he deserves...you horrible, horrible, disfigured thing, you degenerate." He whispered.

Shanaya blinked, unable to feel what she wanted to feel. She saw Vrishaketu, and clenched her fists, grabbing her gown tight, while her crown lay heavy on her head, and her heart was bursting out of her chest.

"Do you have anything to say, boy?" She asked. "You have been accused of crimes that are punishable by death. Is there any remorse, any regret?"

Vrishaketu stayed still, blinking, not even uttering a word.

She knew why. She knew him so well. He was a rebel. Always. Since he was young.

"I sentence you to death again." She announced, leading to a triumphant uproar, while she shed a tear.

For she had just ordered her men to kill her son.

3

They called him the King Killer.

But then he had many names.

He was already overweight when he was born, a burden to his mother, and a painful cry to the skies, like a thick waft of wind. As a child, he ate more than everyone, and grew more than his brothers. He had double the biceps of anyone his age and his crackling thighs would ensure he could lift anyone from the ground, even the biggest men. He grew up to be a seven-foot giant, and was called mighty and great.

His real identity was always the wolf-bellied, because he ate so much and yet remained relatively thinner than his peers.

He went by the name of Vrikodara.

When he was sent to the east to conquer lands for Yudhistr for his Asvamedha Yagna ritual, many whimpered and many were cornered, and many fought back. The latter's heads—kings and queens, princes and paupers—were trampled. He would sever the scalps, or their heads. They said he was good at bursting eyes like a melon pop. They said he was a force of nature, and not even an elephant could trample him.

They said a lot of things, but not for too long, for they didn't live long enough.

But Raja Bhagwant of Mallrashtra was smart. At least better than the clutter. As Vrikodara's army had begun to march towards his kingdom, he knew he would be dead. He had a boutique kingdom, surviving on thick pinewoods that used to grow in the back of his land. He had a quiet life, and he had a penchant for women.

Any ruler of this size would bow to Vrikodara and Yudhistr's might and suffice to say, Bhagwant would do as well. It's the smarter thing to do.

But there was just one catch.

Bhagwant had somewhat of an altercation with Vrikodara, when he was a prince and Vrikodara was one too.

Probably he won't remember, Bhagwant thought. It wasn't a big thing, really. *But should I take my chances?*

And it was better to find the answer to this question by staying alive than by putting his fate in Vrikodara's hands.

But he chose something in between. He staged his kidnapping by paying the river pirates of Mo Chhu River, with a lot of gold, to show he was forced into doing their bidding. But rather, he was to be dropped in the far lands, away from his kingdom, and live a quaint life. He had put himself inside a rubble of a treasure chest, big enough to contort and taken away for godforsaken paradise.

He was glad. He was finally out of this horrible… horrible…fate. He could live now. He could live by hiding. Not the noble life of a king, but still enough. He had to be just dropped at the rendezvous point and from there, he would be taken away to a secret hideout. He would be free…free…

And the treasure chest opened, in the middle of the river.

He took a deep breath, as if it was a sigh of relief.

"Have we reached?" He asked the pirate, who towered over him.

"Yes, my lord, we are reaching the shores."

"Good, good," Bhagwant chuckled, and smiled. "Good job, you lot. Can't believe I have been fighting you all for so long for all the thieving, smuggling and robbing, when I should have just bought you. You get sold for everything, even helping your enemies." He chuckled at the notion. "Won't say it's a very comfortable journey, so to speak," he looked around the moving river, and the wooden ferry on which he was being carried. He had, for major reasons, wore civilian clothes, and the gold and the gowns were left behind in the rooms of his royal quarters.

As he came out, he noticed, he was close to the shores, parked and ready to leave. But there was something wrong. It felt like...

He had returned to the same place from where he had left. He began to shiver with confusion, as the two pirates gleefully looked at him, and he remained confused, till he noticed—the army of Yudhistr's symbol, the elephant of a flag, and in the middle, a man sitting on the ground, playing with sand, as if waiting for something, his head bowed down.

Behind him, rested all the elephants and the cavalry—as if the entire army of Vrikodara, thousands of soldiers and the party, instead of coming to the kingdom, appeared here on the riverbanks.

The man in the middle was not wearing a breastplate,

just a golden dhoti with blue and black marks spread across his stomach as well as his chest, like a badge of honour. A belt hung around the man's waist, with severed skulls of the kings he might have killed during the conquest of the east, and his eyes were black-brown from the dusty roads, his skin bronze, with large sideburns almost crossing the better half of his bulbous face.

From afar, one would say he was a good-looking man, but his face had the deadliness of a marauder and a killer.

He played with sand, putting a waft of it in his hand, then letting it slip.

Bhagwant realised the pirates have been bought off by Vrikodara. He was surprised, wondering how Vrikodara got to know.

Immediately, he fell on the sand, and began to cry next to Vrikodara. "I have given off the kingdom. It's yours. Just let me live. Please."

Vrikodara didn't say anything, while the king whimpered next to him.

"I don't know what you want from me. I am not going to impose any sort of threat. I don't even care about the bloody kingdom. It was handed down from the royal lineage that I am a part of. Please...please leave me alone." He paused, as Vrikodara listened, without a single blink, just staring at the sand, instead of looking at him. "I...I..." he began to cry to the soldiers, the cavalry, "please, please save me...I have done nothing. I have nothing. I have no riches. I have no gold to give. Everything is in the palace. Take it. Take everything. I don't need it. My life is more precious to me than the bloody temptations of the world."

And then Vrikodara spoke, as thunder crackled and the bodies around him shifted. He said: "One wonders, why leave everything behind to go and live a life as a poor man? Unless…there's paradise."

Bhagwant's blood ran cold. Yes. He did have a palace, hidden away. Many wives of his were there too. Less people. And more luxury, hidden in the blankets of the mountains, in the mist, unseen and magnificent. He always wanted to spend his retirement years there, and he was finally given a reason to leave behind the administrative duties of a king. He could be retired from the duties of his late father's impositions.

"You could have taken the kingdom. But you brought your army here…why?" Bhagwant asked, realising his death was close. "To attack just me? Why so many to attack just me?"

"No," he shook his head, as Vrikodara stood up, wiping the sand from the back of his dhoti, "they are here to watch a king cry."

Bhagwant noticed the giant of a man he was, away from the splendour and the tall tales, he was a god amongst men, with curly long hair, and a heaving chest.

He grabbed Bhagwant by the neck and threw him on the ground. A pulsating pain travelled through the former king's body, as he could feel some broken limbs. He tried to scamper away quickly, but he was met by resistance as his leg was pulled back, and thrown again on the ground.

"WHY? WHY ME?"

"Because…" Vrikodara grabbed him by the face and began to squeeze it like a lemon, "because, a long time ago, you had made fun of me once, of my weight, of my height and no one…*no one* except my brothers have the right to make fun of me."

And Vrikodara punched his chest, letting his fist go through the heart, pulling out the pumping organ, his hands replete with crimson silver, as Bhagwant's eyes became lifeless in a matter of seconds.

He lifted the heart towards the skies and everyone began to chant loudly, everyone began to hoot, and the drums began to beat and the ravens cawed in the skies, while thunder clapped in the background.

He heard his name.

No. Not the name that he was given as a young boy. But the name he had earned during the conquest of the east.

"KING KILLER!" They loudly clapped and announced. "KING KILLER *BHIMA*!"

4

They walked on the lonely road, inside a large forest, until they became nothing but dots in a starless sky.

"How long has it been?" Asked the friend, Danube.

"Been a week now," responded the grandson to Adhirath, the eldest son of Karna, Satyasena, "and dadaji returns by now. One can only imagine that something has happened to him."

"Understandable." Danube nodded, as if he cared.

He was mostly intoxicated, and he was one of the close friends to Satyasena. They would gamble, woo women, and probably feast at the local taverns under guises when they must. Danube wasn't as notorious as Satyasena, the opposite of everything that Karna stands for. A rebel of some kind, a rulebreaker, an atheist of the highest order, and yet a perfect, true loyalist to the throne of Anga.

"Heard about your brother," said Danube, "what a travesty."

"I agree."

Their horses winced and moved slowly in the deep, dense forest, where the skies had begun to look like fiery.

"Do you care?"

"No."

"Oh come on, you do. You were close, you lot." He hiccupped.

"No." Satyasena shook his head.

"I remember this one time you both were playing close to the balcony, and he pushed you, right? Something to do with the kingdom and everything. That he wanted the throne of Anga for himself."

"No."

"Then what happened?"

"Sad though, with his skin and the rest of him. He looks like a darn monster."

Satyasena didn't say anything. As a young kid he had always heard about his brother looking like a monster, like a horrible piece of mess. Because of the skin issue, Satyasena used to feel pity as a brother, embarrassed too, until he began to go against the crown. It was the little things. Spending too much time with the children of the Pandavas, talking about the crown kings. He used to be enamoured, until he began to get close to the darkness that was Arjun. He was especially close to the archer, who was after all, their father's rival, and they had so much in common.

Now he had uttered hatred for his brother. Though, of course, he didn't let it show on his face. He managed to simply smile.

Only he wondered if his brother didn't have the skin problem, he would look like Satyasena. Handsome, cherub, high cheek bones, bronze skin, with the long shoulder length hair. Unfortunately, he didn't have the archery skills of his father or Satyasena, who was also an excellent archer. No. Vrishaketu was more of a sword player, but he was a brilliant one, as much as his health permitted him to be.

"What do you think happened to your grandfather? Do you think it was a boar attack? Or was it the Nagas?"

"I don't want to think anything," said Satyasena.

No one had asked him to search for his grandfather, but he did it because he loved him. Probably the only person he genuinely loved. And he had vanished into thin air. His mother was calm about it, said it's fine. His father was absent, as always, probably off wandering with Suyodhan uncle. So, without telling anyone, and out of sheer worry, he left with his friend to search for his grandfather. If his mother got to know he had left the kingdom, alone, without a party of soldiers accompanying him, he knew he would be hung by his mother, for a king's son shouldn't be scurrying around like that.

"And whatever happened with that plan?"

"What plan?"

"About defaming Bhima."

Satyasena was quiet.

By that time, Danube had picked up his flask and was taking a sip of the intoxicant. "You know the plan. The psychological war that you say you were fighting."

"What plan?" He tried to act dumb.

"Where you would spread false rumours, gossips around the entire country. Hire people to tell that he is a big wimp, a mamma's boy, make jokes about his weight and how he eats up everyone's food. You would create all these rumours about him, tall tales, and they would spread them, to piss him off. You also do one thing…" he hiccupped, a bit drunk, "create caricatures of him, to make him look extra fat, and use these images as posters to defame him, to make fun of him. You were angry with him because of the entire yagna, going around, toppling the allies of Anga, and you wanted to have your own sweet revenge against the big man, the giant."

Satyasena clenched his jaw. That was kind of a good way to do it, without being caught, and that just required a little bit of money.

They reached a place where he began to see the dry blood, the corpses lining up, and the horses and elephants just scattered, smelling like dead flesh, rotting up the place, with the flies swarming and what not. He put a scarf around his mouth to cover the smell, and looked at a body which seemed very familiar.

And, of course, to his dreadful, horrible realisation, it was none other than his grandfather.

He scratched his head, and his heart wanted to cry for him. But he suddenly noticed how his grandfather's eyeballs had been plucked out. In fact, the eyeballs of all the corpses had been gouged out, as if taken like collectible tokens.

"This is horrible," Danube went in a corner, and began to retch, "who in God's name would do that?"

Assassins, of course. And a special kind.

Satyasena watched the corpse for a moment, hoping it might flicker, but it had been like that for a while now. And he felt bad for his grandfather, what a miserable death it was.

"I need to go back and tell mother about this."

But Danube was vomiting in the bushes, and in the middle of it he asked, "Why just you? Why not me?"

"Because you speak too much, and you remember too much, and I cannot afford to have big mouths," said Satyasena as he brought out the dagger and stabbed him on the spine from behind. Danube fell on his own vomit, and Satyasena rolled him over, while Danube cried, as Satyasena began to pluck out his eyeballs, to make it look like he died along with the entire crew. "What I did...against Bhima...should never be spoken about, in drunkenness or in haste, otherwise...there will be a war, and a very bad one, and I can't afford my father to be angry."

But he spoke to a corpse now, as Satyasena had completed the surgery, and blood was smeared all over his clothes.

"You were wrong." He said, wiping the blood from his face. "It was not Vrishaketu who pushed me off the balcony. It was *me* who did it to myself, so the blame would fall on him."

5

There's a moment of insanity every man experiences in his life.

Usually, it is accompanied by the simple concept of love.

And just like that, Suyodhan had fallen in love with the princess of Kalinga, daughter of Chitraganda. When he couldn't get her because she had rejected him, for her father didn't want him, Suyodhan did what he had to do.

He kidnapped her.

Oh, it was a simple plan.

Take her and then make sure she falls in love with him.

Everything went according to the plan. He had come to the palace to discuss trade routes, but instead used the back entrance and took hostage of the ruler's daughter.

He stole the chariot too. Very un-royal-like behaviour. And as the soldiers and the guards had reached out to him, he managed to escape in the nick of time. His dear friend had happened to open the doors of the royal quarters and he was out on the streets.

Suyodhan rode the chariot at breakneck speed, through the middle of the bazaar, with Bhanumati behind, her hands bound by a rope. "Are you mad? What are you doing?" she screamed.

"Expressing my love!" Suyodhan yelled back.

"How is this love?"

"You were caring too much about those other suitors who were trying to woo you. I couldn't let that happen." He shouted back.

They had entered a narrow lane, and anytime now the guards would start catching up.

"My father wanted it."

"I know! And I know you want me!"

"Before! Not now, you idiot. You are a criminal in the state of Kalinga."

He turned, with a sly smile on his face. "But I am the king and the heir to the throne of Hastinapur, the king of kings and you'll live a comfortable life with me, I can promise you that."

She rolled her eyes and fell back, her chestnut hair dancing, her olive skin fair and gorgeous. Bhanumati was the kind of woman anyone could go crazy for. And Suyodhan had his fair share of women in his life, but no one could ignite the fire within him the way she did.

As they reached the cross section, a horse appeared, with an archer on top, and Suyodhan could tell that it was one of the suitors.

"By the law of Kalinga, stop or I shall shoot you."

Suyodhan beat his chest. "SHOOT!" And took off his armour. "I have nothing to fear."

The suitor was about to shoot an arrow, when another arrow just struck him, and he fell from the horse, with an intimidating pain on his shoulder.

Suyodhan looked up towards the buildings, and standing there, with his dhoti, a casual yellow shawl, with flowing hair and golden skin, was…

Karna.

Holding his bow and arrow.

He jumped and landed next to the chariot, then pulled himself up with the help of Suyodhan.

The two friends shook hands.

"You were being awfully brave in front of the missus." Karna chuckled, glancing at Bhanumati. "My lady."

"I knew you were there."

"Sure, sure. And if I wasn't?"

"I don't think a scenario like that would ever come in my life."

Karna chuckled, soon after they saw more soldiers appearing from all sides. "You sit back. I'll ride the chariot for you."

And he grabbed hold of the reins, while Suyodhan sat behind, flashing a grin at Bhanumati who just scowled under her breath. They began to move towards greener pastures, away from the bazaars, he knew that there was a small lake ahead which could be crossed and they could be out of the kingdom in no time. Dozens of suitors, their soldiers, their minions were following them, shooting arrows, throwing axes and what not.

The horses moved fast. Suddenly Karna stood up when he saw a group of buffaloes all huddled up and angry, and he shot at the rope which was keeping them tied up. Immediately the door opened, and the buffaloes escaped using all their might.

Karna sped up, moving forward, with the buffaloes behind him to stop the suitors.

"Good job, my suta!" Suyodhan chuckled.

"I'll kill you!" Karna laughed back. "You are turning us into criminals and we are acting like fools."

"We are acting like men in love!" Suyodhan looked at Bhanumati who just shook her head in disbelief.

They moved forward, letting the buffaloes take care of their enemies. When they reached the lake, he saw a man in a dhoti and a turban standing in front of them. He had a moustache, with a sword in his hand.

"I'm going to kill you! You can't take away my wife!"

"Oh dear," Bhanumati shook her head, "he's the one my father favoured the most."

"Then let me do the deed." Suyodhan stood up.

"Oh, shut up! You sit down. And let me do it," Karna said. But there was more to it than met the eye. For this suitor, Suyodhan didn't remember, was the same prince who laughed when Suyodhan slipped and fell in a pond, and all the Pandavas had laughed too during the Rajasuya Yagna. He was humiliated and embarrassed and Karna would never forget that moment, his friend crying, being of such stature and yet be treated like a nobody. He had to show him his place.

"But she's the love of my life."

"That is all right. But I am your friend and I need to take care of this."

Karna pushed him back, and came on his feet, then he moved forward towards the enemy in front. The man came close to him, swaying his sword, which Karna deflected, and brought out an arrow only to plunge it on his back. The suitor cried in agony, as Karna punched and pushed him to the ground.

"Never lay eyes on my friend's woman!" He said.

"Good job," Suyodhan said. "But I could have done better."

Karna rolled his eyes.

"Should we move towards the horizon now, my lord?" Karna asked.

"Absolutely."

Karna reined the horses and moved forward, as the suitor tried to stand up and Karna with a side flick of his leg struck him. He rolled over falling inside the pond.

Glad there's a thing called karma in life.

6

When she was eight, she believed in dreams.

When she turned twelve, those dreams became the things she wanted to escape from.

There was a concept of oracles within the Greeks, and Shanaya's father, who had the Greek blood in him, had a strong notion that his daughter could see the future. At the very least, a fragment of it. Fifty sundowns prior to the death of her mother, Shanaya had witnessed it in the lustrous landscape of illusion.

It haunted her, and she ran from it, hid from it. She stopped dreaming. She started feeding herself opium, to give herself a good night's sleep. But that had to stop when she got pregnant. Even her husband was unaware of her addiction. For a few years, everything was fine.

Until...it happened again.

She began to see them again. She saw a lake. A lake with a deep, enriching redness to it, and whoever stepped inside would be burnt to crisp and slowly withered away in the ashes of time. And she witnessed a slaughter, so horrible that her mind couldn't comprehend it.

Just like the one in the crematorium.

She stood with a scarf covering her face, one hand on

her belly, as she walked around the large, underground facility of corpses, lined up on hard, rocky slabs. The smell was terrible, and the aura was even worse. It felt like she walked amongst ghosts.

Ugra was behind her, her minister of justice, as well as Menander, the embalmer, with his dark skin, being of Greek descent himself, from the party of Captain Archimedes, sent by her father to have trusted liaisons in the city, which was popular for backstabbing.

"I am sorry, my lady. This is…"

"Oh god!" she shook her head, "Who did this?"

And she walked over to the one corpse that she never wanted to see in her life.

Karna's father.

Adhirath.

He was sunken, dried up, almost pale, and looking ghastly…like a fallen king. "He'll be devastated," she murmured. "He should not know."

"We plan to keep him embalmed, so when Lord Karna appears we can carry out his final rites. Have the pigeons been flown?" Ugra asked Menander.

"No." She shook her head. "He should not know."

"What do you mean?"

"He will know when he's ready. Let him return first."

She took a decision. She wondered what'll happen to him. It scared her, petrified her.

"Do you think that is wise, my lady?"

"Telling someone their father is dead is never wise." She responded. "And telling them over a bloody pigeon, that's worse."

She shook her head and looked into his eyes, how cleanly they were wiped out.

"Who did this?"

"I have an opinion." Menander spoke in between with slight hesitance. The man was fair, with green eyes, and a cherub face. Probably a handsome man once, his body and face had been exhausted from handling so much death.

"Pray tell," Ugra said.

"Oh, I'm afraid." He shivered. "I believe it's the Maharogas."

"The Maha what..." Shanaya was confused, while Ugra just coughed in fear.

"Impossible."

"It's the same modus operandi," Menander said. "And I follow the manuals of the Greek travellers who have come to this country."

"But they are dead. Extinct. Purged themselves, by fighting each other."

"Who are the Maharogas?" Shanaya asked bluntly.

"A primordial version of the Naga tribe. While the Nagas worship the cobras, the Maharogas worship the pythons," said Ugra. "But that was not it. They were horrible, disastrous, completely bogus. Myths. Tall tales spoken by the Nagas probably to scare the country folk. They have not been seen for years."

"Why do they take out the eyes?" Shanaya asked Menander.

"A token, my lady," he said. "To show their chief that they have taken the one thing that'll help them attain an afterlife. They believe eyes are the most precious organ to follow through in the afterlife, and they should be protected. But if you take them out...they have nothing to see."

She nodded, wondering if they were imposters, or actually the real deal. "Do you have anything on them?"

"Nothing reliable. Different sources say different things."

"Yes, one said," Ugra spoke again, "they had no heads, another said, they had no feet. One said, they could see from the back of their heads. Another said, they turn into pythons at the night when the moon is up."

Shanaya clenched her jaw, wondering what to do next. "Bury everyone, and do their final rites. As far as my father-in-law is concerned, I will keep you updated. I want to know about the Maharogas, do you know anyone who would know?"

"One person had mentioned in passing," Menander said, "that probably he saw them during his battle campaigns. We talk sometimes."

"Who?"

Menander urged to respond nervously, "Well, your highness, it was your son, who's waiting for his beheading tomorrow—Vrishaketu."

7

Vrishaketu, for as long as he could remember, always wanted Anga to be free of his father.

The hardships of the common people bothered him. The taxes levied were heavy, he recalled, and the alliances were bloody. Out of desperation his father had created enemies out of heroes, and heroes out of enemies. The coffers were empty, and they owed heavily to the neighbouring lands, especially Hastinapur, and his father's friend—Suyodhan. Vrishaketu, as a kid, was influenced by his tutor, who had informed him that Anga only had a few years left, and that it will be destroyed slowly. It needed to be dependent on the supreme rulers of the land, the real heirs. The ones who fight on the side of dharma, who choose violence not for harm, but when it's the only means left.

Vrishaketu learnt a lot from his tutor. He had long hair and blue eyes, and his face shone like emerald. He had an aquiline nose and wore a long gown. It wasn't clear whether he was a man or a woman, but for Vrishaketu, he was a gem.

If he wouldn't have come into his life, he would have never survived. Never opened his eyes.

And then he met the Pandavas, talked to them, allied

with them secretly, and vowed to help them whenever they needed—which they did, to defeat the allies of Anga. He took a handful of rebels with him, and raided those allies, like assassins, they tore their necks at night or hung their nobility by the nose.

Whatever happened to the tutor, he wondered.

One day, he stopped coming to meet him. Probably his mother got him killed for what he used to fill his brains with. But one would never know, for Vrishaketu never saw his body.

He wanted to ask, but the answers were hidden, and he blamed his mother for it. Once, they were close, but not anymore.

"What are you in here for?" Asked his cellmate.

"For treason." He responded.

"Yeah, well, we all are, aren't we?"

"You don't know what it means, right? The word 'treason'?"

"Hell, why do ya think I am in the bloody prison?" He sniggered.

Vrishaketu chuckled to himself. Ever since he was a child, he was the runt of the litter. Kept away from family politics because of his skin disease. He was considered as a backup to the throne, or perhaps not even that. And the only solace, the only silver lining in his life, was none other than his tutor.

The name—he couldn't remember what his name was.

He often wondered if his death by noose would make his father cry. Would even care. He had disowned him when he left to do his own thing. His father had said, "I would break his back myself, if I have to." And now he wasn't here, to see his dreams come to reality.

He waited calmly, as the sun rose, and a figure appeared, in a cloak of brown colour and a darkish hue. He thought his death had arrived, in flesh and bones, as it said: "Vrishni?"

Vrishaketu heard his childhood name, as he scuttled further, and whispered back: "Menander?"

He saw the pale face, and he grinned. He loved the embalmer. As a kid, he would move around with Menander, and learn how to decompose a body, embalm it, and get rid of it by burying it. Menander used to manage the entire crematorium.

"What is it? Why are you here?"

"To help you."

"In what way?"

"I need to know about Maharogas."

He lowered his brows in confusion. "Why do you need to know about them?"

"It is a pertinent matter."

Vrishaketu pursed his lips. "Why do you think I know about them?"

"Because you saw them, didn't you? I told your mother you mentioned me, but it was your Separatist army that had a fun chat at the tavern where I overheard."

"Oh, those fools. They have not been found, have they?"

"No, they haven't been." Menander shook his head. "And I kept that promise of not telling your parents, about this entire bloody thing, about the Separatists still being alive."

"One should, if I can't."

"Still, I feel the sacrifice is stupid."

"I'm their leader, and the head of an organisation sever first."

"There was always a choice to become a priest."

"And join the extremist and horrible council of Surya? No, thank you very much." He shook his head. "Those are bloody mongrels, wearing the capes of Lord Surya's sigil and ruling over people's minds with their iron-fisted rules and doctrines."

Menander clenched his jaw and shook his head, in retreat. There was a pause, before the young son of Karna calmed down.

Vrishaketu sighed. "Maharogas…yes, I saw them. A bunch of them in fact. Haven't seen anyone like them. They had painted their bodies with black paint, and would ride black stallions that breathed smoke. I saw them from afar, and still felt the chill. I didn't know it were them, till one of the lads in my party told me. They carried the symbol of a python, and there were plenty of them. Saw them close to the desert."

"So, it was around this time Adhirath…" he began speaking, and then kind of faltered. "Interesting. It fits well now. Could they be imposters?"

"I've only heard stories about them from Master Keshava," he talked about his tutor, "and I wish I could say they were mere imposters. But they move like hyenas, and they are far too cruel and scary to be imposters. But I can only say what I saw. And I only know what we read about them.

Menander nodded. "I am a man of the dead, Vrishni, and hope to see you in the afterlife."

"It was good knowing you," Vrishaketu said.

And as he went back, Vrishaketu could only wonder, if it was hidden well or not.

The very fact that he had lied.

The very fact that it was *he* who had helped the Maharogas enter the Angan territory.

8

The strongest man alive was afraid of one thing, and one thing only.

But he hadn't let his fears known to everyone. Vrikodara had witnessed everything in his life. Bloodshed, poisoning, darkness, death of closed ones and abandonment. And he had withstood everything, and was called many names.

He was simultaneously eating and feeding his vulture, as the other members of his army circled around him, while camps were being set up. They were a small team, but very effective. They would arrive and sweep and destroy quickly, and soon leave for the next one.

They talked about the wars, the battles, the limbs and torsos flying. They had no remorse. They had no guilt. They were men on a mission. And they followed Vrikodara's favourite policy: don't count chickens when you are killing humans.

Whatever it was supposed to mean, he had forgotten it a long time ago. They talked further about the dynasties, and discussed who would win over whom. There was a war coming, some said.

Vrikodara was a big but quiet man. He would speak only when necessary. But he made sure he sat with his team, and ate with his team. It was important to make them believe he wasn't a king or a ruler, like his eldest brother was—Yudhistr.

"Commander, when do you plan to lay siege on Hastinapur?" Someone asked.

"And what about Anga?"

Vrikodara was quiet. He was a soldier, not a thinker. At least, that's what his brother had told him. Before he could answer and let his party know, he saw a soldier scampering towards him—

"Commander," he was heaving terribly, "a party has arrived to meet you. An important party."

Vrikodara stood up, but felt his legs weaken when he saw in front of him, for the first time in many days, the three charred bodies standing on the opposite side of his tent, looking at him. A feeling of guilt and horror engulfed him...

It was just a vision.

He ignored it, and moved towards the soldier who was taking him. The vulture followed, scooting towards the sky, and then it began to circle around Vrikodara.

They climbed to the top of the hill, where the cliff overlooked a dense forest, and kingdoms and palaces at a distance. They were somewhere in the east.

Vrikodara came close. Two men were in metal armour, with one man in between who was wearing a crimson cloak.

"Brother," Vrikodara knew who it was just by looking at his height.

"How are you?" Asked the cloaked figure.

"To what do I owe this pleasure?"

"My greatest champion deserves an audience of course, after the last demolishing."

"Yes," Vrikodara said triumphantly. "I have planted more flags of our kingdom than anybody else."

"I understand, and I know," said the cloaked figure. "Though it's time to attack the Dasarnas, the Yadava kingdom."

Vrikodara clenched his jaw. "Usually, I get a scroll for this kind of a news. Why demand a personal audience? I'm sure it's more than just a triumphant gift of yours."

"I have been getting reports about your army influencing you to attack the states that are not part of the Rajasuya Yagna."

"And isn't that how it should be?"

"It's more complicated than that."

Vrikodara chuckled. "Brother, you have spies in my army, who feed you ill knowledge. Do we not communicate enough?"

"Eyes and ears should be everywhere."

Vrikodara was deeply hurt, but he didn't want to show his softer side to his brother. "I was thinking Anga," he said, touching the part, where the mark of the poison still resided, on his skin, as a badge of trauma. "It's weak right now. Karna is busy with Duryodhan. His petulant, pregnant wife struggles to hold it tightly. We can take over their timber production immediately."

"I know why you want to attack Anga. It's not professional. It's personal. Don't try to be a politician, big man," said the cloaked figure. "Because you aren't one. You are a brute. And that's how you should act." He spoke harshly. "Gather your men and go for the Dasarnas. I want them obliterated."

"Why not Anga?"

"It's too close to Suyodhan and we cannot make him angry when we are getting stronger. Once we are at our mightiest, that is when we attack."

And the cloaked figure with his two guards, began to move away, after giving the order, when Vrikodara turned around and said—

"What if I don't listen?"

"Excuse me?"

"I serve the throne, the very throne Bhishma Pitamah protects too. You are someone who sits on the throne, Dharma." He called him by his childhood name. "If not you, then probably me, one day. So, I don't think I should listen to you. I should listen to my people."

The cloaked figure sighed, as he asked one of the guards to hand him the stick which contained a chemical that could create fire. He rubbed the stone from beneath, and let the crackle touch the stick, causing the fire to rise.

To anyone, it might just be a child's play, but to Vrikodara...

He fell on the ground, stunned and confused.

The cloaked figure threw the stick on the ground, and Vrikodara noticed that gasoline had been sprinkled all around him, creating a circle of fire. He began to weep. His voice turned into a shrill, and his body became weak. The images of the charred family...they began to haunt him.

"If you don't want your men to see you like that, in the worst possible way, in the most vulnerable way, and you want your men to learn about your weakness, then you do as I say," the cloaked figure said.

Vrikodara cried, and nodded, almost wrapping himself, hugging his chest like a child.

A child…

And the cloaked figure left him like that, letting the fire subdue, as the charred bodies of the family again appeared inside that circle of fire, and embraced Vrikodara, as they said…

"You burnt us, big man. You burnt us."

9

Satyasena was about to do something horrible. Something worse than killing his best friend.

He moved carefully across the lawns of the Surya temple that stood majestically in the corner of the city of Anga, made of bronze, gold and silver. There were large porches, and zigzagged roads meant for the priests and the worshippers. It stood at the bank of a flowing river.

He used to remember running around here, playing with the other dasis, his father used to bring him here, who used to tell him about the idols of seven horses whom Lord Surya rode on. Then it was the idols of the two goddesses that stood tall as well, but not as tall as the murti of Lord Surya.

This was the home to the Council of Surya, a religious organisation which protected the faith of the city, which made sure that dharma persists even amongst the people.

Satyasena moved for the great halls, where he saw the priests from the Council. They were all in yellow cloaks, wearing a sigil of a sun on the back of the cloth. They were bald, completely hairless, and they nodded at Satyasena who nodded back at them in acknowledgement.

Whenever he was frustrated or stressed, he used to

come here, to feel a sense of peace. The rackety life of the city was not comforting always, especially for someone like Satyasena, a king's son, who was perpetually surrounded by an audience.

At the great hall where the priests were feasting on brinjals and what not, he noticed a man who was serving the priests. He walked up to him and said: "Master Ashtar, I need to speak to you."

"I am serving, my child, don't you see?"

"I know. I'll wait. Sorry."

He was sweating, palpitating almost. Ashtar must have noticed something was wrong with him. After the serving, Ashtar handed out water, and then signalled Satyasena to come at the back quarters, where the chamber of the head priest was situated.

The doors closed behind him and the first thing Satyasena said was: "I killed my friend."

"I see." Ashtar nodded. "And why would you do that?"

He looked at the head priest, with his eyes as stark as the grey mountain's peak, his face soft, and his voice softer than the lilies. He was crouched, like a humpback, probably from due to his back pain that accompanied him since he was a child.

"I was afraid he will end up tattletaling what we are up to."

"And what are we up to?"

"To destroy the significance of the Rajasuya Yagna, of Bhima's campaign, spewing rumours amongst people."

"Yes. And your friend knew?"

"Yes."

"When we clearly decided not to speak about it,"

Ashtar said, as he brought out a baton made of metal and immediately struck him on the back.

He fell on the ground. Satyasena spewed blood and cried.

"When the foreigners had come to our land from the east and the west, they attacked our faith."

Another smack on the back.

"We ran. My parents were murdered. Our villages were burnt. We were peace-loving creatures of the sun, and this is how those foreigners treated us."

Another smack.

"Your father, at a very important time, adopted us, gave us a home and a shelter and food."

"So, when his wife was pregnant and she was going through a time of crisis, I came to her rescue. He was happy, and he put me in charge of your safety," Ashtar said. "I am not your priest. I am not your father. I am your saviour." He brought the baton next to Satyasena. "And you need to shut up, generally about things in life."

"I know." Satyasena was bleeding. "I apologise, master. I deserve the punishment you have given me."

"But the deed is done now," Ashtar said. "And I want you to do something for me, as repentance."

"What?"

Ashtar kept the baton aside and moved to the chair. "When a king rules, a good king, it is good for the city. But when the queen rules, it is good only for her. Your mother, for all her graces, is someone who can be a threat to our society, to our ideals, to everything your father believes in. She's a foreigner, she's someone not from this country." His nostrils flared. "And while she's a queen and we all care for her, her decisions could be…not beneficial for the society."

Satyasena knew that he wanted to oppose the queen by doing something nonchalant and something hideous that was going to really irk the queen.

"So what do you want me to do?"

"Save your brother from the beheading," said Ashtar, standing up, and breaking Satyasena's one true dream of watching his brother die, "and repent for what you had done."

10

After a long time, Karna dreamt of death.

And it was not a death he could be proud to dream of. It was not the death he ever imagined.

He looked at his hands, and there was dust and blood on them. He looked around to see where he was. In the dusty, dark plains where his chariot was stuck, and he was trying to pull it out, trying to get away, as the arrows were being blistered towards him. The person who was driving the chariot told him, "It is over."

And he looked up to see who it was.

His father.

He had the same features, the same youngish features, the same bullishness, the same squeaky eyes and enigmatic face.

"What is over?"

"They are coming for you."

"No. They won't. I will save myself before that."

"No, son. They are coming and you can't hide forever."

"No."

He thrusted harder to pull the chariot out, trying his best, but it was not helping. Just then an arrow zapped next to him, shooting him on the shoulder. He crawled away, trying to protect his father, for more arrows came rushing towards him. He took them on his chest, and realised he didn't have his breastplate on. In fact, he had nothing on him.

He fell on the ground, bleeding, as his killer loomed over him, like a shadow.

It was death itself.

Just then he woke up, in sweat and frustration, his chest heaving, the anxiety that once pulled him close to death years ago returned and he wondered why it was like that.

He was in a comfortable fort, close to Hastinapur, where they had been travelling to. He had a bed and a blanket. He had every comfort at his disposal, and yet he felt not enough had been achieved. He felt there was something wrong that he should have righted.

There was a knock on the door.

It was the middle of the night, yet he was unafraid of what was out there. He opened the door to find a soldier, who told him that he has been summoned by his king—Suyodhan.

Karna wondered what it was about, but he put on his gown and rushed downstairs. Had Bhanumati escaped? They had arrived here to rest, while moving for Hastinapur where he would marry her. A kidnapped woman. It was a nice way to tell the elders that Suyodhan would do what his heart wanted. Karna knew it was also because he wanted to irk everyone in that kingdom that had been divided between Hastinapur and Indraprastha, and he wanted to irritate his father, by doing something foolish.

And Karna, being the friend that he was, would agree to all the whims and fancies of his mate.

He moved for the corridor, and the main hall of the fort, where he saw Suyodhan, in front of two individuals in black clothes, knelt down, arms clasped in the back, whimpering. Suyodhan had his arms crossed, and his body looked chiselled and sweaty, his moustache brimming with peculiarity. He was in just a dhoti, and a rudraksh was tied around his arm. Guards circled the two individuals, and then Karna realised that they were Nagas, as amulets resembling a cobra was hanging from their neck.

"What is the meaning of this?"

"They were loitering in the outskirts when they were caught," said Suyodhan. "I presume they are assassins, sent to kill us."

"And what do they say?"

"That it is not true." Suyodhan chuckled. "As if words coming out of the mouth of the bloody Nagas are to be believed."

They looked weak, malnourished, almost to the brink of death.

"What were you doing around the fort?" Karna asked.

"Because...because...master...we were hungry and we thought if we would have..."

"Thieves!" Suyodhan snarkily replied. "Of course. What would I expect of a Naga? Thievery, banditry. They are nothing but outcasts and low-borns."

Karna clenched his jaw. He was certain Suyodhan didn't realise that Karna was himself a low-born and an outcast as well. Probably had forgotten his friend was in the same league as the Nagas.

"We...we...need...food. Please...don't harm us," one of the Nagas said.

"You are going to be killed."

"We have information!" The other said, and the first one tried to shush him.

"What do you mean?" Karna asked.

"About you, Lord Karna. We have heard great tales and we know greater stories around you. We know what happened recently."

"And what did happen?"

"Your father was killed by one of the Maharogas."

For a moment, he was confused and stunned, left in a berserk state. He wanted to not believe them, but he could tell there was some truth in it.

Suyodhan slapped the Nagas. "How dare you speak such lies just to get out of the situation?"

"We speak the truth."

"The Maharogas don't exist. They are tales from the forgotten times."

"They've returned," said the first Naga to defend himself. "And they have returned with a vicious purpose. We don't know what it is. Even we hear rumours. We are not a part of them. We stay away from violence."

Suyodhan glanced at Karna. "Don't believe them, my friend."

But Karna was frozen, in a flux of time, as if something horrendous had just passed him by. "Shanaya would have informed me..." he muttered to himself.

"Don't believe them." Snapped Suyodhan. "They are liars. And they are thieves. Ignore them. They shall be punished." He ordered the guards to attack them, and with one swift swing of the sword, one guard was about to chop off the Naga's neck.

But something stopped him.

And it was none other than Karna, his hand had stopped the blade, letting his palm bleed for the Nagas.

"No." He snapped back at Suyodhan. "Let them go."

"Why?" Asked Suyodhan with fury. "You bleed for nobodies."

Karna didn't say anything, as he pushed back the blade. "If you care about me as a friend, give them food and shelter for tonight. And tomorrow set them free. The wild would eat them otherwise."

And he pulled out his gold ring, one of the many, and gave it to the Nagas.

"Use it when you need food next."

Then Karna stood up and left the room, leaving Suyodhan dumbstruck as he walked out, confused, sad, angry but most of all—

Determined.

Determined to find out what happened to his father.

11

Vrishaketu was prepared to die.

He knew the day was near, and the sun was not favourable, as the thunder rolled and the skies wept, the rain sputtered and the people rumbled loudly.

He was prepared to die because he knew the end was nigh. All his karma, all his actions were leading up to this moment. All the days he had rebelled, and all the important decisions he took against the throne. Vrishaketu wanted to really irk the man for some reason; made him happy.

His hands were tied with a timber rope, as he moved with a dozen guards around him, in the lonely, dingy corridor, while the loud noise made by the crowd was beaming.

The wooden door opened, and he found himself in the midst of an angry mob, that was shouting slurs, and throwing rotten fruits and eggs and what not at him. But he kept a straight face on, and his eyes were dark as ever.

"DEGENERATE!" Someone shouted.

"A horrible abomination." Another person chided in.

Vrishaketu remained steadfast, his eyes fixed ahead, where the gallows were, where an executioner in a black mask waited for him, a cleaver resting in his hand. His neck was going to be chopped with his head.

But as he moved for the pedestal and the rain crackled further, a man appeared, ready to attack him from the front.

The guards were shocked.

Vrishaketu turned around to defend himself, but the assassin leapt on him.

The guards grabbed him before he could hurt Vrishaketu, and he was whisked away.

Vrishaketu was confused by the turn of events, but he had something in his hand now. Something handed over to him by the so-called assassin, who was pulled away into oblivion by the guards.

A knife.

Ugra, like a bumbling buffoon, moved towards the queen's study, moving past the multiple servants, maids and guards. As he neared the large chamber gates, he saw Menander the embalmer, pacing up and down visibly in stress.

"Where is your highness?" He asked. "And what on earth are you doing here? You should be at the corpse land."

Menander, with his charming eyes, looked up, still wearing the raggedy cloak. "She's tad bit unwell today."

"And she would miss the grand undoing of a traitor's head?"

"That's her son you are talking about." Menander carefully warned him.

"Sure. Do you think...she's deliberately trying to miss it?"

"She could be lying." Menander shrugged. "But then, she was coughing and had a bad cold. I am just waiting for the bhisak too."

Ugra growled. Deep down, he wanted the queen to suffer and watch her son die. He had prepared a long testimony against Vrishaketu, as a degenerate and a mixed breed that he was from Karna and Shanaya. And now he won't be able to relish the look of misery on the queen's face.

"Well, tell her, we will miss her."

"Of course, I'll do that," Menander said, with a weak smile.

"Though that still doesn't answer why you are here."

"She fell unconscious in the crematorium where we were studying the Maharogas attack."

Ugra growled under his breath and went on his way, while Menander wondered if his lies had been caught.

He opened the door to the queen's chamber and saw an empty room.

The queen had disappeared on the day of her son's beheading.

And Menander hoped against hope that she doesn't kill herself.

Otherwise, his neck was next.

Vrishaketu moved on the pedestal, as his palms held the knife tightly. The angry mob in front was shouting, while he looked in the distance where the allied kings and queens of Anga sat. They had all come to watch his execution, all from the exiled families and their friends from the kingdoms he helped take over.

But he couldn't see his mother, and his brow arched in confusion. Had her maternal instinct suddenly showed up? How? That seemed impossible since she was and will be always a bad woman, a bad mother, always siding with Satyasena, and responsible for Vrishaketu's skin condition too. If she had taken care of him, and his skin, it won't have come to this. He blamed her, though there was no evidence that it was her fault.

"Kneel down," said the executioner, and pushed him to the ground.

Vrishaketu looked up, "You didn't give me much of a choice, no?"

"Shut up, traitor."

And he made him put his hand on the pillory. The people around him began to clap and hoot in excitement. Vrishaketu also wanted to see his brother, but he was not around either, as if he had vanished into thin air.

Where is my family? Have they developed a conscience finally, after years of mentally and emotionally abandoning me? He thought.

The cleaver was close to his neck, and Vrishaketu's heartbeat had come to a sudden stop, as he secretly was cutting off the rope with the little knife in his hand. The so-called assassin was probably someone who was part of Vrishaketu's rebel alliance, or probably a sympathetic ally. Regardless, he had offered him a lifeline and he had to use it.

But he couldn't see a way out. Even if sets himself free and jumps into the crowd, he would be massacred limb to limb, and getting one's head chopped off seemed better in comparison than getting torn apart.

As the cleaver came up, ready to separate his head from his body, he saw the shine, the water, his entire life reflect in front of him...

And the crowd dispersed. Trumpets were heard, and then the horses appeared. The executioner stopped, looking confused, as arrows rained on his chest, and he collapsed.

More horses, accompanied by black-hooded individuals appeared, killing the guards, throwing the mob into confusion. Fire arrows were shot at those who relented and rebelled.

Seeing an opportunity, Vrishaketu tore apart the weak rope clasp, and pulled his head out of the pillory.

All the ministers, the allied kings and queens retorted, sending their guards ahead, while Vrishaketu's Separatist army fought back. Vrishaketu chuckled. They must have sneaked in somehow and figured out how to help Vrishaketu.

He jumped over, rolling on the ground, grabbing hold of the nearest blade.

A soldier of the state appeared, as the people around them ran away in confusion. There was plenty of pushing and prodding.

Vrishaketu deflected the blade that came towards him, and he stabbed him on the chest, but the soldier just waved him off like it was nothing. Vrishaketu pulled back the blade, but by then the soldier had found his limbs, and went for them, scratching him in the process.

Vrishaketu cried in pain, when the soldier immediately got arrows shooting down on his chest as he fell. Vrishaketu limped, then looked up to see who the archer was, and he saw another black-hooded saviour of his, on a stallion, who had put his arm out for him.

Vrishaketu climbed up, and the individual rode through the mayhem and misery, leaving behind rubble and carcasses. They moved through the zigzags and the topsy-turvy turns of the city, until reaching the gate, which was getting closed by the gate bearers. But the horse moved so quickly that the gate bearers got confused themselves.

Vrishaketu held tightly to the individual, his brain wanted to ask him who he was from the Separatist army.

And as it reached many yards away from the kingdom, the stallion halted.

Vrishaketu dismounted, and looked up at the individual, at his saviour.

"Run!" Said the individual. "Towards the east. The rest of your party awaits you there."

"Who are you?"

He could see the eyes. And they were familiar. The cloak this individual wore was loose and unfitting.

"Run." The familiar voice spoke again.

And the wind blew, letting the hood fall open, and the face of his saviour was revealed. But unfortunately, Vrishaketu could not see, as the figure whisked away in the darkness, becoming a blip.

If only he knew, the face and the voice, the one who had saved him, was none other than his own mother.

12

Satyasena knew he was already late.

By the time he had reached to help out Vrishaketu, he had already received help from his Separatist army, who had sacrificed themselves for their leader. A selfless act, from a bunch of rebels, Satyasena thought.

He regretted for not reaching on time, though he was stuck for a particular reason. He had overslept at the quarters in his lover's arms. By the time he had gotten ready and was about to leave, he had heard that the executioner was ready and then the riots had broken out.

Satyasena knew that perhaps Ashtar would be happy. Even though it wasn't him who had carried out the deed.

With a not-so-guilty heart he went back to his lady love, who lived in a merchant's house, but the merchant was never home, nor would he care about his wife. He knew she was in an illicit relationship with Satyasena, but as he was the king's son he couldn't do much or his business would suffer. But Satyasena was bound, for the woman, Roma, was married. And even if she were to separate, she wouldn't be able to be with him. It would be considered unlawful, unjust in the eyes of the society.

Satyasena spent another day with her, as they lay bare

naked, watching the sunlight enter from the window, and it poured over their bronze bodies. She was older than him, but they were connected as one and the same.

"What are you thinking?"

"I might have done something wrong."

"What?"

Roma looked exquisite. She wasn't from this land, and was a dusky, exotic beauty. She was a mystery to Satyasena, and he knew the more he got to know about her, the less fascinated he would be. So they put words in a basket, and let their bodies do the talking instead.

"I might have killed someone."

"You are a prince. You kill a lot of people and get away with it. Isn't that satisfying?"

"But I'm afraid."

"Of whom?"

"Of not repenting, of not getting punished."

"Who are you talking about?"

"The Council of Surya," he said. "They had tasked me with a job, as a way to repent, but I was unsuccessful because we were inebriated and overslept after a night of passion. I was supposed to complete a deed, and I failed."

"They are just a bloody council, my love."

Satyasena turned and grabbed her mouth, holding her tightly by the chin. "No, they are not." His words had poison in them. "They rescued me when I could have died. They held me together when I was a child. I would have not been here with you if it wasn't for them."

"All right, I understand." She pulled back, a tad bit frightened.

"Master Ashtar is a strict, simple man, but he's a

man of principles and I have been following his orders," Satyasena said, with a remarkable sense of frustration.

"I hope you die right by him, then, because I'm sleeping."

She turned her back towards him and closed her eyes. Satyasena watched her realising he had been slightly rude to her, so he hugged her from behind. "I become quite emotional about the Council of Surya."

She paused. Hesitating.

"What, tell me?"

"Because of them, we can't marry," she said. "Because of them, I can't leave my stupid husband."

Satyasena clenched his jaw. Those rudimentary rules were prescribed by the Council of Surya. Not letting separated women or widows remarry, instead they should be put in exile or worse...death, if their husband had perished.

"I have spoken to Master Ashtar about it, but he's defiant. Hopefully, I'll be able to change his mind and we shall do what we eventually will do. So don't worry."

"All right. And there are other rules too, rules that you as a prince don't notice. The Council of Surya could be quite a mess, even though I'm grateful to them for rescuing you."

Satyasena hugged her tightly. "I am sure, as long as there are people like you who would speak about them, who would rebel, it's going to be fine."

And they both slept, peacefully.

Ashtar wasn't a particularly good-looking man but he wasn't always hunchbacked...once upon a time, before the attack, before the bloodshed, and before that cage where he was bound and gagged, kept like a wild animal without any food, where his back got worse and he turned into a horrifying version of himself. Ever since then, he shifted his ideologies to the ways of living under the ray of Surya. He had become quite oblivious about his appearance, unheeded by the monstrosity that he was.

So when he did see his shadow and his frame, he was indeed surprised by how unwell he looked. The shadows danced in front of him, as his eyes shrivelled, while the fire lingered in front.

"He couldn't do it, master," said a priest next to him.

"Indeed. What was the reason?"

"It's the same woman."

Ashtar was facing a cold wall, pressed against the iron torch. It was his room, after all, and it was an empty one, devoid of any kind of materialistic pleasure.

"Who saved him then?" He asked.

"Probably one of the Separatist rebels."

"How many have been caught?"

"Some of them died and the ones who were caught have been brought here, as per your instructions."

"Did the queen object?"

"Yes. She did. They were traitors and they deserved to die."

Ashtar smiled, as he came on his feet, letting the shadow leave the objectless room. He walked along the priest, exiting the small chamber, to the main centre of the religious place where the shrine of one of the goddesses rested. He bent down and looked at the three

Separatist rebels, all broken, with hands and legs scarred and wounded, their eyes tired and scared. They were not bound or gagged because there were soldiers of the city guarding them.

"You are free here, my children. Once you were pirates and criminals and now you will be the children of this land, and the god," Ashtar said. "Here, you are given a second chance. I have requested your queen to allow me to rehabilitate you rather than murder you. You went against the state, but that is fine, as long as you don't go against your god. Lord Surya's rays are above us, respect that and you'll be free."

The three rebels instantly went for his feet to touch them, weeping. They were just saved from their death by a generous man like Ashtar.

"Though there is an initiation measure to be taken. Something that our gods want from you."

The three rebels looked up earnestly, waiting for a command.

"Good," Ashtar said. "Don't worry, you are doing Lord Surya's bidding."

Satyasena was fast asleep, he had been happy lately so there were no nightmares to give him company. He could picture the perfect dream of Roma and him, together, running through fields, kissing each other, holding their children together, a loving family. He was ready to do a lot of things for her. He would have convinced the Council, in one way or another.

His face turned, and he could feel something squishy, something wet around him, with his eyes still closed he began to trace his fingers across the linen of the bed, and he found Roma's body, all dark and wet, like a crimson pool. His eyes opened, and his body retorted into a shocking glance, as he saw Roma had been stabbed, multiple times, across the chest, and her throat had been slit.

And blood.

It was everywhere.

A knife was in his hand, a knife that he had never seen before. There was blood all over his naked body.

And in front of him, on the wall, in the blood of Roma, it was written with clarity and conviction:

YOU DID THIS.

13

Vrikodara watched the owl looking at him, while the embers of a dying kingdom breathed its last.

He stood there with a mace in his hand, bloody in battle, while his armour was wet from the swampy waters, and the crimson blood of his victims. He scanned his surrounding, and he saw the dead wasteland of soldiers, of victims.

He was able to conquer Dasarana's kingdom and he was looking at the ministers, the nobles and the city guards, all tied up and gagged in front of him, as he contemplated to plant a flag of Yudhistr's kingdom.

He wasn't feeling particularly good about it since the last episode and how his brother used his phobia, his weakness against him. He had to face that trauma alone, until the fire had died and he was whimpering like a child, clinging on to the earth, that he so loved.

His men were around the castle, they had stationed themselves as the usurpers, waiting for Yudhistr's army to come and set up, probably have a satrap here.

But he had to finish one deed, before that.

"Where's your king?" He asked.

None of them said anything. And Vrikodara wasn't

intending to leave without an answer. His vulture circled in the skies above, and he whistled, prompting the vulture to smack down and tear a man's ear off, he cried and fell on the ground, bleeding.

"Someone else will be next. Where's your king?" He asked again. "It'll be easy."

He had to kill the king or subjugate him. He had entered the castle and destroyed the ladders, the walls and the ceilings. But to cripple a kingdom, you need to murder the king.

No one answered even then.

He brought his mace forward, grabbing one of the city nobles, ready to strike him on the head, when he heard...

"YOU ARE A BRUTE!"

It was a woman who said that.

"You are sadistic and horrible and you deserve the worst kind of death."

Vrikodara paused, as if the words had begun to hurt him.

"You do nothing but listen to your horrible brother who will die the horrific death that he deserves too."

"Spoken like a true woman." Vrikodara tossed the man he was holding, approached the woman and grabbed her by the neck. Her hands were behind her, and she couldn't do much but relent and scream. "You have a fighting spirit. I like that. You could be useful for my army."

"Why?"

"If you can humiliate men in power, you can humiliate anyone."

And he whistled, signalling the vulture, who flew down and instantly went for another man's eyes. The woman screamed in shock.

Then he pushed the woman towards his guards who dragged her from there, "Imprison her, feed and clothe her well, like us. I am going to train her to be a warrior."

Vrikodara moved around the lot, when he saw his right-hand commandant appearing, with his pointy beard and venomous eyes, fair skin, and jet black hair oiled neatly, holding a single sword.

"You don't need to bother with them anymore. I know where the king is, chief. Follow me," Pukkusati said, as he returned after searching the castle in and out.

Vrikodara just nodded, waving at his guards. Crossbows were raised, and arrows were shot towards all the ministers, nobles and the people. Vrikodara followed Pukkusati, who was far younger and smaller in size. One could say he was almost a dwarf. Vrikodara had met him a long time ago, during one of his many conquests, and he had proven to be useful since he had what others didn't: mental grit.

"Well, it's funny your brother sent you here."

They were walking up the staircase, and moving towards a big iron tower, which went up to the heart of the sky. Their soldiers were stationed on every corner, and they were all saluting Vrikodara.

"Why is it funny?" He asked in a brusque tone.

"Because it's like he's almost sending you to run a fool's errand."

Vrikodara rolled his eyes. *Tell me about it*, he thought. "What did you search in your study till now?"

"Nothing really. The books show that the treasury is in debt, it was a bad season for crops, and there's nothing of significance in these lands except criminals. You leave this place for an hour, and you'll find bandits scavenging the lands. Dasaras were in a pretty bad shape, and you in fact, kind of saved them from their own deaths."

"Why would my brother send me to such a horrible place?"

"You should know, he's your brother. Is he doing it because there's a strategic value to the empire or do you think it's because he wants you to be busy displaying your brute force while he takes the crowning achievement of taking over the better kingdom for himself?"

"Yudhistr is not a fighter."

"And yet I hear, he's preparing for a war."

"I am his commander."

"And yet you are here, scavenging dirt. One could say not much of a difference between you and those bandits." He sniggered.

They circled their way up to the top as Vrikodara, like an honourable student, listened to Pukkasati, who spoke diligently like a mentor.

"You should be ransacking lands that are of value to the crown. Something that'll help."

"I can see you signal towards Anga."

"Why not?" He shrugged. "It has great money, no debts and best of all—timber. You can really build ships from it and attack the neighbouring islands. Too much power rests in that kingdom. Plus, you can piss your brother off too. That's just an added benefit." He chuckled.

"Have we reached?"

Pukkasati nodded, as Vrikodara paused to catch a breath, when he saw a door, and found a guard dead there. Pukkasati opened the door, and Vrikodara found a cradle in the room, with the handmaidens killed, and the baby dead as well.

"Where's the king?"

"It's the kid."

A chill ran through Vrikodara's body.

"No."

"Yep." He shook his head. "His father died prematurely from dysentery and the kid was supposed to be taken care of till a certain age, before being crowned. But apparently, from the looks of it, the nurses who took care of him, poisoned him, so he wouldn't be captured by the likes of us."

"I would never harm a child."

"I know," Pukkasati said. "And yet this has happened. Didn't your brother inform you that the child king ruled this stead? We would have never attacked."

He played me.

He used me.

Vrikodara frowned, feeling disheartened and betrayed.

"Give the child a proper burial." He shook his head, as he stormed out.

"Where are you going?"

To meet my brother.

14

She walked in secret.

She meant a lot of things to a lot of people. But she held her words tightly to her chest as she swayed in the night, under the bright moon and stars that twinkled and glittered in the ominous sky. The raccoons moved in the garden, and the leaves fluttered in the gushing wind.

Shanaya's secret was something she held close to herself, for she was in an alien country, amongst aliens who didn't understand her. And while she had migrated from harsh conditions from the Greek world, Bharatvarsh had been kind to her and her father, and the other Ionions. But that didn't mean leaving behind herself as well.

There was a large hedge maze through which she walked, a candle dancing in her hands, its light flickering on her face, as she hid under the cowl of her embroidered cloth.

The hedge maze, from far looked like a marvel and a beauty, crafted by the gardeners and the planters. But inside lay the truth, and the hidden visage. She knew her way around the maze as she cradled herself, moving through the shrubs, to find in the middle, what she came for.

A statue of Zeus, a patron, the god of thunder.

She knelt down and began to pray. For a kingdom that worshipped Surya, she was worshipping another god, and in the eyes of the Council, it was considered blasphemous. Freedom of religion was not something that was entertained here.

She wondered, as she prayed, why the three rebels of the Separatist army were taken by Ashtar. She never got a good vibe from the hunchback. He would snide and snigger at her, display a plastic smile and laugh, but there was something unnerving about him that she couldn't put a finger on.

"I have defied my duties as a queen, and became a mother," she told the idol. "For that, I have no remorse nor guilt. A woman can be a mother first and foremost, before she's anything else."

She whispered, justifying herself, when she heard a rustle behind her. She didn't understand what it was, and continued with her prayers. Her eyes were closed…

When there was another rustle.

She waited. Quietly.

She didn't utter a word, and then quickly, a man appeared out of the shrubs, with a sword in his hand, ready to attack her.

She moved, pulling out the dagger she held on to, from the scabbard of her father, and she stabbed the assassin on the neck, moving the knife with precision. She walked up to the corpse, who lay fidgeting now, and pulled out the knife. As she began to uncover the face to reveal his identity…

More assassins appeared.

She knew she didn't have the artillery, and she dodged the attack, rolling over on the ground, swiftly hiding in the bushes. Then she quickly swerved, and reached the other side of the maze, her breath panting as she moved. She heard a whistle, and understood the assassins were whistling to communicate with each other. She caught her breath, held herself against the bush, and kept calm, the bloody dagger against her chest.

First Karna's father Adhirath, and now me.

Someone is plotting assassinations against the royal family of Anga.

But who?

Why?

She knew she had enemies around the country, but so many assassins, around the vicinity of the kingdom, around her palace...

It's an inside job, surely.

Vrishaketu could not be it. He was ousted from the kingdom. It could be any other minister, noble, or worse... merchants. Taxes have been heavy. They must have paid the guards, to allow the assassins to enter.

But then someone who has access to Maharogas as well...

She walked closer to one of the assassins whose back was towards her, who was looking for her, and she grabbed him by the neck, slicing his throat, letting the blood spray on her body too. When she noticed his face, hoping it was a Maharoga...

She saw a man. A simple one. Just a guardsman.

So the Maharogas are not here to kill him. Of course, they couldn't. Anyone would know of their presence in the kingdom, if they even exist.

As she moved quickly to the other side, her hand was grabbed, and an arrow swerved next to her hair, but she was pulled in the bushes, and managed to escape from the other assassin, to be close to her muscular, high cheek-boned, long-haired husband, with eyes like olive and the nose of a god.

"Vasu," she sighed. "You are back."

"Quiet."

Karna grabbed her by the arm and led her towards the exit. She followed, crouching, moving like a stealth cat. When they reached the exit, an assassin was standing there. Karna used his bow and arrow to shoot him in the head, and then he moved outside. Suddenly Shanaya was grabbed by another assassin and thrown on the ground.

Karna used his brute force, and shoved the man down using his bow, breaking his head apart. Then he grabbed hold of Shanaya and picked her up.

"How are you?"

He touched her belly.

"I'm fine."

He carried her slowly, away from the hedge maze. "What is going on?" He asked.

Shanaya could feel the tremor in his eyes. "I don't know. But someone is ordering hits on us."

"My father?"

A chill ran down her spine. "You know?"

"From a bunch of thieves, but yes. I meandered in the city, with a secret identity, so not many realise I have returned. Why did you not tell me?" There was pain in his voice.

"I'm sorry. I wanted to, but you were with Suyodhan. I didn't want you to be distracted."

"And Vrishaketu has escaped."

"Yes."

"And you have assassins behind you," Karna said, shaking his head. "Ashtar told me everything."

That snake.

They reached the main gate, when the soldiers of the palace noticed her, they immediately rushed to help her, as Karna said one last thing, which hurt her more than the fall that she had just experienced—

"I was wrong about you," he said. "You cannot rule this kingdom anymore. You are not fit to rule his kingdom anymore."

15

Vrishaketu was in a delirious maelstrom of illusions and dreams, he woke up sweating like a swine.

He was in the middle of the woods, amongst the shrubs and the leaves. A few tents were stationed, and a fire was burning at night. His wound hurt him in the leg, as he limped. He opened the dressing on his wounds as he came close to the lake, looking over the moonlight that shimmered over the water. He wished he was in a quiet land. He wished he was somewhere else.

There was something that he always wanted to do. He wanted to become a rancher for cattle. Taking care of god's own animals. He wanted to own a farm, and wanted to use his bullock carts to go to the local village. He never wanted an expensive, extravagant lifestyle, rather a quiet one.

It had been few days since the attack, and they were still formulating what their next step should be. Some Separatist rebels were caught, and thrown in jail, some turned over to the Council of Surya, and some faced a bloody death. He had scolded the rest who were with him, that they should have not done what they did—saving him—but his group of rebels, they loved him like a leader, and a god. They believed it's better to kill dozens to save one, for he will inspire thousands.

He kept sitting by the lake, when his eyes fell on something. A boat appearing, with a torch hanging in front, light shining over two individuals who were standing while the boatman rowed towards the shore. Vrishaketu was taken aback, and he reached for the scabbard, which had no blade, and he immediately cursed himself.

The person in front, stepped down from the boat, and handed some coins to the boatman, while the other person, a girl with emerald eyes, followed the first one.

"Who are you?" Vrishaketu stood up, almost tripping but ready to be in action.

The man removed his hood, revealing a handsome face, but with a glass eye and a scar, running from the top right of the face to the bottom, long hair and a chiselled jawline to accompany.

"Babhru," he spoke to his partner, "that was quite a surprise."

"I take it you haven't received my pigeon."

"No."

"Your commandeers were pretty all right in sharing your location with me." He smiled, as Vrishaketu came forward and embraced him.

Babhru had been kind of a strange friend to Vrishaketu and his Separatist rebels. He had been their looter, thief, spy and a supplier of weapons too. He had met Vrishaketu through the soldiers of Yudhistr, when they both had too much of madeira and the friendship had begun. He considered himself a freelancer and had even done odd jobs for the Pandavas, helping the ones who fight the feudal systems of the country, for he doesn't believe in any god, any culture, any kingdom. He only believed in himself.

And he was the one who had asked Vrishaketu if the Maharogas could enter the domain.

"My grandfather was killed by the Maharogas," Vrishaketu said. "And it is a matter of extreme grief. If I had known they had bad intentions, I would have never given them backdoor entry to the kingdom."

He shrugged. "Oh shush, those are rumours. The Maharogas who entered wanted to be at peace and seeked solitude. You met them. You saw them. They were a hapless gay couple, who ran away because their doctrine doesn't permit their love. You can trust me on their character, and you know I would never lie. Your grandfather must have been killed by someone else, I'm sure. But not the Maharogas, that I'm sure of as well."

Vrishaketu wanted to believe him, and yet there was something he wasn't sure about.

"Their reputation precedes them. They were a myth until they became a reality now."

"All myths are based on reality, my friend. You should know." He smiled, with a quick twist in his mouth, as he chewed on something, probably betel leaves. "I will investigate your grandfather's death and hopefully find the culprit, but how are you? Good to see you alive."

"I am good. I am waiting for Dharmaraja's orders now."

"And you will continue to wait." He shrugged. "He's quite busy ever since he's been running that bloody kingdom of his. Your mother actually wanted to nick you, right?"

Vrishaketu nodded, glancing over at the girl.

"Oh, my bad behaviour! This is Tripti, my associate, and a colleague. I have got too much on my hands nowadays, so she helps me from time to time."

"Business is growing, I believe."

He chuckled. "When you are good at something, business definitely grows, which brings me to the point why I am here."

"Why?"

"I am sure you want to stab your mother in the heart."

Vrishaketu sighed. He had no hate for what she did as a queen, but there was a sting. He wanted something to happen that led to her demise, and be done with her, for sure. No more problems. He wanted to stab his father too. The hate his parents would make him feel would shake his knees. He would go back and remember the time when he was born and his parents had abandoned him for almost forty nights and forty days just for the way he looked, the colour of his skin. Master Keshava was kind enough to speak to him about it, to tell him the truth during his infancy.

"And while you wait for Dharmaraja's consent, I have an offer."

"What is it?"

"Do you often wonder why he doesn't attack Anga?"

Vrishaketu nodded. "Because he would have to cut the trees around the kingdom to release his army and that's the most important resource of this land."

He shook his head. "Oh no, that's mostly gossip. The real one being, when Indraprastha was set up, the land used to belong to the Nagas, correct?"

"That's the rumour, yes."

"A genocide had happened, that's what they say."

"People vanished overnight." Vrishaketu had heard this.

"Now apparently, what I have learnt is that your father, Karna, knew about it. In fact, he had spied over them. The Nagas were wiped out from their lands, probably murdered too. We don't know. And people don't care too, for they mean nothing to us, right?" He chuckled. "Tribals. Outcast. Bleh. Though when they were wiped out, allegedly Dharmaraja had happened to steal their Mani, their shrine, as a kind of triumphant booty."

"Okay?" Vrishaketu arched his brows, surprised that someone as noble as Yudhistr would do this.

"Your father and your uncle Suyodhan had stolen that shrine from Dharmaraja, and used it as ransom. Dharmaraja won't attack, because if he does, your father has the shrine as proof to show to the Nagas and their tribal lords, and Dharmaraja would have a huge war looming large on himself. Not just that, he could be imprisoned, for all we know, for committing such mass genocide. He can't let everyone know till he becomes the Maharaja of Hastinapur, and he wants to stay quiet till then."

"Okay, so where do I come in?"

"You come in where you help our Dharmaraja." He smiled. "Be in his good books. You take away the leverage. Find the Mani and return it to Dharmaraja, and then he has every right to attack Anga. No holds barred, leading for you to finally lead the campaign and eventually kill your mother."

Vrishaketu clenched his jaw. "What's in it for you?"

He looked at him innocently. "War profiteering. If Dharmaraja attacks Anga, all the weapons will be supplied by me. He would need a lot of them, I'm sure. And unfortunately, he's my only client."

"So money, is it?"

"Yes." He gleamed.

"Does Dharmaraja know I will be doing this for him?"

"He wants you to lay low, as far as I'm concerned."

"Yes, he hasn't contacted me. I sometimes wonder whether he is disappointed I got caught like a fool."

"Only one way to know. Meet him with this gift, and you'll be in his good books again."

Vrishaketu folded his arms and looked at the girl again. With her bright green eyes, and a striking pose, she watched him like a hawk. "This genocide, you say... these were rumours. The Mani, everything. So how do you know that there is a ransom, there is a Mani, and there is my father stealing from Dharmaraja?"

"Well because, unfortunately, they are not rumours," Babhru said. "Because I know where the thief, who stole the Mani, lives."

16

Vrikodara moved with purpose.

He sat on a bison with long horns, a mace dangling from his large frame, as he walked through the foggy landscape. The mist had covered most of his vision, but he had soldiers around him, guiding him through. He moved along with the dwarfish Pukkasati, who was on a mule, like a shorter muse to Vrikodara who was triple his size.

"Have you made up your mind?"

"Yes." Vrikodara responded.

The fog cleared and he found himself in a dry, deserted wasteland, just miles away from the kingdom of Anga, but there were barren corpses of animals, vultures circling around them.

He found two men waiting for him with their stallions. He didn't recognise them, but he also knew why they were there.

They were summoned to this place.

By Vrikodara himself.

"Halt." He called to his soldiers, who stopped moving at his command, but he remained steadfast, and moved ahead, before climbing down from his bison, his mace still with him.

He came close to the two soldiers, whimpering in the mist. The soldiers held the flag against the shoulders of the elephant, the very flag that Vrikodara had been plantimg on the earth, for its throne and its king.

"Lord Vrikodara," the two soldiers bowed, "it is a pleasure to hear from you."

He looked at them, feeble, and armoured, with their swords close to their chest, as if afraid of Vrikodara, as if the blades would penetrate his flesh with ease.

"Tell your king, messengers, I am going to Anga and I'm coming back with its throne, which I shall rule."

"Dharmaraja, Lord Vrikodara, knows of your intention."

Spies. Spies amongst his mates.

He had decided to plan Anga's downfall, along with his teammates, but he was not aware that there was someone who would be sending pigeons to his brother.

"He has told us to move back. To leave Anga alone." One soldier said.

Another began, "He believes there's a lot of diplomacy involved which he doesn't want to get into, and Anga right now, must remain unharmed."

"When he sent me to the east, to conquer kingdoms for him, he never specified a territory to avoid. And now, all of a sudden, the most lucrative territory, the one that will benefit the crown—he doesn't want that. I call nonsense. There's something he's hiding, and I don't care what it is. I serve the throne, not the puny man who sits on it," Vrikodara said.

"He has specified more instructions about the kingdom in this scroll." The messenger said, pulling it out.

Vrikodara looked at the scroll but didn't touch it. "I will only take Anga on my behest and it'll be under the rule of Indraprastha and not Hastinapur."

"Lord Vrikodara, you must understand that we have no choice, but to inform Dharmaraja of it."

"I know. And I don't want that. Because he will send armies back to stop me."

He grabbed hold of one of the messengers and broke his neck. He went to grab the other messenger, who escaped from his clutches, but he used his mace to break his back, bleeding him dry on the ground. The blood sprayed from his neck.

"And now there will be no message to him for a long time."

As he moved back towards his bison, he heard something. Arrows. Launching. High in the sky, as they began to fly through the mist, cutting it like flesh and landing on the ground. Unfortunately, those were flaming arrows and they began circling around him, the flames increased, and the wind didn't help.

The moment he saw the flames and the fire, he felt a pang of guilt, his knees shook and he fell on the ground. He felt petrified and horrible.

He had no idea, where the arrows were coming from, but they were thrown with such precision, that he knew who was behind them.

Arjun.

But he couldn't see his younger brother anywhere around him. He was unseen, unheard.

Yudhistr doesn't want at all—for me to chase Anga.

He sent Arjun and he knew Vrikodara would never harm Arjun.

He began to avoid the flames, closing his eyes, but more arrows lined up, and he fell on the ground, before he saw the family—the burnt family—in the shadows of the fire, and he began to feel it's the end of the world for him. Shouting, he growled under his breath, letting his men hear him as well—

"YOU CAN'T STOP ME! I WILL TAKE ANGA. SO NO POINT DELAYING THE INEVITABLE."

There was silence at the other end. No words were spoken, no sound appeared.

He grabbed hold of one of the flaming arrows that were stabbed on the ground and broke it into two. "STOP USING MY WEAKNESS AGAINST ME. I HAVE NO WEAKNESS ANYMORE."

But he did. He showed prowess, but he was held weak.

There was no answer again. Arjun didn't do anything. There was no response to it. No arrows, at all.

He crawled himself up on the bison, when his curiosity piqued him, and he moved towards the scroll again, next to the corpses he lying there, and flipped it open.

He turned back to see Pukkasati, who remained steadfast with a clenched jaw, witnessing his weakness, which many didn't know he had. Only his brothers did. But Vrikodara didn't pay heed to the entire moment.

He unravelled the scroll, and read what was written in it:

I know you won't listen to me. Arjun was my last resort to threaten you to back down. But you have made a decision, and like the brute you are, you would not understand the sense of diplomacy that comes with my position.

So be it then.

I shall not stop you.

His eyes grew bigger as he read the letter further, which was not at all what the messengers thought it would be. It had no mention of any kingdom that he should be targeting, rather it was a mission, to do something far greater.

If you are going to Anga, and you plan to attack it—then complete the bloody job.

Kill Karna and destroy his family. Don't let him or his men exit the kingdom. Capture them.

And he has a material of vital importance to me, before he breathes his last breath—

Take it from him. That is of utmost urgency.

Good luck.

I am sending more men to you.

Vrikodara grinned.

He finally got his brother's permission.

He finally got his blessings.

I am coming for you Karna.

For my revenge.

For what you did to me.

17

Whenever Satyasena's mind was in turmoil, he would always veer towards his first love—sword fighting.

He would practice it alone, letting off the steam, bringing his anger drown. But that day it wasn't helping, as whenever he was in the middle of a stance, his mind would go to Roma, and her headless corpse. It began to traumatise and trouble him. The people of the Council of Surya did it, and while his anger had no bounds, he had no power to do anything. Not just as a prince, but as a student of Surya too. They had made him who he was, they had made him survive the toughest of winters when he was small. And whatever they did—probably, they did for the best.

His mind had begun to draw the horrible picture of murdering everyone. To dispute his power too. To show that he was indeed a king. The wooden puppet in front of him stood still, as he slashed and tore it apart. As he lay sweating, his muscles were tight, his thin beard greasy with sweat, bangles hanging from his ears, his chest heavy, and his tight abs in a formation of six to eight.

He was by no means a handsome man, but he was an incredulous one. A charming fellow, and a fit person unlike his albino brother, who was meek, small and extremely discoloured.

"Anger should be the last resort of a great man." A familiar voice boomed in the sword room.

Satyasena turned to see who it was, a familiar grunt came too, and a smile later on, as he found his father entering, in his dhoti and a sherwani covering his chest. He was not aware his father had returned.

"You know who told you that?" Karna asked.

"You."

"And you know who told me?"

"Who?"

"Dronacharya."

"The guru who threw you out."

He came on the pedestal, getting rid of his slippers. "True, he was a cruel man and we had our differences. Worse, I was in love for a long time, and I did something out of love. Always remember, practicality should be what you should look for. Any decision taken emotionally is a decision that leads up to a prosperous death."

"You had vanished for months and now you have returned to speak to me?"

"I was missing you, my son."

"Sure." He shrugged. "Threw me to the wolves, the last time I met you."

"To train you against ferals, so to speak."

Satyasena chuckled. "Pick up the sword. I want to see how you perform now."

"Surely, my son."

He grabbed the nearest sword.

"You met mother?"

His voice deepened. “Yes, I did. I have asked her to rest.”

“What do you mean?”

“I’m going to sit on the stead till her pregnancy is complete.”

“So you are not going back to Uncle Suyodhan?”

Karna came quickly, zapping like a current and smacking Satyasena on the cheek, who fell on the ground. “Be fast, my son. Be fast.”

Satyasena spat on the ground. “You are being an ass, father.”

“You are talking to the king.” He kicked him on the ribs and he rolled over. “And you should respect that.”

Growling under his breath, Satyasena leapt forward, lurching ahead to attack Karna, who deflected his attack with the sword.

“I am not popular for this weapon and yet I am defeating you. You should have learnt archery as I had asked you to.”

Their swords clashed, when Satyasena said in a venomous tone: “I find archery a coward’s man game.”

“Ah yes, because being a brute is more important to you than being a strategist.”

He pushed Satyasena down.

Satyasena grabbed him by the feet and bit his toe. Karna growled, and kicked him on the nose, as he began to bleed. Satyasena grabbed hold of his face, as the crimson pool gushed.

“You should follow the rules of warfare and biting isn’t a part of it.” He shook his head. “You have so much to learn.”

"You should be here to teach me probably, so I can lead this kingdom when you are gone."

"Why do you think I am going?" He narrowed his gaze. "And why do you think you will lead? You haven't displayed a single act of courage till now."

Satyasena sighed. "I am the oldest. I belong on that throne, more than mother."

"Shut up. You belong to the dogs."

"What makes you say that?"

"You bedded a married wench, to start with. I know your dilly-dallies, Satya." He shook his head in disappointment. "Probably find someone of your age, a princess of a minor kingdom, who we can partner with and grow our empire."

He continued to bleed, and he could taste the blood in his mouth, but he stood there in horror, as he hadn't realised his father knew about Roma.

"Your grandfather is dead, your betrayer of a brother has escaped, and you are having fun keeping every responsibility away. Be a romantic, but not a fool." Karna growled. "I want you to take a small party and leave for the outskirts of the empire. I am sure, they must also be behind the assassination attempt on your mother. See potential whereabouts of the Maharogas. Or are they really Maharogas? I want intelligence on them, so we can act accordingly. If the Maharogas have returned, and the myths are true, then we have a big problem. The Nagas will rise, and we have nothing to protect us from… except…" he paused, remembering something. "Yes, that's the only thing."

"Why are you so afraid of the Nagas?"

"I am angry, more than afraid," he said. "But in the ancient times, the Nagas were the ones who used to control the water, before it was taken by the men. They used to worship water, and the men began to use it to wash their asses. The Nagas have hated humans, and as their numbers reduced, probably because their women were murdered before they could have children, they have always held grudges against the humans, the citizens. And the Maharogas, according to the myths, would rise against men. They were berserkers, creatures and beasts of different kinds, who had python blood in them or something." A shiver ran down his spine. "We need to figure out more about them, and you lead that party, and for once, prove me wrong about something. Don't be your brother."

Saying that, Karna left the scene, and he called for water, and began to wash his face till the water in the bowl began to turn red, and he remembered what his father told him about the Nagas and the water. He smiled showing his bloody teeth and in his delusional mind he thought:

He believes in me. He wants my help.

18

"Where are you taking me?"

"To the truth."

That was what Menander's response to Shanaya was, as they meandered through the twisted groves and intertwined shrubs. Shanaya had never been a part of this kingdom, and though it was outside the palace boundaries, it felt safe, to be in the woods, and away from her life as a queen, which was tiring and where she felt bound.

Menander was wearing his cloak, the same brown, tainted one, with a hood that covered his prickly hair, riding a mare that was tired and guffawing. Shanaya followed him, in a hood as well, so her appearance was deceiving and one would not know instantly who she was. Because there were fanatics, and conspirators waiting to stab her in the gut.

Shanaya knew she wasn't a good queen. She thought she could be one, but she was not of this land, was unaware of the customs, and was hated by the religious order that protected the city. Worse, she was not a diplomat, but a warrior, who earned her keep by eating sourdough and putrid wine as a grown-up.

Her father used to take care of her as a child, and

while she was one of the many daughters he had given away to different people for partnership and expansion purposes, he was very close to her. She had a fighting spirit that he could see none of his other children possessed. He was ostracised from his country long time ago due to his penchant for violence and disobedience towards the leadership there, and to achieve the riches here he began to work from the ground up.

But his reign had problems, for there were other Greeks, especially Kalyavana of the Ionions who was close to a lot of kingdoms here. They used to call him the Black Greek, for he was dark as an unripened jamun. Kalyavana was a menace, and a tyrant, a horrible miscreant to the entire Greek race, until he was defeated by Lord Krishna of the Dwarka. He was trapped and burnt alive in a cave. After that, the Greeks had begun to die slow and painful deaths and diminish in number. Shanaya, being married, survived so long because of Karna. Otherwise, she too would have been hunted or worse, incinerated into oblivion. The kingdoms were against aliens of foreign nature. And she thought her father would be safe, of course. He was smart. He had given her a ribbon that she carried along with her, a red one tied around her ankle, like an anklet. And it was a sign of an Aprodhite, a symbol of protection and love.

Whenever she would feel dejected, she would look at it, like the last week when Karna gave up on her. But she knew it was out of grief. He was broken from inside.

"I had managed to establish contact with your father. He hadn't been answering my letters, and even yours, which you used to secretly send through me," he said.

She remembered she had asked him for a favour. Long

story short, her father had betrayed Karna at the last moment during the fight against Jarasandha. And while he hadn't done anything about it out of respect towards Shanaya and his marriage with her, Karna had always held a grudge and made sure that she or his children would never meet their grandfather.

Though, she used to miss him, and she would often send letters through Menander, and in the beginning would get responses too, until recently. A few months back the letters stopped coming, and she was afraid, wondering if everything was all right.

"Until I got to know the truth," he said. "After Jarasandha's death, the plea bargain that he had with him also died alongside. Your father rode for a few years with his band, but foreigners in this land have always faced persecution, especially the ones who don't become royalty," he said, remarking to her. "And I was beginning to worry, so I sent some of my messengers out there in the wild, hoping they don't bring back bare bones and flesh, and what I found in return was something horrible."

"By the time I reached, it was too late."

"What do you mean?" Her chest became heavy.

She reached the circling around a clearing, where the greenery was dead and the plants didn't flutter or speak. Rather, they circumvented in horror, as in front lay a naked man, ribbed and boned, with long hair, grey in colour, tied up in chains, against the large trunk of a tree. The man's guts were spilling out, and there was blood all over. The corpse was of an old man, and decaying in colour, as if left there a long time ago, the maggots had their fill, and the vultures too had taken whatever flesh there was for them to take.

"He was tortured here."

Shanaya jumped from her mare and ran towards him, but Menander grabbed hold of him, and pulled her back.

"I have to take him first, clean him and then you should visit him," he said. "Otherwise, we don't know the infections that you might catch from it."

"It can't be him."

"It is," he said. "I have checked."

"Where are the others? His men?"

"Dead," Menander said. "They either left him, or perished."

Shanaya couldn't hold back her tears and fell on the ground, while Menander held her tightly against his chest.

"It's all right. It's going to be fine. He's…he's in a better place now."

"I should have taken care of him." She wept like a child. "I should have let him see my children. He always wanted to meet them."

"It's okay, it's all right, it's fine."

Shanaya looked up at him, with anger. "Who was it?"

"Who could it be, my lady? I found this here when I found him earlier."

Shanaya saw the bracelet he carried in his hand, and it was a bracelet with a sun symbol.

And she knew who it belonged to.

Karna.

19

Karna knew what had to be done.

To repent.

To atone.

To forget.

And to be forgiven.

But that was what he had intended to do when he had approached Ashtar, and begged him to be given a reason—as to why his father was stolen from him, why his empire crumbled around him, and why his family was torn apart. He wasn't sure where to go anymore. He wanted to meet his friend Suyodhan, and he had sent a letter too, but the pang of frustration rested on his chest like a big rock. He wanted a way out of this feeling.

He was kneeling down in front of the large idol of Lord Surya, under the dark, stormy skies that blurted an occasional thunder. Fire torches were risen on either side of the pathway on which he knelt, while the yellow-cloaked priests were chanting a hymn that he couldn't understand. Before this congregation was created, nothing was as it seems. Lord Surya's temple stood, but not as flamboyant as it was now.

Ashtar was right opposite of him, looking down on him, with a bowl in his hand.

"He's angry," he said. "He's angry at you."

"Why?"

"Because you don't listen."

"What do you mean?"

"Drink the blood of Surya."

He brought the bowl of liquid down, and he placed it near Karna's lips.

"Sip it. And you shall know your answer. And you shall have repented."

Karna nodded, and he took a long sip.

"Finish it."

It was sour. Dirty. Felt like something was off.

But he had to do it.

"Fine."

"Listen to him. Feel him. Make him a part of you."

"He is a part of me."

"No, he's left you."

And he sipped out of rebellion, out of proving the man wrong. As he did that, for a moment nothing happened to him, but he experienced a revolting feeling in his head, as he began to feel lightheaded, confused and delirious. He couldn't kneel anymore and fell flat on the floor, blurting out nonsense. His mind began to crisscross and when he opened his eyes, he found himself on the cliff.

Far away from everyone.

He saw a kingdom in front, very akin to the land of Anga, but it had perished, broken and destroyed. He was frenetic, and confused when he saw Ashtar, with his hunchback by his side.

"For so long, you've tried to fight back the kingdom for the sake of your mother, to keep her word that

Anga should always be yours, you are the true heir, and yet it continues to destroy itself from within," he said. "This is what will happen to your favourite land when you wouldn't do anything about it. Decrepit. Broken. Destroyed into a thousand pieces."

The scene began to shift, as he ran away from the cliff, and found himself in a village, where there was a hut, and when he peeked inside that hut he found his wife Shanaya and an indistinguishable Greek man. They were in an intimate position.

"Your wife goes behind your back to be with someone else. Your third child is not yours. In fact, none of your children are yours. The son of Surya wouldn't have children as degenerates, as disappointments and yet she produces with the coldest of her hearts—all inbreds, and horrors."

"No, that's not true. My children are mine. They have my nose. They have my..."

"And yet they don't act like the children of Surya, do they?" He asked.

Karna was shocked, his eye bags began to deepen, and his face had maneuvered into a horrific reality. "My children...no...can't be..."

And he turned back, running into the forest, only to land up in front of a white ball of sky, where he saw a large metallic creature, with a head resembling a crown with a sun symbol engraved on it, holding on to him, raising him, its eyes buzzing with electricity and its face wide opened.

The voice of Ashtar echoed in the background.

"Allow him in. Allow him to be your vessel and reclaim

the kingdom that you deserve."

Karna tried to escape. Tried to push away.

"What do you want me to do?"

"Let him eat you."

And the metallic man swallowed him, and when he entered his mouth he was in a vortex of darkness, falling down, but not dying. He wanted the fall to end, but he couldn't do anything about it. He found different images swirling around him, different scenes from his life being played out—how he was abandoned as a child, to facing persecution as a suta, as the charioteer's son, to him finding out about his mother's death, to finding Jarasandha and winning the day, to meeting Shanaya and finding a long-lost friendship in Suyodhan…

He saw everything.

He saw his life flash in front of his eyes. And he thought he would die, and probably the pain inside him would vanish too.

But he woke up sweating, and confused.

"What did you see? Did you hear my voice?" Asked Ashtar, smiling.

"What did you give me?"

"The drink of truth. Did you see the truth?"

"I saw so much." He shook his head. "I don't know what to believe."

"Believe what you see, and what you hear," Ashtar said. "Lord Surya never lies. For your kingdom to perish, you must do what he asked you to do."

"But…but…" he shook his head, "I saw something I should never have. I don't know. Should I? What is it?" He was whimpering.

"And what would that be? What did you see?"

Karna blinked, horrified, as he spoke the next few words: "I saw me strangling Shanaya's throat."

20

"Are we on the right track?" He asked.

Vrishaketu had been staring at Tripti for a while now. She was holding her spyglass, as she watched the waves in front. They were on an undulating plain, and from far they watched a river that flew with harsh winds, and louder waves. They were alone, under the watchful sunny skies, hoping to find the thief as was told by Babhru.

"I don't think the coordinates were right. We are under the bloody sun and nothing is out here. And we were told, that's the bloody..." He paused, as he saw that Tripti didn't even bother looking at him.

He had been travelling with her for quite some time, and she spoke very little often, and cared even less as well, but there was a story that he wasn't sure of. Something that was within her, hidden in plain sight.

She was a beauty of a different kind, something that not many would ever witness, but only few could possess. She was a part of the air, of the winds and the skies, and she was not held by the world under her feet. She wouldn't use words as her weapon, but her actions. Her eyes spoke volumes, watching, blinking like an owl under a watchful gaze of infinite vision. Vrishaketu had never been smitten by a woman who spoke less, but here she was, and something drew him towards her strongly. Something somersaulted in him, and made him wish to forget his cause, and probably live a life that only few could ever hope for.

But Vrishaketu had to focus on his mission. After all, he had been working on it for quite some time now.

"There," she said in her lustrous tone. "There is someone."

Vrishaketu grabbed the spyglass from her and looked at a man, holding buckets of fish probably, as he put them in a boat. There were other boats too, possibly belonging to the villagers around, tied to the store.

"Do you think it's him?"

"It's him," she said with conviction.

"How do you know?"

"Because I was the one who found him in the first place."

"So what's the plan?"

"Torture."

They began to walk towards him, as he was preparing his boat.

"No, no, I mean, really what?"

"Torture." She stopped and said it again, this time slowly, as if Vrishaketu didn't hear her the first time.

"Are you serious?"

"I thought you will ask him kindly."

"There's no kindness in what we do."

She began to walk, with her twisted dagger in her arms, while her mouth was covered, with a tight red cloth, and her eyes dense, her body moving like a snake...

When the man looked back at them.

And instantly made a run for his boat, pushing it out into the water.

"Oh great, he's running now. We should have just done it in a better way. I know how to barter with thieves..."

And his voice drawled, when Tripti went for the other boat.

"Help me!"

She shouted, and Vrishaketu realised what he was signing up for. As the boat got pushed out into the river, she jumped inside it, while the thief in front was rowing hard towards the currents.

"This is not a good idea. This meets at a larger river, and that river is not safe."

"JUMP!" She screamed at him, almost hissing.

He did, out of fear.

She began to row, chasing after him.

"How does he know you? He knew you that's why he was scared. Have you approached him earlier?"

"I tried to catch him earlier."

"This is not catching! This is scaring someone to death." He paused. "How do you think this plan will stop him?"

"Because I have you now."

"I am not a thief, god!" He shook his head, realising what an absurd statement that was.

They raced behind the boat, and were making headway, as Vrishaketu began to yell at him, asking him to stop rowing, so they could talk. But the thief, bearded with scrawny hair, was all over the place by then. The boats began to collide with each other, almost adjacent...

When a huge wave rocked it ahead, nearly spiralling both of them out of control. Tripti fell on the other side, while Vrishaketu grabbed her by her waist, and pulled her back up. Tripti growled, trying to jump to the other boat, but the thief pushed away from them, and rowed even faster.

They were about to close in on him, when Vrishaketu saw the horrible current downstream that was about to rock them hard.

And it fell flat, as he got beaten by the logs on one side. He pulled himself up again, but that's when he saw the river culimnating in a waterfall. Even the thief saw that, and out of fear he jumped out of the boat, trying to swim away, but the currents were too strong...

And they both fell. Their boats and their bodies crashing in the middle, as they dropped in the large puddle of water. Vrishaketu felt his entire life staring back at him, while he swerved and swam out of the rubble, and moved towards any sign of life. By then, he had seen that Tripti had managed to grab hold of the thief and had pinned him against the rocks, punching and kicking him, while he begged for his life.

Vrishaketu leapt forward and pushed her away.

"Let me handle it from here," he said. "Why did you escape?" He asked the thief.

The thief, with fear in his eyes replied, "I thought you are assassins trying to kill me."

"Why would anyone want to kill you?"

"I did a lot of bad things in my life."

"And what do you do now?"

"I hunt and scavenge."

"Interesting," Vrishaketu said.

"Who are you? Why do you want to hurt me?"

"We want your help in finding something, that you stole a long time back," he said. "And in return, we might actually give you food and clothing which you desperately need, and of course, money."

He looked at him for some time, confused. "Really?"

"Yes," Vrishaketu said, raising his hand to help him, while Tripti simply rolled her eyes. "What's your name?"

"Jara," he began, "Jara the hunter."

21

Satyasena marched towards his death.

Or so he thought.

It was pretty uneventful to be acting like an investigator of sorts, of finding clues on where the Maharogas were. Instead, bringing the head of the killers of his grandfather would have been better. His father would have been impressed by him. He would congratulate him, probably pat him on the head, and hug him. He knew his father's heart was broken after his grandfather's death.

He did manage to find a lot of leads, and inquired, until he learnt about the last location where the Maharoga assailants were. The people he talked to were all afraid, scared like a whimpering child, relating that they saw death in the Maharogas' eyes, and their soul carried sharp blades with them, and they reeked of corpses.

Satyasena was arrogant enough to believe that they were tall tales, all wished and washed to hide the skepticism and the spiritualism that came along with him.

By the time he found out about it, the skies had gone turbulent, and a blizzard had appeared in the distance. There was wind, and mist, and the occasional rain, as his band of men of a dozen soldiers, along with him, moved for the caves, ahead.

Those were the caves where the Maharogas were last seen, but Satyasena was warned by his crew—

"This is the area of the mountain dwellers, the worshippers of darkness, the ones who live in the shadows."

He had heard about the mountain dwellers, a sect of people who never progressed technologically, lived like scavengers, and used to eating rotten stuff, probably exposed themselves to cannibalism too. They were the Pisach! And they came from those who were ostracised, who were created out of inbreeding, incest and infidelity. The mountain dwellers were fiendish, dark, and absolutely gory in approach. They were considered bandits too, for they would steal the occasional caravan, not for money or gold, but for the flesh and bones.

"Why did the Maharogas come here, to the Pisach land?" Asked another crew member. "They would be eaten alive."

"If their skin is made of from what we are made of," another chuckled and guffawed, as if it was a laughing matter. "I've heard they bleed poison, and anyone who bites into their skin dies an instant death. One should kill them from afar."

"Where did you hear all of that, lads? From your nanny's bedtime stories." Satyasena chuckled. "The mountain dwellers are idiots, they are stupid, afraid of light. Just show them the blades and the fire, they'll scamper away." He had never met them though. Only heard stories, but his tutors used to teach them about fighting all kinds of evil in this world.

"Where do they even come from? They just happen to

inhabit these mountains. Lord Karna should do something about it." One of the crew members said.

"Indeed," Satyasena responded, "we should wipe them out, remove the dirt."

"No, he doesn't do it," another said, an elderly soldier, "because he doesn't want to harm them. The Pisach as a community were a product of bad choices, and it's not their fault that their ancestors put horrible practices in place, causing their progeny to follow it. Though many eat animal flesh, the ones who do eat human flesh, if found, are put on trial and executed in the land of Anga. But they are sneaky, and we don't get to know about them much."

Satyasena didn't say much anymore. He wasn't sure of the history, as there was no one alive to talk about it.

As the winds began to grow worse, they stopped their mares inside the cave, and moved further, with their swords out.

Satyasena was having doubts. He had a hard time believing that there would be people. The fire was lit on a large log, and they moved carefully, as the caves leaked water, and the sound drip, drip, drip could be heard.

"If worse comes to worse," Satyasena whispered to his crew, "we find a place to rest, till the blizzard ends."

They all agreed in unison. They continued to move, realising it was a sophisticated cave which opened to multiple pathways and clearings. They walked ahead, only to find dry blood around the walls, around the ceilings, and on the ground.

"Your lordship, there's something you must see."

Satyasena went towards his soldier, and he looked at what he was showing, in the glare of the torch. There, he found weird paintings, made with blood, symbols depicting a story, probably.

"The Pisach, since they lack language, speak with drawings, and what I see here is nothing but a tale."

There were symbols of two men appearing, and there was a cluster of people, and then there was a fight ensuing, during which the people in that cluster were getting murdered, and the two men rejoicing over their dead bodies. Satyasena's eyes widened, as the two men's faces were coloured in white chalk, and they had snakes drawn over them. It looked like there were more drawings, but they ended up fading, or were not completed by the person who was making them. It looked like a message.

"Your lordship, here." A voice echoed.

Satyasena followed the voice, and he heard the same soldier say:

"You don't need to worry about the Pisach here, lordship," he said. "The Maharogas, they must have come here to rest, and well the Pisach, they must have attacked, and well..."

And Satyasena understood why. For, what lay in front, made chills run down his spine.

Almost dozens and dozens of corpses, all Pisach, reeking and smelling of shit and piss.

All slaughtered.

All dead.

The Maharogas had done the dirty deed, that Satyasena's father *never* could.

22

There was a time when the entire family would sit for dinner together. They would take out time, within fifteen sundowns, to come together and have a meal.

But Karna began to see that Vrishaketu had backed out, and betrayed the family, and Satyasena was idiot enough to not follow through.

And that night, it was only Shanaya and Karna.

They sat at opposite ends of each other, as food and delicacies began to arrive for them. Karna watched her, as she looked pretty, just the way she used to be before. A long time ago things were different, when they had married and he had won Anga, and handed it over to her.

And she ruled for many years, and many deaths had followed in between, and so much had gone down.

"How are you feeling now?" He asked.

"Petrified," she said.

"About?"

"That you hate me."

"I don't hate you, Shanaya."

Shanaya was looking at him with utmost disgust and there was so much going on, within her eyes that Karna was not able to figure it out.

"Do you want to tell me anything?" He asked.

"Nothing." She stared away from him, as she asked further: "Do you remember my father?"

"The one who betrayed me, of course."

"He did what he had to do to survive."

"Sure. That's what he did. You can't justify him after many years."

"I don't. I just...do you know where he is?"

Karna shook his head. "What have you been up to? There have been rumours about your infidelity."

"Oh, you came straight to the point."

"Is it my child?" Karna asked.

Shanaya spat, with venom. "You are a horrible man, you know that, asking me such nonsense."

"I have to ask, no?"

"And you ask this to your wife. I have been nothing but loyal, while you on the other hand, are stealing wives."

"Suyodhan liked her."

"And you kidnap her? You are a bloody king! You don't do all this nonsense, doesn't suit you."

Karna clenched his jaw. "I did what I had to do for my friend."

"Yeah, you do everything for him and not for your family. If you would have just given your children some time, they wouldn't have turned against you, and against us."

"Satyasena is fine. He's just an idiot."

"That's exactly what I'm talking about, Vasu! You say things like this, since childhood. You don't treat your children like that."

"I treat them, the way I was treated. Discarded, thrown

away, I still stood up. My children were free to make their choices, and that's what they did," he said. "It's not my fault their choices were shit."

"Those choices may be shit, but you need to be there for them. They are your children, and now one of them is plotting your demise and another one is probably going to make a mistake in executing that plan."

Shanaya was about to say something out of anger, her eyes were burning with frustration, but she paused, controlling herself. "I have to tell you something."

"What?"

"I am scared of having another child with you. I wonder what'll happen to him or her. I am so afraid. And I am learning things about you, things that you have hidden from me."

"You have hidden as well."

The food appeared in front of them. The tasters appeared, and took a bite from Karna's plate. Chewed it. And then nodded in approval.

"Since when have you started keeping tasters for yourself?"

"Since we have begun assassinations."

A taster came on the other side of the table and went for Shanaya's food, but she objected.

"I don't want to live in fear."

"I fear for our child. Let him taste it. You can't trust anyone in the kingdom." Karna's voice made it sound like an order.

She looked at him and then nodded slyly, before letting the taster approach the food. He chewed on it, and for a moment nothing happened, but then he began to cough, and cough...and slowly his eyes turned red, and his skin turned purple and he fell on the ground.

The servants came and instantly cleared the room, while Karna and Shanaya looked at each other in horror.

"I told you," Karna said. "There's someone out there, trying to murder you. Why? Why is it that?"

The servants were in a fluster, one said: "My lady and my lord, the food that we gave you...we mistakenly and accidentally switched. That plate was yours." He looked at Karna.

Karna arched his brows. "Who had access to my food?"

"No one, my lord. Only the cooks. And they all have been making food for you for a long time now. So we have doubts..." the servant just seemed confused and worried. "There was something though, that we had noticed. Something that was off. It didn't make sense for that particular person to come to the kitchen of the palace, but we didn't take heed, but now when you ask me in such a way, my lord, I begin to wonder."

"Who was it?"

At that moment, a familiar person entered and Karna's face lit up seeing his old friend.

"I was there in the kitchen," Suyodhan said. "It was me."

23

Vrikodara watched the kingdom of Anga from the cliff, ready to let it burn under his mighty fist.

And he laughed.

He was excited. It stood in the middle of a deserted landscape, with large forests as tall as gigantic mountains that acted as gods of this world. Vrikodara had his spyglass, ornate with the bones of a mule, as he watched with a clear, piercing gaze, a cloak of red colour hung on his back, and his feet were bare, only a loin-cloth around his waist, and a breastplate shining like gold. His beard was trimmed, cut by him with a dagger, and his hair was long. He stood tall, towering just like the mountains, and he chewed on the food in his mouth, almost grappling with a sense of excitement that the war would bring.

He turned back to look at his army, and he found them all sharpening their swords on whetstones, checking the crossbows and the arrows, wearing the necessary armour, eating food, and drinking goat milk while getting excited and feeling energetic. The red earth around him was dusty and splattered like a bloody desert. There were horses, mules, dogs and elephants, all living, and thousands of soldiers, all in their red capes.

He saw the dwarf appear, running towards him with small steps, until he asked, "Do you have time?"

"I have all the time in the world."

"What do you gaze at?"

"The world below." Vrikodara smiled. "I'm excited about the carnage that's going to unfold."

"Yeah well, the Angan army is ten times bigger than us. How do you plan to fight them?"

"We are brutal and we play by no rules. They've never met a beast like me," Vrikodara said.

"And yet I am trying to find alliances. Your brother's armies would never reach on time, and I'm hoping I can strike with some mercenaries around the villages and towns, to get us some backup," Pukkasati said with an exhausted grin.

Vrikodara flared his nostrils. "Do what you have to do, my friend, but keep in mind, I'm going to bash Karna's head."

"I never asked you why you hate him, and especially why you hate Anga. You have this undeniable reason to come here, other than the economic and political ones."

Vrikodara contemplated to say something further. "It's been a while."

"Good. Then you tell me after I tell you. I have some news for you."

"Tell me."

"Walk with me."

Vrikodara did, and followed the dwarf towards a large tent.

"I was getting piqued by the nature of the word going out against us to your brothers and I often wondered how that was happening. Who was talking. Who was the whistleblower? And I began my research. I began to pretend I was a spy too, and I happened to find the person, the culprit who had been feeding intel about us to Dharmaraja."

They entered the tent, to find the man knelt down, with his arms and legs tied up, naked, with his face burnt from every corner.

"Who is he?"

"Infantry, one of the many soldiers," Pukkasati said. "I found him delivering a letter to the messengers."

Vrikodara looked at the man, he had been beaten up brutally by Pukkasati and his men. Vrikodara felt somewhat awful about it. He had started his regiment a long time ago, handpicking these men, so they would never betray him. His regiment was called the Brute Company, and it would have the finest of warriors. They weren't conscripted from the civilian quarters. They were wrestlers, gladiators, prisoners and killers. They had pledged to the Brute Company. And they were then marked with hot iron on their skin, with the symbol of an elephant.

"You know I started this regiment primarily because I couldn't trust the tenacity and the ferociousness of our company soldiers," he said to Pukkasati. "Our crown's soldiers. They were weak. They were tired. They were fed poorly. When I started the Brute Company, I fed everyone the best of roast, the best of clothes were given to them and the best of women were supplied to them. They lived and dined like kings, primarily because they were the best of the lot, and that's why we have the highest kill streak when it comes to winning kingdoms. With a little army, we have lost less, and gained more. And when I see my own man, sold for...I don't know...it hurts me."

He looked down at the soldier, who had a cloth stuffed in his mouth, and he pulled it out. The man was sweating profusely, he gasped and immediately began to apologise.

"Why did you do it?" He asked. "What did Dharmaraja offer that I didn't? You lived in glory with me, so what was it?"

He couldn't speak, it was then that Vrikodara noticed that he had no tongue so he was just crying and whining.

"When did he lose the tongue?" Vrikodara asked Pukkasati.

"As a kid apparently, is what I learnt after talking to some people."

"Strange," Vrikodara said, "As a soldier, and an infantryman, I would never enroll a cripple or a dumb guy. Which makes me wonder, who approved his entry?"

Pukkasati shrugged. "I can investigate more."

"Send him back," he said, feeling forgiving towards the soldier who was just doing his job. "And put a letter in his hand so he could deliver it to my brother."

"What do you want to be written in it?"

Vrikodara turned to see his army ahead, and smiled. "Tell him, I am not here to win his kingdom. I'm here to bludgeon Karna's head. For revenge. For myself."

24

Vrishaketu didn't trust Jara.

But he had no choice, than to follow the thief and the marauder. Jara stank like a hundred, dead swines, and he would spit often. He hadn't bathed in what felt like years, and even the mare they had given him to ride was getting uncomfortable with him sitting on it.

"Can we trust him?" Asked Vrishaketu, whispering to Tripti.

"You tell me. You didn't let me beat him."

Vrishaketu shook his head. Wrong person to ask.

"Why do you like beating up everyone?"

"Because he deserves it. He has done a dirty deed of hiding a genocidal maniac's true evidence and your father partake in it."

"Before we come to the conclusion that my father is a horrible man, can we talk to him?"

Jara was whistling, as they moved from one clearing to another, through the thick lush greenery, they could hear the music coming from the local ravine. The sparrows fluttered and chirped, while the butterflies swung through the skies. It was the beautiful southern part of Anga, where the timber woods ended, and the different varities of trees came into being. Anga had always been a beautiful part of the country, but unfortunately, after the naval production caused the forestry to die, a large part of Anga turned arid in nature, with storms and dusty plains.

"Where are we going?"

"To the place where I hid the Mani."

"What's the story?" Vrishaketu asked.

"You don't need to know. You just need to know where the Mani is."

"I would like to know what happened."

He shook his head and spat on the floor. "I am a Nishadh, outside the boundaries from the land of the men, and into the land of the animals. I used to cut trees and hunt animals for food. I was a simple man. But then circumstances forced me to become a thief. To survive, I stole, and I kidnapped and I did everything in my power to remain outside the realm of men until the kingdom people appeared, with the sigil of a sun, and asked me for help. They said Lord Karna wanted my help, and they wanted me to steal something from Hastinapur, and it had to be done discreetly. I was talented in this art, and so I did the dirty deed. I brought what I stole here."

"But did you know what you were stealing?"

"Yes. Lord Karna knew what he wanted, and why he wanted it. The Mani is the only evidence of the Naga people, that there was a genocide of their kind by the men of the Kuru clan. Every Naga clan has a Mani that they worship, and it is indestructible, and it is unique in its own way. Each Naga clan knows about the uniqueness and where it comes from. If the men have that Mani, that means they are behind the violence—for a Naga clan and the Naga chiefs shall never surrender the Mani, as it belongs to Lord Vishnu's Shesh Naag. If that evidence is handed over to the Nagas, there will be a war, a war of all wars. Why Lord Karna stole it was something I had no idea about."

Vrishaketu though had an idea, of course. Karna wanted to use it as bait, and instead of actually handing it over, and being a decent person, he let it remain hidden in his kingdom, so he could use it as ransom. Vrishaketu wished there were at least a few moments when he could respect his father, but there were none, and he never gave those opportunities to him.

They reached the land where it was supposed to be.

"The last I knew was that the Mani was here, ahead of these tall groves. I keep coming here, to check on it, and it is well-guarded," said Jara.

Vrishaketu dismounted from the mare and moved forward, looking through the bushes, and he found a small hut, right in front. And there was a family living in it. A man, a woman and a child, as they were cooking food outside, and laughing and enjoying.

"This doesn't make sense. It's just an ordinary farmer family," Vrishaketu said.

"Well…"

But before Jara could explain, Tripti went through the bushes, and with her dagger out launched herself at the family. They got scared momentarily. Vrishaketu instantly ran after her, so she won't harm the poor kind, realising that Jara was playing some kind of a sick game.

"Where's the Mani?" Tripti asked, holding the dagger in her hand. "Give it to me."

The farmer was confused, shielding his family, horrified by what had just transpired.

She growled, "Give it to me!"

Vrishaketu pulled the dagger from her, but she fought him and pushed him on the ground. In that altercation, Vrishaketu noticed something. Another knife coming out of the farmer's hand and reaching for Tripti, as he stabbed her. Even the child jumped on Vrishaketu with a knife, ready to attack him, but he kicked him on the ground. While the wife grabbed the nearby pot and tried to hit him on the forehead. They were skilled warriors. The kid ran inside the hut and appeared with a crossbow and shot at Tripti, but Vrishaketu jumped in front and took the arrow on his own body. For some reason, he wanted to protect her, every time.

He pulled out the arrow and instantly flung it across the man, whose eye got stabbed. The woman tried to hit him again with a boiler, snarling at him, but Tripti by then had shoved the dagger inside her. The child flared his nostrils and tried to shoot the crossbow again, but by that time Jara had appeared behind him, and knocked him down with a stone.

"He's one irritating kid," he said, with a frown.

"So this was what?" Vrishaketu stood up, wounded, while Tripti who had been stabbed was bleeding from her shoulder.

"A disguise in plain sight. If they put actual guards, it looks like something is hidden in the hut. But when it's just a farmer family, it's nothing. It's just a family," Jara said. "Even I was confused when I first came here, but they were trained soldiers, even the young kid."

Vrishaketu limped inside the hut, as Jara guided them, to see the Mani. But what he witnessed inside was surprising, as he found...

Nothing.

"Is this a joke?" Tripti asked.

"Hold your horses," Jara said, and he knelt down, opening the small compartment on the floor, which looked like an underground tunnel.

They began to descend into the dark terrain and a small galley, until they saw the light at the end of the cave. Vrishaketu moved precariously, as well as Tripti who was groaning with pain, and by the end of the path, they saw what they had come for.

The Mani.

But instead of a sapphire stone that was expected, Vrishaketu saw a man, with raggedy hair, chained and bound to the wall, food kept in a corner, with a chiselled body and a scarred, injured frame. The man, looked up, and Vrishaketu saw his forehead.

It had a Mani on it.

He knew who the person was. He had seen him in the courts, a long time ago, and he had seen him in the yagnas and the regal events, and, his name came out of him like a whisper in his heart—

"Ashwatthama."

25

Satyasena rode back in the cold dusty desert, hoping that he might reach the kingdom gates at the right time.

The skies were bluer, and the desert was shrouded in darkness, sending a chilling, vibrant feeling down his spine. But he wasn't sure whether it was what he had witnessed that brought him to his knees. He couldn't believe the entire escapade with the Maharogas. How were two defiant beasts able to corrupt and maraud and destroy the livelihood of such cannibalistic inbreds. How were they able to do it? It seemed impossible, and then his crew had begun to cook up tall tales that the Maharogas might be anything but human.

Satyasena had told them to shut off, not because he had begun to agree with them, but because he was afraid. He was one of those kids who wanted the milk of the mother till he was seven years old.

He was prematurely mature, but he was a child at heart. He was a rebel too, and wanted to fight everything, but a coward when it came to actions. As he rode in the high desert, he looked up and saw a vulture circling over them. Satyasena was confused for a moment, until an arrow zapped close to his ears, and went and hit one of his mates on the head.

The soldier fell on the ground, so did the others, as more arrows came flying. Satyasena got thrown off by his horse which was shivering in fear, and he fell on the cold sand. The horses began to neigh, and Satyasena was in a frantic, confused zone, unable to comprehend what had just transpired. He saw the other soldiers, most of them dead, while some others had their shields on.

Satyasena grabbed hold of his shield too, to defend himself, waiting for more arrows to come.

"Who's it?" He shouted, but in the bluish darkness of the desert, he was unable to see the enemy.

Satyasena moved closer to the surviving crew mates, who were gasping.

"This is bad. This is really bad." One of them said.

"Calm down."

Satyasena lurched on the floor, and began to move, with his body against the sand, trying to stay away from the enemy's peripheral vision. He continued further, as his teammates followed him, whispering to him:

"The Maharogas have learnt that we saw their massacre. They want to leave no witnesses and thus want to kill us. I don't know...I am scared."

Satyasena growled under his breath, in fear and then in anger he slapped his soldier to shut him up. As they crawled further ahead, Satyasena saw a horrible sight in the distance. Majestic too, in some sense.

Standing at the edge of the desert, where the moon rose, and the land ended, there was a buffalo and on the buffalo was seated a tall man, a towering figure with a mace, resting. Alongside him were archers forming a semicircle. All with crossbows aiming at him. The buffalo man rode towards them while Satyasena stayed where he was with his soldiers.

"Protect me! Protect me, you little pigs!" He kicked one of the soldiers, who stood up with his blade to protect their prince, and the buffalo man charged towards him and hit him with his mace, knocking his head off from his body.

Satyasena saw the other soldier running away from the scene, but the crossbows got to him, and he fell dead just few yards away. Satyasena stayed on the ground, like a corpse, hoping he might not be recognised. But the buffalo man got off and walked towards him, swinging his mace.

"Little boy, show your magnificent face," he said.

Satyasena was crippled with fear, unable to move properly, but the buffalo man turned him over to see his face, then lifted him up in the air. He was small, like a dwarf in front of the giant. Satyasena looked at his face, and his regal, brutish features. He had seen the man in many chariot races, in many of the gladiatorial fights, often destroying the deadliest animals.

He knew who he was.

"Look who we have here." Vrikodara smiled, showing his broken teeth. "The suta's own son, isn't it? My luck! And I thought I was just attacking a convoy, so I could get some intel about the blueprints of the kingdom."

Satyasena tried to fight, and tried to push back, but then he gave up, as Vrikodara continued to grin continuously. "You are the normal one, aren't you? The other one services us. Services your father's enemies. What do you plan to do?"

"I shall not be disloyal to the throne."

"That's foolish of you. I'm going to decimate that throne. So you better help me out, or eat the ashes of your iron throne." He grinned.

Satyasena licked his lips, his heart pumping. He had heard stories of the great Bhima. He could crush skulls with his bare hands, break spines with just his fingers, and his gaze would be enough to put the fear of a thousand gods in anyone.

"What do you want me to do?" He asked fearfully.

"Nothing." He smiled.

But it was not nothing.

It was never nothing.

26

Karna was quite happy that his friend had come over to meet him. But he was also alarmed, wondering what he wanted that needed him to be in Anga.

After the entire scenario at the dinner, Karna brought Suyodhan out for a walk, as they strolled around the palace gardens, mulling over in silence.

"You might be wondering what's the reason behind me being in the kitchen?" He asked.

"Were you trying to poison me?" Karna said.

"Oh, I wish. You would stop to torment me then." He chuckled. "But no, it was something else. I had been hearing reports of assassination attempts on the royal family's head."

"Yes."

"And I often believed that the best way to kill someone is to poison them, so I went to do an unregulated inspection of the kitchen but found it perfectly fine. It has the right security, the right rigmarole. The cooks are passionate and loyal to you. Everything seemed tip-top."

"And yet, there was poison in the food."

He nodded. "Yes, that makes me wonder why. Even after all the inspection. That means it was done after the food had left the kitchen."

"Indeed."

"By a servant then, perhaps," he had a cane in his hand, made of gold, and a hood to cover his face. "Or perhaps a handmaiden, or the cleaners. It could be anyone."

"Are you here to play investigator?" Karna chuckled. "Because you seem quite an inquisitor."

"I worry about my friend's life, of course," he said, shaking his head.

"Even though you put my life in peril on multiple occasions?" Karna grinned.

"Yes, of course."

"Have you heard about the Maharogas?"

"Of course. Apparently, they have returned," Suyodhan said. "But then, our men had gone out to search the Naga settlements, and they act as if nothing is there."

Karna shook his head. "I feel something is brewing. I feel the Nagas are lying."

"Could be. They have always been derogatory by nature, chose violence and horrors over sanity and civil." Suyodhan growled under breath. He had a fiendish disgust towards the kind. "I still feel they are tall tales and the supposed Maharogas who were behind the killings, weren't actually Maharogas but copycats. It could also be the Nagas trying to frighten the men. You know how this scare of the Maharogas started, right?"

Karna pursed his lips and shook his head with a no.

"Well, it did because they wanted to put fear into the men. So they created the Nagas, a violent, horrible maelstrom versions of themselves, ones who would bleed poison, and who had white faces from the ashes of their victims, and pythons as their commanders. They were meant to frighten the men, and many did too," Suyodhan said. "But many saw through the facade and took over their lands, and destroyed their vegetation. It's said that the Maharogas would return when the Nagas would be relinquished from the earth's reservoir, when they would be in peril. I don't know. I doubt all of this. Seems like an old dame's story." He smiled.

"Probably. Why are you here?" He asked.

"Because I need your help."

"Bhanumati ran away?" He smirked.

Suyodhan punched him lightly on the shoulder. "No, but I am kind of done with the entire plan that was brokered. I don't want Yudhistr to be the king of Indraprastha. That land belongs to me too, and he has to give it to me. Soon, the way he is performing his Asvamedha, he will have most of the kingdoms under him, and Indraprastha would be bigger than Hastinapur in its reach and trade, and he would definitely attack me then. He wouldn't care about ethics at that time."

"Dharmaraja never lies." Karna repeated the statement that reverberated across the entire Kuru clan. Yudhistr apparently never lied, but that didn't mean he always told the truth.

"I know, but everything is already done. We can't fight them anymore. That was a part of the deal."

"Probably. But...there's a way." He smiled. "He could give it to us."

"And how would that work?"

"You know he's a gambler, his entire brotherhood is. I suggest, we bring him to the table and wager his kingdom."

"And we will wager?"

"We don't have to. We will win," Suyodhan said with an earnest certainty.

"How would that work?"

"I know someone from Gandhar, who has dices that will play along with him. But we need to bring them now, and we need to strike now."

Karna flared his nostrils, unable to understand what to say. He was at a crossroad, and they both had halted close to a fountain. "I would never say no to you, Suyodhan. But I would have to excuse myself from this plan."

He arched his brows. "Why?"

"I have too much going on here. And I would like to first work on that before I jump on to something with you."

Suyodhan clenched his jaw and nodded. "I can put one of my brothers to rule your stead, while you come with me."

"It is not the kingdom I'm afraid to lose. It is my family." Karna sighed. "I am afraid, I have not been a good husband, good father, or a good king. And I have to work on it. I might have twisted ideas of parenthood, of marriage, but I need to sort them out. But once I do, I shall surely return to you and we shall execute the plan. But if you can't wait, I would understand and you are free to do as you think is right."

Suyodhan charmingly patted him on the back. "I can't do it without you, my dear friend. Unfortunately, you are the only one who would give a shit about my ideas."

And they both laughed.

"I will wait." Suyodhan spoke earnestly. "But if there's

any help you require, anything that would be…"

"Nothing is needed. I have the biggest army in the east. I have food and I have all the entertainment one could dream of. So no, thank you. I don't need your help. Go back to Hastinapur, and wait for me."

"Remember, if you are in peril, I'll be there." He hugged his friend. "Even though you would not call me, I will come. I have my eyes on you, my dear friend."

And they remained hugging, smiling and Karna, after a long while, felt truly happy in his heart.

27

Shanaya knew she was being followed.

Between Suyodhan returning and then leaving again, Shanaya got some time to sneak out and reach for Menander, as she wanted to have an important conversation with the man himself. But by the time she managed to escape, hiding under a cowl, with her pregnant belly slightly visible, Shanaya noticed that the brown cloak-wearing followers of Ashtar were around. And wherever she turned, they were there.

Shanaya knew that Ashtar had her back against the wall. He never liked her in the first place. He had a crazed fascination towards the natives of the country, and he was xenophobic about the foreigners, which were people like her.

She moved towards the bazaar where there was a heavy traffic of people, all shouting, laughing and bargaining, and as she turned around she found the two cloaked followers moving in speed, trying to not let her be aware that she was being followed.

Was Karna behind this?

But then, how would they know she had escaped? She had sneaked out, like last time, when she tried to protect her son.

When the bazaar ended, she saw a crisscross of roads, and she turned. Held back against the wall, waiting for them to see their reaction. She peeked over, and found the followers to be casually moving away, as if they weren't following her at all. She was confused. For a moment, she thought...

No.

She was being paranoid. She wiped the sweat on her face and took a deep breath.

What have I become? She asked herself.

She went where the rendezvous point was, towards the crematorium, which was at the edge of the town. She took the local carriage and looked at the city around. There was less poverty and not as many beggars. The soldiers walked on every junction, the merchants sold their clothing or their sweets. There were factories where weapons were made. There were carriages of the nobles, and there were artist performing on the street, either singing or playing with a monkey showing people various tricks. It was a kingdom bustling with energy, had wider roads, tall houses, and an ever-growing hustle.

She reached the crematorium and carefully entered the dungeon, descending into the underground lair, where she saw Menander preparing a body for it to be sent for antyeshi.

"I want us to stop."

"And stop what?" He turned back. He was gloved, and he was busy in his process.

"Stop our plans."

"That's why you came all the way? To tell me that." He wiped his hands, after throwing away the gloves. "You must avenge your father's death. And you fear now, after one attempt on his life. If the foolish servant would have not caused a confusion, he would have died."

She clenched her jaw. Menander had put poison in his food, and it was supposed to kill him, not the taster.

Shanaya came forward and saw the corpse he was working on, and it looked vaguely familiar.

"I was surprised how a server could make such a horrendous mistake. We have to plan something else," he said.

Then she realised why the corpse looked familiar. It was, after all, the corpse of the server who had served the food wrong. She watched Menander prepare his body.

"How did he pass away? He was so young."

"Someone poisoned him," he said, showing her its stomach which had turned blue, as well as its throat. "Human life in Anga has become quite an unexpected ride. The one who was supposed to die is alive and the one who should be alive, is dead."

Shanaya had a feeling that he had a role to play in it, for some reason. And she had a very stark intuition about it, but then why would that be the case?

"I will think of something."

"Menander, we are done. I do not want to hear any more of it."

"He killed your father. He killed your only father, and he hid from you."

"Yes, and I...I want time to think. I was distracted when I allowed it for the first time, my emotions got the better of me, but I want full inspection of my father's death to happen before I come to a decision, and then too it won't be death, but imprisonment of a king, for murder," she said, sternly.

Menander had an edgy side that he had been hiding for quite some time. "Fine, your highness. You command, and I shall listen."

Shanaya nodded, swallowing a lump. As she departed from the crematorium speaking to Menander, the only thing that she could think of was—what she had done in the first place, something that was true to her character, but something she had hidden from Menander.

That it was not the server who shifted the dishes, but it was she who took the poisoned dish when it was offered to her.

She didn't want Karna to die.

She couldn't fathom the idea of the love of his life, to pass away.

28

Karna awakened to loud horns.

He was sleeping in a separate room from Shanaya after their fight, but he had been keeping a check on her through the handmaidens. But these horns were loud and crackling. He was sweating as he rushed to the door, and at the door was Commander Agastya, who took care of the royal guard, and essentially worked as Karna's right hand man.

"What is going on?"

"Your highness, you should see it yourself."

Karna sighed in anger.

"They came out of nowhere, riding through the arid side of the kingdom, and they began to attack."

Karna moved towards the top, as all the soldiers were rushing in, the horns were blaring, the drums in the city woke everyone up. Karna leapt for the terrace where more soldiers awaited him. Agastya handed the spyglass to Karna as he watched what lay ahead.

"Which flag is it?"

"That's the point sir, they have no flag. They just have the red capes."

Karna growled under his breath. "The Brute Company." He whispered to himself and looked through the spyglass, and found all the watchtowers close to the kingdom burnt down, destroyed and empty.

"It's Bhima," he said.

Commander Agastya instantly felt a tad bit worried, and creases appeared on his forehead. "Your highness, but Indraprastha cannot attack us."

"I know." Karna thought about the Mani that he had been using as ransom. "But I guess Dharmaraja is desperate."

He looked through the spyglass again and found the army, stationed a few yards away from the kingdom, setting up their tents, making sure they were working as one in a large huddle, blocking the main entrance to the kingdom.

"What should we do, your highness?"

"Prepare the elephants and the cavalry and barricade all the gates of the kingdom. Bring all women and children inside the palace, don't let anyone get harmed. We stay quiet, and we let them die in the desert." He announced.

Vrikodara couldn't look at the destruction he had caused in the watchtowers, so he ignored it and concentrated on eating the fish his vulture so dearly had brought for him. He was sitting close to his tent, kneeling, eating like an animal. All his men were happy that they were able to destroy the watchtowers with ease, catching the attention of Karna. He knew he had to wait now, for Karna to appear with his army. There was no point battling a guarded kingdom. It would be difficult to penetrate, so best to bring the person out.

In front of him, wounded and tied up was Satyasena, the younger son, who looked laughable, the way he looked and spoke. Vrikodara felt a tad bit awful for Karna, that he had produced such a weakling for a son. Vrikodara had wives, but he didn't father anyone till now, and he chose not to let his seed die with such a horrible progeny. He wanted a demigod, and he wanted someone he could work with.

"What is your plan?"

"Do you know why I want to attack your pitiful kingdom?"

"Because of our trades, our manufacturing, our resources in timber."

"Gah!" He tore apart the flesh of the fish, looking bored, "All these things matter to my brother, the Dharmaraja, but to me that's all bogus. Utter nonsense."

"Then what is it?"

"A long time ago, your father used to study with me. Now I didn't have a problem with him, but I had a problem with his company. And he was a bit of an asshole, to be honest," he said. "But you know, I am a bully and I wouldn't stand anyone being an ass, so I used to pick on him, trouble him, even hurt him. I used to have a lot of fun. Until…" he grinned. "Until one day, while eating my food, I happen to get poisoned, and I vomited, and fell ill and all the Bhisaks of the city couldn't do shit about it. I was in a lot of pain. And yet I survived, like a vulture." He gave some flesh to his friend bird. "Now, I really thought I had something horrible, because as a child, you do end up eating the occasional bad fruit, only to realise that no…it wasn't my mistake. It was your father's."

Satyasena narrowed his gaze, confused.

"To help Duryodhan, Karna had happened to find a poison from the Naga settlement close to our Gurukul, since he was so friendly with them, and Duryodhan handed the poison to me. They both worked in bloody unison. I got to know this much later."

"How?"

"Through ways and means." He chuckled. "But all I know is, he did it. He was after my life. I was embarrassed. I was retching and shitting everywhere and all the kids made fun of me. That embarrassment, and that humiliation, and that pain...oh that was somcthing. To reclaim Anga, to defeat your father, to really piss off Duryodhan by attacking his best friend, that's when I'll get a good night's sleep."

Satyasena was taken aback. "You still hold such grudges?"

"When you have lived like a king all your life, and then comes along two people who make you feel otherwise, you got to do something about it. I would have my revenge. In one way or the other."

Satyasena was quiet. He couldn't fathom what to say at that moment, and Vrikodara could see why.

"What is my role in all of this?"

Before he could answer, two soldiers appeared and one of them said, "Commander, they don't plan to exit the palace."

"Great, I'll give them a reason to."

Karna stood quietly on the terrace, while war plans had begun to take shape, meetings were going on, armies were being allocated, the livestock and ration were being checked to see if they would be enough or they would require help from their allies.

"The good part is," he told Agastya, "they are a small army and they could be easily defeated, if we just go brute against brute."

"But they are vicious, your highness. Our soldiers are freshly trained, children of farmers and merchants. This lot run by Bhima, they are…marauders, and crazy."

Karna wiped his sweat. "Hope he doesn't do anything crazy. Just hope."

And then he looked through the spyglass, only to find out what they all had been gasping about. Karna saw there was an elephant aiming for the door, and on top of the large-tusked elephant, was Bhima, laughing gloriously, he had his mace, and his vulture was flying above.

But Karna realised why he looked so full of life, for right next to the elephant's trunk, tied to the animal, crying and wailing…

Was his son.

Satyasena.

29

Vrishaketu watched Ashwatthama hog all the food, as they circled around the fire and covered themselves under the shrubs and the canopy of the tall trees.

Water trickled down from the sky, and even the wind was howling.

Vrishaketu had heard quite a bit about Ashwatthama, and knew him quite well too, although from afar. He would come with his father to Hastinapur for functions of different kinds, and Ashwatthama would be there. He was older than Vrishaketu, and was also the king of a local land that his father had won. What he had heard about him, though, was that he was a spoilt brat. He would get everything from his father, and would be considered for any role available, plus all concessions were given to him.

Vrishaketu would get jealous because he always felt marginalised. All his life, he had sought to gain acceptance from society, and this was the man who achieved everything. Which made Vrishaketu wonder—

His father had kidnapped a man and kept him within the premises of his kingdom. That was quite a crime.

"Will you tell us now?" Tripti asked, after prolonged silence.

Jara was biting his fingernails, unbothered by the shenanigans. As far as he knew, his work was complete, and he was here for the gossip.

"Tell you what?" Ashwatthama asked, raising his brows.

"We came in to get a stone, and we found a human. So I think we can start from there?" Vrishaketu asked.

"Stone." He pointed towards the forehead. "It's right there."

Vrishaketu studied the scar that he had on his forehead, and felt the cavity there, before putting a stone on it which glimmered.

"How did you happen to get that?" Tripti asked. "For the Nagas, a Mani is the most sacred thing out there. They'll kill themselves before giving it up."

Ashwatthama nodded. "I know about it. I was with them."

"Whatever do you mean?"

He finished the food. "Why should I tell you, son of Karna? You are nothing but a kidnapper's progeny. For all I know, you could be a ploy or a trick of your father to take more intel out."

"Why would he need that?" Vrishaketu asked.

"That's what he did, no? He kidnapped me using this man here." He signalled at Jara, frowning at him. "So the suspicion wouldn't fall on anyone but an independent contractor. His men asked me questions, beat me up, tortured me, to know more about the Khandava forest."

"Khandava?" Tripti raised his brows. Her mouth still covered with a scarlet muffler.

"What is now Indraprastha," Ashwatthama said, "it

used to be a lush, beautiful forest, full of games and hopes and children and women. There was a civilization that lived there peacefully."

"Why did he want to know about the Khandava?"

"To use it as a blame against the Dharmaraja, for allowing such a genocide to happen," Ashwatthama said. "He wanted to tarnish his image. Wanted to erase the word dharma from his life. But he wanted evidence and I gave him none." He sniggered.

"What's your role in all of this?"

"I was the one who was told to go there and do the dirty deed," Ashwatthama said, reminiscing. "Bring the army, burn the forest. That was the idea."

"So the Pandavas knew what they were doing?"

"They knew there was once a civilisation present, but it was so long ago that it was not a surety. But we had to act fast, so I finished the deed, only to realise there were people. So we went in, trying to save them, and I saved plenty. One of them happened to give me this Mani, to deliver it to the other settlement. I made it my job to do so out of guilt and I went to the Pandavas, and told them I would do what I was asked to. But after learning they had just massacred an entire civilisation out of desperation and lack of knowledge, they instantly tried to stop me and convince me not to do so," he said, contemplating. "They gave me gifts, food, madira, you name it. Even my father was on their side, telling me that I should not deliver this Mani to anyone, otherwise the Nagas would know what has happened. I kept quiet until I couldn't bear it any longer, and I could picture the Naga who had promised for this Mani to be given and I was ready to leave, sneak out, until the entire incident with Jara happened."

Ashwatthama growled. He instantly attacked Jara, as if the energy from the fruits and vegetables he had just consumed prompted him to do so. He began to strangle Jara, close to the fire, when Vrishaketu came and pushed him.

"I have been trying to stop fights for so long." Vrishaketu shook his head. "Calm down, both of you. This is enough. We are all on the same side."

Ashwatthama sighed. "My mission has failed. And I have been used as a toy by two kingdoms."

"I have been tasked to deliver you back to Dharmaraja," Vrishaketu said. "I will convince him personally that your odyssey must be completed, but please, you need to come with us."

Ashwatthama looked at Vrishaketu. "You are a pawn, playing a master's game. We all are. The only game master is out there, and we dance to his flute."

And instead of fighting further, he skid and ran towards the other side.

Vrishaketu roared and ran after him, while Tripti was racing too, leaving Jara behind, holding a rope in her hand that she got from her rucksack, and lassoed it around Ashwatthama's feet, pulling him and throwing him on the ground. She hogtied him, while he grumbled and howled.

"I feel bad," Vrishaketu said to Tripti, who was gagging him. "From one prison to another. He just wants to do the right thing."

"He can, once we deliver him to Dharmaraja. Once we enter those gates of the city of elephants, and he's our key to any door opening."

Ashwatthama's mouth was gagged by a cloth, but Vrishaketu took it out, and spat: "You have no idea what you are doing."

But before he could say anything else, Tripti shut him up.

"Let's go," she said.

Vrishaketu looked at him being dragged by a girl, he was almost double her size but she easily pulled him away. By the time they reached, Jara had departed, and was nowhere to be seen.

And of course, their food had been stolen, along with their clothes.

"It's true what they say," Vrishaketu said. "You friend a thief, you get thieved."

30

Karna got himself prepared.

His squire appeared, putting on the golden breastplate on him, the kundalams that he was born with already adorned him, his crown was placed on his head, a red dhoti was wrapped around his waist, with a large girdle that had the symbol of Surya—the sun. His gauntlets were put on, and he felt his hands tighten, his boots were tightened and fastened over his feet, while kohl was put around his ears.

He was being prepared to go out for all glory, and as he did, he saw a familiar figure enter the tent that was set up in front of the palaces.

Of his wife.

She was weeping, a complete wreck. Karna rolled his eyes. That was the last thing he wanted, before he would go on the field and fight against the horrible Bhima.

"What is your plan?" She asked, her eyes were red.

"Take care of the women of the city."

"Don't act like that. I want to know your plan. I was a queen for a long time, now don't treat me like one of the wenches of the city."

Karna grabbed hold of his dhanush and his quiver that

he slung on the back. "Stop being hysterical, Shanaya. I will bring back our son."

"I have my doubts. You have been disappointed in him for a long time."

He flared his nostrils. That's the last thing he wanted to hear. "Fine, I won't. Let him rot. He's useless anyway."

Immediately she flung at him, using her nails as a weapon, scratching his cheeks, making him bleed. He grabbed her by the arm and threw her down.

"Enough, woman! You have gone mad!" He wiped the blood off his face and realised she had scarred him.

"You don't let my son die. You have killed one! You don't let another die."

"I didn't do anything with the other. It was his choice to go against us."

"You let the villains of the other kingdoms corrupt his mind. If only you were there, not perpetually absent, he would have respected and honoured you."

Karna squared his jaw and nodded. "You have become a faint mirage of a woman I used to love, Shanaya."

And her face contorted into a scream. He left her inside, the screams grew louder, and she cursed: "YOU WILL BE DAMNED! YOU WILL BE DAMNED!"

Karna pursed his lips and ignored everyone, as he walked across the tents. He moved for the chariot, where Commander Agastya was waiting.

"Your highness, you are going alone?"

"Yes. He's alone too. I can fight him."

Agastya looked more aghast than impressed. "Off you go then, your highness. Off you go."

Karna took hold of the reins, and moved for the

battlefield, passing through the trenches, and onto to the arid fields, where he saw the elephant, and the man on top waiting for him. The three-horsed chariot maneuvered and swung across the desert, until it reached the destination. He hadn't brought his weapon out.

He saw his son, tied up with the trunk of the elephant, and his lips were chapped and he had gone unconscious, as the hot winds slapped his cheeks. He was bruised badly, tortured. And on top of it was Bhima, grinning at him.

"Finally, you have come. I like that the plan worked."

"That is playing dirty," Karna said. "Why did you involve my son?" He shouted, holding the bow in his hand.

"Is that your son?" Bhima looked over mechanically. "I was not aware. Oops!"

Karna wiped his face. "Let him go and deal with me directly."

"I don't think so." He chuckled. "I won't leave him at all. In fact, now that I'm seeing you, you look a tad bit worried. You have lines under your eyes. You seem exhausted. Last time I saw you, well, it was at the swayamvar, isn't it? Where you went to take Draupadi's hand and failed when she openly declared she won't marry a suta. Funny, no?"

Karna remembered it very well, but he didn't wish to recall those memories. Draupadi was the love of his life, but she broke his heart, not once, but many times over.

"Hasn't the Dharmaraja told you, you cannot attack us? We have a deal with him," Karna said.

"I know." He nodded. "That is why he said—'If you go out to attack him, make sure you bring back his head.' And that I shall."

Karna sniggered. Fool. *He doesn't know what I have.* That's why he was the brawn of the bunch. But it was surprising for Yudhistr to make such a clumsy move.

And yet, the deal was closed. And now he could use it to his advantage. And what wrath would befall him, only Yudhistr would know. Clumsy, stupid move.

But for now, Karna had to focus on his son. The one he had to save.

"How do we do this? One on one duel."

"Pfft!" Bhima shook his head. "Take your son, if you want. I mean he has to help himself but. At sundown tomorrow, I will let him go on my terms."

"Why are you doing this? Why these games? Just attack us and be done with it."

"No, no, that'll be too simple." Bhima retorted. "I want this to be fun. This is the one kingdom I'll love stabbing my flag into, and hopefully in your heart too."

Karna didn't say anything. "See you tomorrow."

And then he turned his chariot and moved back to reach his settlement, where the trenches opened, the cavalry welcomed him, and he dismounted in the clearing. All the soldiers, helpers, porters and servants were watching him, as he appeared close to Agastya, who bowed at his presence again.

"Your highness, any update?"

"Prepare a small party and leave for the forest behind, search for the Mani, and bring him to me," Karna said, as he turned and looked at the elephant and the man atop leaving. "If he wants to play dirty, *so will I.*"

31

Shanaya had been hysterical for quite some time, and she had become worse by the time Menander had appeared and told her everything that had been happening back in the kingdom.

Grabbing hold of her mare, and her guards and her handmaidens, she made her way outside the palatial gates, where a nice lake was situated. Menander followed her diligently, moving through the barracks. Shanaya couldn't help but wonder what had happened to Karna, and seethed with rage. She didn't want to feel this way, but it was all pent-up anger. She was afraid Satyasena would die by the hands of Bhima, because she had heard stories of him. She had never met the vicious giant, but she knew that he and Karna were never on good terms, and that would lead to more problems between them. Satyasena would be a dead man in the crossfire, and Shanaya knew that Karna had to choose his son before his kingdom.

But she had high doubts about that.

She reached the city, close to the lake she saw almost hundred women, all naked, self-flagellating with whips in their hands, turning their own bodies red and bloody. They wept, since they were being forced to do so. There were followers of the Council checking up on them, their crossbows ready, while the women hurt themselves.

"Ashtar had brought down all the women from the lower strata of the society and made them strip and flog themselves," Menander said, from the corner of his mouth. "It is considered an art of redemption in the eyes of Lord Surya, according to him, since we have offended him and thus the bloody war has come upon us. If the women beat themselves till they are exhausted and dead, the war will dissipate. This is the kind of twisted logic, your highness, Lord Karna supports."

Shanaya didn't speak anything against her husband, as she ordered her men to go and cover all the women with blankets. As they followed her order, the council followers appeared, and soon a riot broke out with all of them fighting each other. In the commotion, the women managed to escape—having covered themselves up, some throwing themselves in the water to soothe the burns on their body, while some fled.

Shanaya was on her mare, looking from the top, watching the scene unfurling. She couldn't believe that the city was burning from the outside and from within with so much rage. There was internal strife as well as outside enemy. They were cornered from everywhere.

"Tell me something," she said. "Did Karna know about this?"

Menander shrugged, "I'm sure the king knows whatever goes on in his constituency."

Shanaya clenched his jaw. His ability as a king had begun to waver the trust that she had in him. Not only was he not a good father or a husband, he wasn't a good king too. The riot soon stopped as the followers gave up, being no match for the trained guards and began to disperse. Luckily, not a lot of blood had been shed, except a few broken noses here and there.

"Your highness, if I may speak?"

"You may."

"I have a solution to your problem."

"And how do you know what my problem is?"

"You want your husband to listen, isn't it? He does everything behind your back, and I know your trust falters in him," he said smoothly. "I would suggest you to get hold of his finances and grab him by the gold."

"How do you intend to do that?"

"Siege of the treasury," he said, with a simple smile. "We take over the money that funds the war. The king would have to then reason with you and us, and we can demand anything, such as—him focusing on your son instead of his ego, isn't it? To win the war, he would have to save Satyasena."

"He would do it regardless."

"Do you think so? Have you forgotten, my lady, it was he who directed Vrishaketu's execution by your hands while he dilly-dallied across with his friend?" He asked. "He thought about his allies more than about his family. He killed his father-in-law. He ordered the death of his son. And now, for all we know, him sending Satyasena on a wild goose chase to find the Maharogas was a part of a ploy to get him caught by the enemies. He must have heard that Bhima was coming, and he did the needful."

"Why would he do that?"

"Because he's a vicious man, a ruthless adversary to

our kind." Menander shook his head. "Anyhow, whatever decision you make, remember, one has to have leverage."

"How do you intend to do it?"

"Your father had friends and I know a group who can help us. They enter quietly tonight and control the treasury for you. All we need is a way to enter the gates of the kingdom, and I know the front gates are guarded with all the shenanigans, so we need one at the back. And you have the keys of the soldier's entryway."

As a queen, she did have the keys, it was kept in her study, untouched, in safety.

"I don't know if it's such a good idea."

"Do we have a choice? Your son's life is in peril. After the death of Adhirath, your husband has indeed gone mad. Listening to fools like the Council of Surya, to carry out such absurd nonsense." Menander sighed. "At the end, it's your choice, my lady."

Shanaya took a deep breath, and her entire life with Karna flashed in front of her eyes. She had begun to see her husband in a different light. Of course, he wasn't the same person that he used to be, but was he really the monster that he was being portrayed as?

Probably not.

But his mind had gone astray. And he had to be curbed. Even if it meant his wife had to do it for him.

"I'll get you the key," she said. "Do it."

32

Satyasena was stripped naked, to be freed on Bhima's terms.

He felt violated, as cold water was thrown at him, and he was confused, unable to comprehend what was happening to him. He felt dishonoured and broken, left in a hapless state, while his naked body was witnessed by the entire army of Bhima, who laughed at him and ridiculed him. He had scars on his body from the injuries he had endured in the past.

He was made to wear a loin-cloth and an iron mask which had grills in front and worked as a helmet. He kept asking what was going to happen to him.

The sun had already set, and the time had come for him to be taken. A blade was shoved in his hand, a feeble sword merely, almost as if they wanted him to lose to whatever he was about to fight.

While the soldiers dressed him up for the part, it was a dwarf who had entered the scene, to escort him. While in the middle of the plains Bhima waited, on a throne that had been placed for him. On the other side, he could see his father's army, waiting for the poor lad.

He was pulled by the dwarf, who sat on a small mare.

"You must wonder what I am doing here," the dwarf said. "It is after all, a Brute company and I am anything but a brute, no? You must be surprised."

"Shut up, inbred."

"You know, it's laughable that even though I hold the chains of your freedom, you abuse me."

"Dwarves are inbreds, no?"

"And you are a mixed breed too. Son of a Greek woman and a Bharatvarshi man," the dwarf said. "You know, all my life I have been ridiculed for being a disappointment. I was born an orphan, or so I was told. I believe my parents left me on the streets because they saw something was off about my size. At least, that's what the world makes me believe. But I was of a humorous kind. My tricks with words brought me in front of the local king, who was very happy with my demeanour and the way I spoke. I made the king laugh whenever he would be in a glum mood. I almost became like his wife, for I was the only one who could make him laugh. It was pitiful really. But it gave me a lavish lifestyle. He gave me the quarters, the best of women, and the best of food to eat. For a degenerate, I was quite a lucky lad. Until, it reached to a point that my jokes and my humour began to die, for I was inebriated most of the time, and out of anger and galore, I made jokes about the kingdom and the king. I was exhausted of making others happy. When would *I* be happy? Being a trickster, is quite a giving job you know."

Satyasena carefully listened, as the dwarf spoke with such wisdom. He had never thought that his own journey would be so similar to an inbred's.

"I have heard dwarves are born if the woman has bad karma," Satyasena said.

"Probably. I never knew my mother. And you know what happened after that? The king grew tired of me joking about him. He planned to execute me after the last joke, but I got to know of it so I never finished the joke, and he was left in suspense. The joke continued to haunt him..."

And they continued their walk, reaching close to the arena where Satyasena would be handed off.

"Until he asked. I would let you live, he said, but in return you need to finish the joke." The dwarf smiled. "I knew he won't let me live, but you see, I was buying time. Because while all of this happened, I was able to ally with the local king's enemy and I said, "I would tell you the joke under a peepul tree. He went there, little knowing that his enemies waited for him at the peepul tree and he was murdered in plain sight. The enemy offered me a job in his company, said I was quite a brain and he needed minds like mine. He had too many brutes already. That enemy was none other than the great Bhima, and I owe him my life."

"What...what..." Satyasena was thirsty, exasperated. "What was the joke?"

"I don't know," the dwarf said. "I didn't know the ending either."

"So what was the point of the story?"

The inbred chuckled. "The point of the story is, you can really kill a man with suspense. So remember those words, lad, you might require this advice, if you survive that is."

He was pushed into the arena, his chains taken off, and he was in the centre, when he saw the luscious eyes of Bhima, who was directing him to go in the middle.

"Off you go, off you go. Nothing is going to happen."

But Satyasena had his doubts. He had a feeble sword, and he moved towards his father, who waited, and was worried.

"Off you go, faster, faster."

Satyasena tried to move slowly, seeing through his peripheral vision, gazing at anything that moved around him, but it was an empty desert. After a moment of strolling he noticed that nothing happened. He began to run as quickly as he could, until Bhima whistled loudly.

The whistle made a large vulture appear out of nowhere from the darkness, and claw at Satyasena's shoulder, scratching his skin. He fell hard on the ground, and whipped his sword to defend himself, but the vulture flew away.

Another whistle could be heard, and the vulture dived again, and this time it clawed his hair, making his face bleed.

Satyasena whimpered as he ran towards his father, and threw himself on the ground, curled up like an infant.

Satyasena heard a fit of laughter coming from behind him, he knew it was Bhima who was clapping and chuckling at the sight of what was happening.

"A coward's son, is of course, going to be a coward!" He yelled loudly, humiliating everyone, even the guards and soldiers who saw the prince of Anga feeling frightened of a vulture.

A bird.

Satyasena sighed, realising what had just happened, and he looked up at his father, and looked into his father's eyes.

They were stern, cold and hard.
But most of all…
They were disappointed.

33

Vrishaketu had a long journey ahead, and it had already been an arduous one.

He wasn't sure what he should do, and what he should not. He was going with the flow, appeasing the lords of Hastinapur, unsure whether they would be appeased or more so, whether they are worth impressing even.

He rode on his stallion, with Tripti sitting behind, while Ashwatthama was near the tail of the horse, tied up and gagged, so he won't spew any more nonsense.

Tripti was quiet as usual, and they had had no food, or new clothes to change, and they had to take rest somewhere soon. He shouldn't have saved Jara, now that he thought about it, and Vrishaketu could only wonder, what more would lie in Jara's life further, as a hunter and a thief.

The only thing that helped him ride through the forest and enter the misty areas, towards the outskirts of Anga, moving day and night, were the words of Guru Keshava, who had helped him when he was young. While he was dissuaded and disappointed by everyone, hurtled in a corner for his skin colour, Guru Keshava had told him: "In life, you shall be hurt and broken, but always remember, choose what's right, and what you feel is right."

"How do I know what is right?"

"We all know." The man smiled, and he had the sweetest, most comforting one. "We just choose not to pursue it."

Vrishaketu thought about all the knowledge he had received from Guru Keshava and how it had shaped him, to choose the side of Dharma, which according to him his father didn't follow. His father followed his emotions, not practicality of situations. He went by his friend's suggestions when he should go towards what's right. Vrishaketu, thus, had begun to have issues with him.

But there was one incident that had really shaken him up, and he had begun to hate his father since then.

He could hear Tripti, talking in her sleep behind him, almost whispering.

"Maa...paa...no...*no*." There was fear in her voice, which was indistinguishable.

Vrishaketu stopped, he was feeling sleepy too nearly losing control of the stallion, letting Ashwatthama roll over to the ground. He had been snoring as well, and as soon as he fell, he began to yell and scowl.

"Okay, calm down." Vrishaketu dismounted, while Tripti was still asleep on the stallion. "Sorry, my eye caught the wind and I was well..."

But Ashwatthama came on his feet, and instantly made a run.

"There's no point. Your arms are tied. You cannot run fast."

But he continued to run. Vrishaketu woke Tripti up, who shook herself instantly.

"What happened?"

"You were talking in your sleep."

She ignored him. "Where's Ashwatthama?"

"He ran."

"And you are staring at me," she said, as she leapt from the horse, and rushed towards the direction that Vrishaketu pointed towards.

The stallion followed, as they made their way to Ashwatthama, only to exit the forest and finding themselves in front of a large bridge that connected two parts of the land. The bridge was made of bamboo, and underneath it was a large water base, and rocks, one would probably die if one fell. They saw Ashwatthama had no qualms about running over the wobbly bridge.

But suddenly he stopped.

Even Vrishaketu and Tripti stopped, as they saw that on the opposite side of the bridge a small party of soldiers had appeared.

And they looked quite familiar.

"Agastya," Vrishaketu said in a frustrated tone.

"Who's he?" Tripti said.

"Father's commander. He's the son my father always wanted to have, but he got me instead. A traitor and a degenerate."

She looked at him blankly. "Do you care about him?"

"I want to kill him. He used to trouble me as a kid."

"Good. We are on the same page then."

But why was he here?

Ashwatthama was stuck in the middle, as Agastya glanced over to the other side and began to laugh.

"So it was you, who caused all the mayhem? The kid

told me, who you happen to knock around like a coward." Agastya pulled out his sword. "I should have had an inkling that you had a role to play in it. Ashwatthama is ours and so are you. You are wanted in the state of Anga."

Agastya came forward with two of his soldiers, and instantly the bridge began to shake. Ashwatthama squeaked: "For the love of a thousand gods, please do not step on it. Otherwise, I will die."

Agastya stepped on it still, carefully, first with one foot. Ashwatthama was getting afraid.

"You go," Tripti said. "I have the rope if something goes wrong."

Vrishaketu nodded. "I have a feeling if you had to choose between saving me and Ashwatthama, you will save him."

Tripti looked at him indignantly as if there was some truth in what he had spoken.

He moved forward with his sword in hand. They both did, and the bridge went topsy-turvy. But Ashwatthama tried to regain control.

"What's the point of fighting over me? I have no worth. Let me be and my father will teach you how to wield the Brahmastra." He tried to barter and negotiate, but Vrishaketu, along with Agastya, didn't care a hoot.

As Vrishaketu neared, he grabbed hold of Ashwatthama, but by then Agastya had appeared, and he swung the sword across which Ashwatthama dodged, kneeling, and Vrishaketu deflected. He jumped over Ashwatthama and pushed Agastya on the ground, while Ashwatthama found some leeway to run, and he ran towards Tripti's direction, but the bridge turned wobblier as a result.

And it twisted.

The bridged went upside down, and soon they were all hanging from it, somehow grabbing hold of the half loose bridge.

Ashwatthama, since his hands were tired, was holding the rope of the bridge with his teeth, and he was really struggling.

In that hanging state, Agastya attacked Vrishaketu with his sword, and they both sparred, and kicked and punched, while the water underneath them rollicked and rolled. Until Vrishaketu did the unthinkable.

He kicked Agastya in the groin. The hand that had been holding the bridge came loose and Agastya had nothing to grab on to, as he fell deep into the water, cursing and screaming.

Meanwhile, Tripti had been trying to keep the bridge steady by twisting it ahead, and bringing them on the top again. But seeing their commander die a horrible death, the soldiers began to slash at the bridge.

And it broke apart from one end, making the bridge fly through the middle of the skies, and they all screamed, and held on to their lives on the bridge, falling flat against the rocky walls which was close to Tripti's side.

She pulled down the rope, so they could catch it.

It fell towards Vrishaketu, and he grabbed Ashwatthama too and pulled him up. When they reached the top, Vrishaketu looked at the skies, exasperated.

"Why do you need to make it so difficult for me?" He asked Ashwatthama. "Just let us take you."

"You idiot! If you take me…" Ashwatthama began, but at that very moment Tripti kicked him on the face, knocking him out.

Vrishaketu looked at his saviour, with her scarf around her face, as she asked him to stand up.

"He was trying to say something," he said.

"All lies, as you know," she said. "Ignore him, we have a long journey ahead, and there's a town close by, which is an alternate route to the city of elephants."

Vrishaketu, confused, lay there in a dream-like state. But he decided to not think too much. Though, Guru Keshava's voice rang in his ears:

"*Never trust the one who speaks less. They have a lot more to hide.*"

34

Karna watched his son, Satyasena, with a look of disdain, as he lay on the bed. Exhausted.

"I am sorry, father," he said. "I was…erm…I was scared."

Karna didn't say anything. He was quiet. He listened intently though, just watching his son.

"He wanted to humiliate you, and what better than to make the prince of the kingdom feel ashamed in front of his troops." Satyasena kept speaking, and got no response from his father. "I want to gut him. I want to kill the fat man and his dwarf. I want to murder him, sever his head, and do unimaginable things."

He paused. Looked at his father. No response.

"I went to see the Maharogas, by the way. They had killed the entire Pisach community that resided here. Dozens and dozens of them," Satyasena said. "They are quite powerful. Probably they were attacked by the Pisach and they retorted. But if two Maharoga assassins could cause such humongous damage, I wonder what the entire community is capable of?"

Karna sat next to his son, and spoke, after a prolonged silence, "There was a time, though, that I believed you could really take over the throne. You had the skillset, son. You were energetic. You were out there. You made mistakes. But somewhere along the way, you were burdened by the state, by the people around you and you began making stupid decisions. I don't know when that happened. I wasn't there to witness your downfall. Probably your mother was behind it. To turn you into a weakling, because as long as I was here, you were strong. The Greek blood in you, has indeed made you weak."

Satyasena was confused; albeit horrified by these words. "Father, give me another chance and I shall do what you expect of me."

"You do nothing," Karna said. "Because you can't do anything. And I don't expect anymore or anything out of you. Go back to the kingdom and serve the palace and its ministers. I don't see a warrior in you anymore."

Karna came on his feet, and began to exit the tent, when Satyasena cried out in frustration: "How are you so sure about it?" He snarled.

Karna didn't say anything. He let silence prevail. He began to move towards his tent, as they prepared for the next form of attack that Bhima had planned for him. His commander hadn't returned until then, and there was no update even. It terrified him a bit. He moved to the royal tent, where his war room had been set up, and he found none other than Ashtar waiting for him.

"Why is the man of religion here?" He asked.

"Your wife is creating a ruckus in the kingdom, your highness," Ashtar said, with disdain. "She has to be controlled. I was trying to help the state, in appeasing Surya, but she stopped the procession, which led to bloodshed."

Karna sighed. Exasperated, he fell on his chair, where in front the table were kept maps and blueprints of the war, board pieces which acted as makeshift enemy figurines. "I don't know what to do."

"Lord Surya guided you in your trance."

"I am not sure about that. I cannot murder my wife with my hands."

"Then let someone else do it." He snided.

Karna grabbed hold of Ashtar and pushed him against the tent walls. "You never speak about murdering my wife, you hear me!"

"You hurt the man of Surya, your highness. Surya..." he spoke breathlessly. "He proclaims you as the son of his...his cion, and you treat him like that."

Karna released him, and immediately began to regret his anger. "I have no idea what to do."

"What bothers you?"

"My son." And he began to narrate whatever had transpired.

As Ashtar listened, he began to create his own theories in his mind and he spoke, "Lord Surya tests you. He tests you mighty. Your son has potential."

"But not as much as I do."

"Probably, but he can be far more than you could ever imagine."

"Is there a way to reach that potential?" Karna said. "I might not outlive this war, and I know Satyasena seems appropriate to take over, but I'm afraid, the lifelong dream of fighting for Anga, for my mother, would all be washed away by the ignorance of Satyasena."

"When do you think he achieved such mediocrity?" Ashtar asked. "What was the trigger?"

"When he was young, he had suffered from tuberculosis and ever since then, his mind has gotten rotten," Karna said. "He has become more docile in his approach. Vrishaketu has more courage, more brains, but he was a traitor. He stabbed me on my back when he went against my allies, and went against Anga. And nothing is worse than that."

"I understand," Ashtar said. "Your highness, I totally get your pain. You are in peril. You are confused. Lord Surya sees your pain, and that is why he has sent me to you. When you saved me from the foreigners, you had given me a new life, and for that I will always be grateful. I have a ritual, that can safeguard Satyasena and give him the strength you desire. He will do what you expect him to do but that ritual demands pain. Do you think he's capable of handling it?"

Karna looked at Ashtar, and there was definitely hope in his eyes. "Even if he's not capable of that pain, Guru Ashtar," Karna said, "I will *make sure* he is."

35

She was practicing the art of being a traitor against her crown, against her husband.

Shanaya and Menander, walked in silence, as he comforted her, and spoke to her in a low, hushed tone.

"It's going to be all right," Menander said.

He looked mighty different today. He was wearing a tunic, and long, baggy pants with boots, and a scarf tied around his neck.

They were in the underground sewers of the kingdom, Shanaya knew there was a way out from there. Once upon a time it was meant to smuggle prisoners, but now was used as a way to exit the kingdom. To open it, of course, one had to have key to the two doors. One to enter the sewers, and one to exit it. The sewers hadn't been used for quite a while, and it was left barren and empty.

"This is an interesting outlet."

"You do what I say, all right?" She added. "I do not want anything going out of hand, and if I see that happening, I will pull out of the plan."

"Of course, your highness. They are your father's people," Menander said. "They respect you more than they respect me or anyone else."

"So brief me about the plan then."

"We enter the city and we take control of the entire treasury. Lord Karna will come to sort it out, and you have the keys to the entire plan, so he has to negotiate with you. And then you display your terms," he said, repeating whatever she had said.

"Yes, and no one else would know. You are discreet. You are quick. I don't want the entire city to hate me."

"Of course."

"I will lay down the negotiation terms, and I will offer myself to Karna. No middle person."

"Of course, my lady."

She opened the gate to the sewers, and there was a large drippy tunnel right in front, where a huge light was shining as a beacon. They waited in silence.

"You know, I am sure you don't know, he had sent me here to take care of you," Menander said.

"Take care of me?"

"Yes. He felt you would be in danger of some kind. He doesn't trust the Bharatvarshi, for obvious reasons." He smiled gleefully. "He thought they will dampen your spirits, stab you in the spine and be done with you."

She scoffed. "He underestimated me. He was always like that. Underestimating his daughters. You know why he wanted me to get married to Karna? It was, after all, for the throne. When he saw there was resistance, and that I was happy, he kind of let go."

"Why did he want Anga for himself?"

"We had ships, so many of them. We even do now. He wanted to use them to attack his opponents back in his native land," she said. "There were those who exiled him for his actions. He was ruthless, after all, and he was exiled by the councilmen, and he was about to be imprisoned before he got fired. So he wanted to use the chance to take the ships and be done with it. But he found no support from Karna, and he let it be. He also thought his daughter is no more his daughter, which was quite a surprise. He replied to my letters. That was nice of him, to let bygones be bygones."

Menander nodded and bowed a little. "Your highness, I'm at your service."

"How did you find these men of my father?"

"They reached out to me," Menander said.

She didn't trust Menander completely. He had been acting funny. And he had been acting all nice, but at the same time he was manipulative. There was obviously a sinister reason behind his words. But she was confused, and she was at her wit's end, not sure who to trust anymore.

They both saw a dozen soldiers appearing, in their raggedy outfit wearing animal furs, and cloaks, and hoods. They had no symbol, no sigil, nothing. They were bulky, and all large in their frames. The moment, she saw them, she was shocked by their apparel, and by their way they wore their ornaments.

"I have never seen these men with my father," she said.

"We are new," one of the hooded Greek soldier said. "Let us through."

Shanaya was a little confused, and then she allowed. They began to move, when the hooded Greek soldier turned around and with a quick movement of his sword slid the blade across the sky and tore apart the chest of

Menander. He screamed and fell on the ground. The other man closed the sewer gates, and pushed Shanaya towards the back, so she was on the other side, while Menander's body contorted in pain, and cried in horror.

"What...is...what is going on?" She asked, exasperated, as she went towards Menander, who she couldn't trust but had then surprisingly become a victim himself. "Who are you people?"

"Oh, we are bandits," the hooded man said. "And we just wanted a way inside the kingdom. And now that we have it, we know what we must do."

"To steal?"

"To do more," the hooded man said, as he pulled back the hood, and a chill ran down Shanaya's spine.

"Father!"

And she saw the older, murkier version of Captain Archimedes.

36

There are some moments in a man's life when he decides he would live through carnage, even if it is to achieve a moment of true happiness.

And that was the day for Vrikodara that day.

The battle had begun, and his men had gone forward to deal with the skirmishes, while he geared up for the war. He wore his helmet, and put on his breastplate that had the symbol of a skull, plus he had his huge mace with no gauntlets supporting his arm. He had no knee pads, or any girdle that would hold his dhoti. He was naked in the war, just like he would be walking as a stray man. He came upon his chariot, and held the reins of the horses by himself, not letting a charioteer control his vehicle.

By the time he was about to launch himself after passing the barricades, he found Pukkasati approaching him, with his small sword hanging on a side, dangling from his girdle.

"Lord Vrikodara, we might have an issue."

"What would that be?" Vrikodara asked, focused on the war.

"Anga has a much bigger army than us."

"So be it, I don't care." The brute responded.

"You should. Our people are dying, and we need a supplementary army."

"They are dying because I haven't entered."

"And that is fine, and that is mighty of you, of how graciously powerful you are, but we need to be strategic too."

Vrikodara grimaced. He hated these conversations. "What do you suggest?"

"We have identified a local Rakshas colony, a few miles away. I would suggest, we parlay with them, and get them to come on our side and become our mercenaries. Having the Rakshasas with us, we will have a far greater chance of winning the war."

"Rakshasas? They are not reliable." He growled, under his breath, talking about the warrior race of people who worshipped Lord Shiva but had their own rules and ways of living. They were those who absconded from the city life and lived a life in the forest, worked for the forest, and followed the warrior mentality of Lord Raavan—their ancestor. "I don't think we should do any kind of business with them."

But there was indeed a reason of following through with him for Vrikodara. He had a past that he didn't want to explore with the Rakshasas.

"I have heard the settlement has thousands of warriors that we could use," Pukkasati said. "We just have to convince them."

Vrikodara shook his head. "I know how they are, and I don't believe them. So let it be."

And having said that, his chariot broke past the barricades, leaving the dwarf behind, entering a battle under the hot sun and the red skies—bodies were being mangled, human parts were dispersing in awkward directions. There was bloodshed and horror of every kind. But in that carnage, Vrikodara thrived.

He opened the flaps of his wheels of his chariot which released large incisive blades from each side.

And he began to attack them. They stabbed, and pulsated and torched and did all kinds of damage to the opposite army. When Vrikodara leapt from his chariot, with a mace in his hand and smacked the ground, the men of the opposite side fell down.

As more soldiers appeared, he began to smack and destroy and plummet them. He shoved and pushed and got them to their knees, and he laughed, as the blood of his enemies sprayed all over his face, a laugh so maniacal that one would consider him as a madman of some kind.

The moment he found refuge in all the blood, he saw a large ball of fire appearing out of nowhere from the sky, the moment his eyes saw that fire they immediately shrivelled.

He turned back, and the ball of fire crashed close to them, as he instantly ran away from it feeling his heart sink.

A soldier appeared and tried to stab him, but Vrikodara grabbed him by the throat, lifted him up, kicked him in the shin, and tossed him away. Then another one appeared, but he smacked him with his mace causing him to bleed profusely. And another appeared, as he battered the man's head with his mace till it was nothing but pulp.

While all of this was great, he saw another ball of fire, being shot by catapults, and then they started coming in quick succession. He found them hitting the ground around him lighting up the whole place.

Vrikodara shied away, until a ball of fire hit him on the back, rolling over him and burning him from top to bottom. He felt a pang of horror and his body became numb.

He used his remaining energy to whistle at the horses and bring his chariot, and quickly sat on it to return to the mainland where they were stationed earlier. In fact, all the soldiers, began to retreat too, after a succession of catapulted Greek fire had begun to haunt them. He took a deep breath, trying to come back to his senses, as he was burnt in patches, and his arm was covered in blood.

He lay there, yelling loudly, feeling betrayed by the gods of war who seemed to have turned their backs on him.

Pukkasati appeared out of nowhere, and he ordered the servants to pull Vrikodara up, until he was dragged and put in the medics tent.

"What happened out there?"

"The fire…the fire…" his heart was still burning and his mouth was grim. "They are using the catapults."

"Then we use them too."

"Retreat for now."

"All right, not an issue." And Pukkasati commanded one of his guards to pull back.

A battle ranges for months and even years, these skirmishes last until one party gives up and raises the white flag. And he had never expected, that during the first conflict itself he would give up.

"What do you want to do now?"

"We attack tomorrow."

"And we lose more."

Vrikodara looked at his strategist and gritted his teeth in frustration. "Fine, get in touch with the Rakshas colony."

"Good, thank you. I thought you would be more stubborn, and it'll take longer."

"You always get your way, so what's the point of stubbornness?"

"Good. You get it." He smiled. "There's just one caveat to the entire Rakshas discussion."

He grunted. "What now?"

"Oh, it's erm…nothing, it's led by your pregnant wife," he said. "Hidambi."

37

Vrishaketu had always craved for a family.

And he never got it.

But that same longing, that similar sense of loss, was also pertinent in Tripti's life. She had abandonment issues. They had entered the town, which was close to the city of elephants, and had gotten themselves some fresh clothes and food. They took turns to bathe and got ready to set off for their journey towards Hastinapur.

They didn't speak much except for the occasional grunts and rants of Ashwatthama, who was always cribbing, crying and trying to say something.

They halted in the woods, where they began to light a fire, and set up a camp planning to sleep there. The woods, though, often had been a bone of contention when it came to loafers and marauders. They had to be careful, especially with someone like Ashwatthama with them. One can never tell how many more soldiers from Anga were following them for the Mani.

"What are you thinking?" Vrishaketu asked Tripti. He wanted to begin a conversation with her, but she was a quiet woman.

"Nothing," she said.

But the word itself had a lot of definitions that he was not aware of, and he wished he did.

"You know, we should get to know each other," Vrishaketu said. "Like what's your background, where have you come from? Who are you? I have no idea. And I'll be asked these questions when we enter Hastinapur."

Ashwatthama mired in between, wriggling on the mud, with his hands and legs tied up. Tripti opened his gag, and he immediately said, "The boy likes you, lass."

Tripti growled and stuffed his mouth again. "He must say something stupid!"

Vrishaketu almost blushed at being called out.

Tripti glanced at him, and there was a look of snideness and trust on his face, but she just glanced away, her ears pricking, as she silenced Vrishaketu from saying anything further.

"What happened?" Vrishaketu whispered.

Tripti began to climb up, and move towards the other side, Vrishaketu followed, and he could also hear little whispers coming from the other end. They broke free through the shrubs, and under the moonlit canopy they saw three men, sitting around the fire too, but they looked like raggedy, battle-worn ex-soldiers. They had cages in which young girls were sleeping, as if it was their home.

"Slavers," she said, with definitive clarity. "They are going somewhere to sell these women for a high bid."

Vrishaketu had heard about women slavery and the child abductions, but it used to never happen in Anga. Now, once they were out and in a wasteland like this place, where no other kingdom presided, they saw the rule-breakers of society. It was considered the gravest of sins, for these young girls were impressionable and they would become slaves of much older people, or the kings, or the foreign emissaries who would take them back to their native lands. It was common practice, and these girls mostly came from poor households, poverty-stricken lands, and they had worries that only few could solve.

"We need to help them."

"Look at those men. They are tough as a nut," Vrishaketu said. "We might get backup and we can ask for help later."

"No," she said.

"Why?"

"You wanted to know about me. So here it is—once upon a time, I was one of those girls, in an exact same cage and I had no idea where I was going. My slavers were nice and they were kind, until I became a part of an insidious kingdom which exploited me for the way I looked," she spoke with disdain and hurt. "So no, thank you, I want to help those girls."

Vrishaketu couldn't say much after this revelation.

"Distract them."

And she vanished before Vrishaketu could say anything more.

Vrishaketu was unsure of his next step, when he heard Ashwatthama still humming a tune and he pulled him back.

"I need your help."

He removed Ashwatthama's gag and he nodded. "Anything for my freedom."

"You won't get any freedom."

"Then why in the heavens would I help you?"

"Because I am the only one who can make sure of your safe return to your father."

"You don't understand, boy. There's a conspiracy brewing," Ashwatthama said.

"I don't believe anything you say. You are the captive and I'm the captor," Vrishaketu said. "You can do or say anything to escape. If you help me, I will give you madeira."

"Well, that's quite a nice barter. All right then."

Vrishaketu dragged Ashwatthama after disclosing the plan to him, and they entered the line of sight of the slavers who immediately rose from their seats, as they ate their mutton and beef. They saw Vrishaketu and drew their swords.

"I am lost, lads." Vrishaketu began. "I have to escort this prisoner to Hastinapur, and I seem to have lost my way."

The slaver arched their brows, not speaking a word. Meanwhile, as their backs were towards the cages, Tripti was going to the cages and quietly opening them with her dagger, letting the girls out, as silently as she could.

Ashwatthama, tried to overact, "I am a prisoner of very high value. If you take me to a local Naga colony, they will pay you handsomely."

Vrishaketu cursed under his breath, as he went against the plan. The slavers were confused, and Tripti made some noise back there, when the slavers looked at them and began to chase them, realising they were duped.

Vrishaketu pulled out his sword, and instantly went for one of their necks, while Ashwatthama bit the other person's toes. Tripti leapt on the third slaver and began to hit him mercilessly. The prolonged fight went on for some time, until Vrishaketu finally ended it with a stab on the heart of the slaver.

"Well, that is done," Ashwatthama said, as Tripti took care of the girls.

"That is why I don't trust you." Vrishaketu said. "You will use every sleazy way to escape the bloody mess." He held him up on his feet.

"Then don't trust what I say next too," he spoke. "You are going to regret the moment you set foot inside the kingdom, I swear to every god out there."

38

Satyasena heard his brother had created more ruckus than he was supposed to.

The entire camp got to know, once the two escaped soldiers from Agastya's party returned and began to narrate how Vrishaketu caused a commander's death. It created a big scene, and he knew his father would hate it. In one hand, he was disappointed with Satyasena, in another he was frustrated with Vrishaketu.

They weren't ideal sons.

Satyasena had been resting on his bed when the news reached, and he was quietly absorbing it, when he saw Ashtar enter his tent too.

"Guru Ashtar," he spoke, recalling the murder of Roma his anger was at its peak, but he could not do much, since he was limp by actions and was absolutely coward by soul. "How come you are here?"

"Your father has sent me for you."

"To take me back?"

"To take you to a new land."

"What do you mean?"

"He wants you to be a man," he said, as two followers appeared from behind. "He wants you to discard the foreign blood in you and embrace your nationality."

Satyasena was confused. His body still hurt. "I don't know what's going on."

"Come with us."

"No. You tell me, what is it?" His panic was getting the better of him, afraid and scared, bile was forming in his throat.

"Come with us, Satya."

Satyasena remained there, frozen on his bed.

"You know you were named by me," Ashtar said. "I saved you too. I saved you from the disease and your father is in debt of me for that. He respects me too much for that. And I too have a lot of respect for him," Ashtar said. "Your name, it came from truth. It came from his guru, his uncle Satya, who was a great general, and helped him fight Jarasandha. He thought you would be a reflection of his great soul, but you went towards your mother's side, and he knows it's going to be tough, but it has to be done."

Satyasena saw the followers of the Council appear, ready to grab him, but he tried to push them away, shove them aside, when he was grabbed by his legs, as he fell down, thudding on the floor, then being dragged up.

"Don't make it more difficult than it has to be."

Satyasena relented a little bit, before being pushed out in the night, the moon was sparkling and the war ahead seemed numb. It looked almost empty, as both sides of the party planned and plotted their next move. Satyasena saw there were people looking at him curiously from a distance, as he was dragged in front of a log, where a man in a mask was standing with a cleaver in his hand.

"What are you trying to do?"

"To sacrifice for Lord Surya, you must give what you love the most."

"No, no..."

"And in return, he will give you everything," Ashtar said, with a gleeful smile.

When Satyasena realised what was happening, he began to pull and prod, but he couldn't do much.

"You fools! Stop them! FOOLS!" He yelled at the soldiers who were under his command, but they resorted quietly. "FATHER! FATHER! LOOK WHAT THEY ARE DOING TO ME!"

He scowled and yelled.

"Apologies, child," Ashtar whispered, as his arm was rested on the log, and the cleaver neared it. "But you told me you don't want your father to be disappointed in you."

Satyasena stopped revolting after that, his eyes melting at the thought. "Yes."

"Do this for him, and he shall never be disappointed. Lord Surya will make sure of that," Ashtar said with a smile.

Satyasena clenched his jaw. He let go of the followers and gave up his sword arm willingly. It was the arm that he was proud of, the arm that would protect him against his enemies.

And now he was giving up.

He watched his father, who had been staring from far. He was in his tent, and he looked a tad bit afraid too.

"Do it," Satyasena said, as his eyes locked with his father, who nodded from the distance.

The cleaver dropped sharply and cut his arm off till the

elbow. Immediately, blood began to spray out of him, as he cried loudly. The medics came and began to control the bleeding, while he yelled and sobbed, in excruciating pain. But the pain of not being able to participate in sword-fighting again—that hurt him more.

He fell on his back, on the mud, his eyes straining. He looked up at Ashtar, who knelt next to him.

"It is good you did what you did." Ashtar smiled, patting him on the shoulder. "Now you will rise and you will grow with such power. You will have everything at your disposal. And I have some news for you."

"Wha…what…" he was a bit delirious with the blood loss.

"I have been informed by my sparrows that the Greeks led by your mother are planning something. No one knows except me and Lord Surya. Go back to the kingdom and destroy them. Come back with their heads and your father would be the proudest."

Satyasena smiled through his pain. "Thank you. And I shall not disappoint Lord Surya."

"Yes. And he has given you another life, another opportunity," Ashtar said. "And when I say you deal with the Greeks, you deal with *all* of them."

Satyasena knew what he meant.

Lord Surya…he wanted his mother to be killed.

39

Shanaya had stopped the bleeding, but looking at the bloodless face of Menander, she knew he wouldn't survive for long.

His head was on her lap, and he was shivering, holding himself back. His hands were clasping her arms, and the crimson liquid was drenching her clothes.

"What happened?" She asked him, as he bled. "What went wrong? What is going on? You showed me my father's death and he is alive."

"I-I...served your father," he faintly said. "He had sent me here to spy on you."

"Why spy on me?"

"Because he wanted to know what was going on, how he could benefit. I always served him, and he betrayed me." He looked at his wound.

"Yeah, that's my father. You should have asked me before trusting him," Shanaya said. "What else?"

"He had been living off on the other king's money for quite some time, but after being ostracised on multiple fronts for being Greek, his position began to get lowered. It became worse when Jarasandha had abandoned their deal with Archimedes and he cursed himself for it." He coughed blood. "He thought, I should have partnered with Karna. I would have not gotten betrayed then."

"Yes. That is true," she said proudly with a smile.

"He thought. It is best to go home. Back to Greece. Back to his homeland and actually live there. But for that, he needed army, coins and ships. He began to reach out to me more, trying to get a sense of how else he can benefit from us but Karna was reluctant, of course. He didn't pay heed. He knew his neck would be on the line if the one he betrayed was approached. But he also knew that Anga was his only salvation."

"He knew the only way to enter was to kill Karna, so he pestered me into manipulating you to do so," said Menander. "That is why I persisted and asked you, but he always got saved for one reason or the other. Captain Archimedes got angry, and he asked to let him enter the kingdom and that is what I did, with your help."

Shanaya shook her head, feeling disgusted that she got manipulated into doing such a thing.

"Who was the man who had been killed? Who resembled my father?"

"Oh, just a poor farmer, who looked a tad bit like him," said Menander. "That is why I didn't want you to see the face, because otherwise you would have recognised."

"So Karna never attacked?"

"No. He always stood by your word," Menander said, pale, losing his light. "He didn't attack him, even though he easily could have. But he loved you. No matter what."

Shanaya flared her nostrils.

"I don't know why he attacked me. I did everything he asked me to do."

"I know," Shanaya said. "You've done your job and he doesn't need you anymore. And frankly," she spoke, as she twisted his neck, "so do I."

Menander's body was rested, as she began to walk towards the other side of the tunnel, to see what was at the end of the sewage. She found a ladder which led to the top, but that top, unfortunately was closed off, blocked by something. She used her strength and tried to push it, and eventually succeeded in opening the door. She twisted her head out through the little clearing, and saw a wide desert around it, and the kingdom was paces away, but she was outside it. A forest lay on the other end, and it was the perfect way to enter the kingdom, but many didn't know of this path and thus, it had remained a mystery.

She heard something within the sewers, so she closed the door and went back to where the corpse was lying. By the time she had reached, she saw her father staring at the body from the other end of the grilled door, a malicious grin pasted over his face. She continued to watch the corpse, as he said, "Oh, and I thought you would be soft, living with the Bharatvarshis." He chuckled. His hair was shorter, and his teeth crooked as always. Once a handsome man, he had now become rotten to the core. "But I'm glad, my daughter still lives inside of you."

"I hate you," Shanaya said, with gritted teeth. "You only ever cared about your money and about your status, never about your blood."

"To be fair, lass, you were procreated to be used as a commodity and nothing else. We had to build strong relations with the Bharatvarshis here and what better way to do that than to give your women. The unfortunate part is, your husband fell in love with you." He shook his head, as if it was a sick joke. "I just can't believe it, and I still can't understand how he had to come to me for help during Jarasandha's war, and he agreed to take you for my army and then I kind of pulled back."

"Yeah, because you got a better deal."

"To be fair, my point was never to side with the weak side. That's how you survive."

"That's how cockroaches survive. Not kings. And my husband is a king."

He rolled his eyes. "I was wrong. You are soft. But regardless, if you listen to me, you keep your crown and your man, and let us be." He opened the grill gates, while one of his men grabbed her by the arm, and pulled her in.

"What do you want?" She snarled.

"I want to enter the treasury and apparently," he said, "you are the only one who can help us enter."

40

Vrikodara hated the idea of meeting his wife, since it hadn't resulted in healthy repercussions earlier.

He ordered his army to attack from every corner, kill their archers, fight their cavalry, use guerrilla tactics to buy more time. And avoid the catapults, since they were the real problem at that point.

Vrikodara and Pukkasati moved for the Rakshas colony, and the news of their arrival had already been sent. Mostly the Rakshas were a cannibalistic tribe, like the Pisach, but they weren't a result of inbreeding. They ate human flesh because they loved it, because they felt consuming another man was giving them greater control over themselves.

As they moved on their mare, Pukkasati asked, "What had happened with Hidambi?"

"Well." He pursed his lips, "I happened to seduce her and kill her brother."

"Erm...yeah, that's bad." Pukkasati rolled his eyes. "You probably shouldn't have done the latter."

"Oh no, she was fine with the latter, it's the former she has a problem with. The Rakshasas believe death is a part and parcel of this world, and death in the hands of a mighty warrior like me is an honour greater than even life." Vrikodara smiled. "Oh, I love that woman. She's feisty and crazy."

"Then what happened?"

"It was the seducing part, definitely. A Rakshas cannot wed a citizen, not outside their circle, basically. A Rakshas is ostracised from the community of men and they consider others like...well...food. They believe everyone is useless and they are all mighty and powerful." Vrikodara explained. "I had the best time with Hidambi, but she was really really bothered that I tried to bring her to my side, to be part of a community. She couldn't leave her Rakshas brethren and she chose them, though officially, we are married. We never spoke again, because otherwise we would end up missing each other. It was a surprise when you said she was okay with meeting me." A smile continued to waver on his face.

"You seem distracted," Pukkasati said. "I hope her involvement wouldn't be a problem with the battle. We need to win Anga, for your revenge and for Hastinapur."

Vrikodara shrugged. "Of course, of course...for my brother. My so dear, lovely brother." But he was indifferent.

And as they moved through the crevices of the large mountains, through the rocky terrain where the canyons greeted them, he noticed he was entering a different world together. The canyon opened inside the mountain, hollowed out spaces inside the hills, and there lived the people. There were bridges built on top of more bridges, each floor of the large-ceilinged colony shaped like huts and houses. The residents went berserk, greeting Vrikodara and escorting him. He looked at the Rakshas, who were wearing jewellery made of human bones, and had large bodies with humongous strides. They looked Vrikodara's size. And he felt like one amongst them.

He saw in the middle of the coveted colony a stadium-like place, where people fought with each other, with animals, and also with creatures of different kinds. Men were being ripped apart from head to toe, and Vrikodara even cheered the kind of violence that he was witnessing, while Pukkasati tried not to vomit. The Rakshas didn't know about him, but they knew what he had done. Killing Hidamba wasn't an ordinary feat. He was a Rakshas chief, a giant amongst men, who terrorised the local villages for food. He would steal infants to fulfill his appetite until Vrikodara put a stop to it.

"That's the arena," Vrikodara said, pointing at the bloodshed. "That's where the fun happens."

"I think you were born on the wrong side of the world. You belong with the Rakshas."

"My heart does, at least."

"What did you just say?"

"Nothing." Vrikodara was defiant.

Pukkasati though, was being met with frowns and giggles, since he was small in height, and didn't really resemble the kind of a person one had to be in the land of the Rakshas. They reached the top of the mountain, from where the entire gladiatorial arena was visible. Pukkasati said, "We have a meeting with Lady Hidambi."

"Lady?" The guards chuckled. "She's a riot."

They let him come, and Vrikodara saw his wife after a long time. Her back was visible as she watched the fight happening below. She was wearing a long cape, tied around her thick body, while her curls were long and tied in a bun. She was as tall as any man out there, her muscles and thighs hard as rocks. Vrikodara felt a lot of emotions in a second.

"Hidambi," Vrikodara said, "it's been a while, my love."

She turned, raising her brows, so beautiful and gorgeous she was.

"My dear Bhima," she smiled lusciously, "and you must be the person who reached out to us."

Pukkasati nodded. "It is a pleasure to meet you, my lady."

"I am not your lady. I am his lady." She winked at Vrikodara, who giggled in return. "You want my help, big boy?"

"Yes," he said confidently. "That would be nice."

"Great, come here then." She brought her hand forward.

"We should have never stayed apart, you know," Vrikodara said. "I don't know why we at all separated. We should be together forever."

She held his hand and smiled. "Because, my dear love," she said through gritted teeth, "you cheated on me."

And she pushed him inside the arena.

41

They waited near one of the ravines of the River Ganga, when they saw a familiar boat appearing. Just like last time, a boatman came, and in front there was a man in a black cloak with a hood on. The boatman was singing a lullaby.

"And you have completed your journey." The hood came off, to reveal the face of Babhru. "Interesting, that it has taken you all so long."

"Lots of obstacles along the way," Vrishaketu said, with an exasperated sigh, showing off the Mani that they had brought along. "But we have managed to get him." Ashwatthama had been gagged, and his face was covered with a black sheet, so he didn't get recognised in Indraprastha till they reached there.

"I was expecting the Mani to be...well...smaller in size," Babhru said. "Rumours do have a tendency to be lies."

"Come on the boat. I know the way to go."

Vrishaketu and Tripti did so, recalling what had happened back at the forest.

The little children had been handed off to an orphanage in the local town before they had appeared here, closer to

Hastinapur, as well as the newly famed Indraprastha.

The boat began to move in the water, under the silvery moonlight, as the lullaby continued. Ashwatthama tried to resort to fighting back, but he couldn't as he was held back by Tripti and Vrishaketu himself.

"Erm, I am sorry about what happened to you," Vrishaketu said to Tripti.

"Hmmm."

"I think our journey ends here, but I'm not glad about it. It was a pleasure knowing you along the way."

"You're such a flirt."

Vrishaketu blushed. "Oh no, I have no experience in that department at all."

She looked at him. "What I told you, I have never told anyone, so I would like you to keep it that way."

"Of course, of course. Mum's the word."

Babhru had not been listening, looking ahead at the stars and the incoming bridge, which was long and somewhat broken down. As they began to enter a kingdom where palaces and bazaars all stood at a high pedestal, staircases that led to the top, and rivers intertwining between the cities, to be used by boats for travel. Stallions were less in number, but probably because it was night. He was in splendour when he saw Indrprastha and how beautifully it was made.

"Spectacular, never been here."

"Created by Lord Indra himself, they say," Babhru said. "Designed by Maya, the Rakshas architect, a maverick."

There were orchids all around, while a slight mist prevailed because of the high altitude.

"It is small, but there is a dispute going on," Babhru

said. "Lord Krishna had brokered a deal for a land of five villages, and this is just one of them. The other four are disputed. Duryodhan doesn't plan to give it to them. He is vehemently against it. Now, I don't know about him, but I think why he's being so sassy about this entire scenario is because he was laughed at by Pandu's children when he fell near the fountain. It's rumours again and probably baseless, but could that be true?"

Vrishaketu raised his brows. These kinds of fallacies and these kinds of reasons, definitely do make sense for the adults to fight on. He knew uncle Suyodhan, popularly known by this side of the family as Duryodhan, as a whiny brat. He would not listen, and was entitled and privileged. And he knew, keeping in mind Suyodhan's power, that if he became the leader and the king of the entire land, he would be unstoppable and he would perish any dharma there ever was.

"So who do you think will win the war?" Vrishaketu asked.

"The smarter one." He winked at him.

Vrishaketu didn't understand what he meant though. They had reached a local shoreline, from where the staircases opened into a large castle.

"We have just infiltrated Indraprastha, from the back side."

"How do you know about this?"

"This is where I clean the dirty laundry for the Pandu brothers." Babhru chuckled.

"What exactly do you do?" Vrishaketu asked, getting off the boat.

Babhru shrugged. "We shall talk soon about that.

Where I come from though, I believe we both have a very similar story to tell."

The staircase had guards, but seeing Babhru, they resorted to laughing. Tripti and Ashwatthama were getting dragged. By the time they reached the gates, Babhru had to relent.

"I wouldn't be joining, but best of luck to both of you. I am sure the rewards would be plenty." And saying that, bowing, he left.

Tripti's face was covered, and her expressions were placid, as the man was being dragged. They were told to go downstairs, where the battle room was located, and they followed the guards across lanes, passages and finally to the battle room, which was filled with books, scrolls, and other reading material.

And in front of them they saw a man, holding a book, in a dhoti and a small scarf around his naked body, memorizing something.

He didn't turn towards them, but Vrishaketu heard the booming voice, and he was excited to finally meet the great Dharmaraja. He had heard so much about the man, a personality to reckon with, and he could feel the weight of that personality.

"You must be wondering why a battle room has so many books," he said, in his smooth, marbled voice. "Because you see, your greatest weapon is your mind. And that must continue to be sharpened, from time to time."

He turned his face, revealing his handsome features, his smooth hair, and his aquiline jaw. "So tell me, Babhru says, you have brought me a gift that I can't refuse?"

Vrishaketu nervously brought the man forward and presented him.

Taking off the mask.

Revealing the man himself. Muzzled. Beaten up.

Dharmaraja looked at him for a moment confusingly and said: "You both brought him here?"

"Yes." Vrishaketu said, while Tripti was quiet.

"You are Karna's son, right?" He stood up and moved towards Vrishaketu, putting his heavy hands on his shoulder. "The one who works for us."

"Y-yes, my lord. I serve you and the true king of Kurus."

He nodded. "Good. Good. The only problem is, kid, you have made a big, stupid mistake and so has the bloody Babhru. He played me."

Vrishaketu arched his brows. "What? He's Ashwatthama. He's the one who led so many Nagas to their death."

"Yes," Dharmaraja said. "That did happen. But he's not Ashwatthama."

Then he pulled the cover from the man's face, and he turned to see Vrishaketu and Tripti.

"Well, I told you to not bring me here." He grinned sardonically. "I am Arjun. Nice to meet you all."

42

Vrikodara was confused for a while, and petrified too.

He was standing in the illuminated arena, where people shouted and cried and gambled with each other for flesh and money, to achieve the ultimate feeling of winning. Vrikodara hated being in the arena. The last time he was in a similar situation, he had killed Hidamba.

And now he was here.

He wiped the mud and dust, and looked around at the corpses and bones left behind. He had no idea what kind of a beast was about to attack him.

But he looked up from where he had been thrown off, and saw Hidambi grinning madly. Pukkasati, on the other hand, was scared to death to see his general in this position.

"Who do you want me to challenge?" He slapped his muscles. "I am ready to do it."

She looked at him. "Here we announce our new contender!" She shouted looking at all the other Rakshasas, her hair frizzy and wild, grey in colour. "The Rakshas killer!"

Everyone began to hoot, and some began to boo.

"He wants our help in his puny battle!" She shouted.

"He wants to call on to his brethren. We will give him that if he survives the arena."

"I'm up for it," Vrikodara said, no fear resorting in his bones, though he did wonder why she said he cheated, because he never did. "Let's do it."

"So I will give him the contender that he's looking for."

And the cave in front opened, letting a tiger out, ready to lash at its enemy with its claws, still in chains.

"Oh, a simple animal!" Vrikodara screamed in glory.

The tiger gnawed and snarled, roaring.

"No!"

And Hidambi jumped from above, landing on the tiger's back. "You are fighting me."

Vrikodara paused. He hadn't been expecting this. He couldn't attack his wife. He couldn't kill her. She was his...love. But he pulled out the mace from his girdle and prepared himself.

She launched herself forward, he rolled over letting the claws of the tiger scratch him a bit. More hooting followed that.

"Why do you think I have cheated on you?"

"You married that woman!" She scowled.

Vrikodara was confused. Who was she talking about? And then it hit him. "You mean, Draupadi?"

"Yes."

"It is purely a political play. I had to do it because she can't be married to one person. She can only be married to five, as her pandits and her astrologers have told her. If she doesn't, she will perish. Though her true love, and her real husband is none other than Arjun. Our marriage is nothing but simple politics."

"You manavas and your puny politics!"

And she launched herself again, he fell on his back as he couldn't roll over. The tiger was on top of him, somehow he was able to grab hold of the mace which acted as a barrier between him and the beast. The tiger attacked, roared, clawed at him.

"Eat him! Eat him!" People shouted.

But Vrikdora's strength was more than the tiger's, as he began to push the tiger away, and then tossed him like a toy. Along with him, Hidambi fell on the other end with her weapon too.

The tiger, noticing she no more had reins over him, plunged at her now, while she tried using her sword to defend herself.

"Calm down, boy! Calm down!" She yelled.

Vrikodara came from behind the tiger and grabbed it, breaking its arms and twisting his neck, leading the animal go lifeless and fall dead. He punched his chest and immediately shouted every slur he knew and roaring how he remained undefeated.

"You didn't have to save me. I am not a damsel in distress!"

"I love you, Hidambi. You are my only true love." He said.

"You are a liar and a thief."

"Thief?"

"Thief of joy."

He laughed.

She attacked him with her sword, which he deflected with his mace and returned with a swifter attack, but she managed to roll back. And jumped over his body, startling him. He fell on the ground. And she went for the sword to stab him. But he didn't revert, and she stopped.

The crowds hissed and yelled.

"Kill me," he said.

"Can't!"

"I should see you more often." Vrikodara smiled.

"I like my freedom."

And he pushed her against the floor, and kissed her.

The entire crowd continued to boo and began to disperse.

"I am a crowd-pleaser, but I don't care anymore." Hidambi smiled. "What do you need from me?"

"I need your help. I need you to fight with me."

"There are those who might oppose me," Hidambi said.

"As if you care?"

"As if I care."

And they both kissed, drenched in the tiger's blood.

43

Vrishaketu remained frozen at the sudden realisation, while Tripti on the other hand was quiet as a preying bird.

The soldiers had arrived from behind, and were circling around Vrishaketu, while Dharmaraja stood there with a snide smile on his face. Arjun was drinking gallons of water. The more Vrishaketu looked at him, the more he realised the resemblance between Ashwatthama and Arjun. They had the same nose, same eyes, and the hair… it looked identical. Anyone would be in a pickle and get confused.

He definitely felt like a fool.

"What do we do with both of them?" Arjun asked, as he finished drinking the water. "They had been quite kind with me during the journey though. The woman, I still feel holds a lot of secrets."

"What is going on?" Vrishaketu asked.

Dharmaraja looked at him. He was a handsome man, and a calm, composed individual. By the looks of it, a fair thinker, and a strategist. He wasn't as tall as Arjun, or as broad as Bhima. But he was something different altogether. And his only vice, as Vrishaketu had heard, was that he loved to gamble, and during that he would become a fiery monster, incapable of being stopped.

"What's going on is that your ignorance has led to my plan getting flopped," he said. "You see, when the genocide of the Nagas happened at the Khandava forest, on which this very land had been built, it was not Ashwatthama who did it."

Arjun raised his hands. "Guilty."

"His arrows ignited the fire in the jungle."

Vrishaketu could imagine the long-haired man, using the archers with him, to attack the forest, burn the people within, and destroy everything.

Privilege is a curse in the hands of the dishonourable.

"Realising it'll lead us into a lot of heat ourselves, we made a deal with Ashwatthama. We gave him drinks, money and women and offered him to scoot away till we figure it out. Ashwatthama took the blame, grudgingly."

"He enjoyed it."

"Brother, I have a feeling he might come back and attack." Dharmaraja instantly nudged Arjun in the right direction. "Anyway, we realised it was a great opportunity."

"Hey, you realised." Arjun chuckled.

Dharmaraja blushed a little. "To learn about the most prosperous kingdom of Bharatvarsh after Hastinapur. And that was Anga. Beautiful and seductive from outside, Anga stands as an important testament, of course. So now, we had to know what was going on from within. And, of course not just that, but also attack it from within when it was necessary. So with my sad, pitiful face I went to Suyodhan and gave him a deal. Help me hide Ashwatthama from the world, he's the only evidence out there who can harm my reputation. Suyodhan, thinking it was a great opportunity to use against me, went to Karna, and they just fell right in my palm, like a bunch of organised puppets." He laughed a little. "Because they think straight. They think like brutes. They think like warriors." He commented. "Anyway, instead of Ashwatthama, it was Arjun who was sent, and of course, the vermins that they are, especially your half-breed father, they turned on me. Said, it is a ransom like situation. We would keep Ashwatthama, so he could be used as ransom down the road, if we ever attack. My poor brother." He shook his head. "He was now kidnapped, of course. Tied up. And I had no idea how to help him escape."

"But!" Arjun continued, "I could figure my way out, of course. I was glad I was in Anga, if Yudhistr needed me."

"And thus, I couldn't attack Anga. Because my brother was there, and he would be caught in the crossfire."

Arjun looked at Dharmaraja. "Well, we both strive to protect each other, from each other too."

Dhamraraja smiled. "And Babhru did what was needed. He brought in an inside help, to escort out Arjun. While my other brother, Bhima, was using his means to attack Anga. Now they don't have any ransom, nor do they have the brains to support and fight against Bhima. Anga is going to be ours, the one powerful stronghold for Hastinapur will perish and we'll have a better chance of reclaiming my throne."

"Though," Arjun began, "where Babhru did falter, involves a girl."

And both the brothers looked at Tripti who was standing there. Silent. In a corner.

"We had of course, asked for you," Dharmaraja said to

Vrishaketu. "Since you know the lands of Anga quite well, but the girl was never a part of the plan. How she entered we have no idea."

"You can trust her." Vrishaketu gritted his teeth. "And we are doing your job. It would be better to not be in the dark from next time. I am on your side."

"No," Arjun said. "You are your father's kid. You are just a rebel and a tool for us."

Dharmaraja continued. "Shush, brother. He's valuable. But forgive me for this, boy, as five brothers, we have enough on our hands. So we cannot extend that trust towards you."

"I have given everything to you and your cause..." He began to retort and looked frustrated. "But, but..."

"It's all right. Time will heal the shock," Dharmaraja said. "Now, we will keep you under supervision, both of you, till we figure things out."

And in that moment, as the soldiers had come to take them, Tripti launched herself, revealing her face, tattoos adorning her neck, and her jaw, very similar to that of...

Snakes.

She launched with her dagger, and stabbed Arjun on the shoulder, who yelled in pain. Tripti began to shout and scowl, "MURDERER! MURDERER! I WOULD HAVE KILLED YOU IF I KNEW IT EARLIER!"

Vrishaketu looked at the mostly calm Tripti in a different daze altogether, a woman who was frenetic and furious.

And he was surprised, that she was none other than a...

Naga.

44

Karna entered the war, with his bow and arrows.

The skirmish had turned into something far bigger than he had anticipated. He had a chariot and a charioteer who rode with him, skidding and swerving on the battlefield. Karna wanted to concentrate on the battleground, all dusty and muddy, and covered in blood, ready to be its tamed beast.

In quick succession he had been shooting arrows, back-to-back, hitting his enemies in large numbers. He had almost shot a hundred arrows, and penetrated a hundred skulls.

They fell like comets from the sky, massively corroding the grounds, and destroying half of Bhima's army. He was losing definitely, and Karna for a moment did love and relish the beauty of the arrogance he possessed within him—at the thought that Anga would prosper.

Always.

And then the comets halted, for some reason, and the skies were clear as day, except the winds. One of the soldiers stopped next to the chariot, breathing heavily, scarred.

"My lord, the catapults have been disabled," he said.

"What do you mean—disabled?"

"They were attacked by…beasts."

"Beasts?"

And before the guard could speak further, a humongous warrior appeared, wearing animal fur on his back, and throwing him down, he pounded a large spear on his chest.

"RRRRRR!" He yelled like a beast and jumped on top of the chariot, throwing Karna off it.

He stabbed the charioteer who tried to fight back, and then threw him off it too.

Karna used his bow as defence to deflect the enemy's attack and kicked him on the chest.

"You…you…"

The Rakshas had teeth, that he had sharpened using the knives to make them look like fangs, and he was trying to bite Karna with them. He punched the Rakshas and moved away from the chariot, pulling out an arrow and shooting the enemy while mid-air.

He fell back on the ground, rolled over, and looked at the battleground around. There were multitudes of warriors appearing out of nowhere. And these warriors in fur carried long spears, and they were rowdy, riding large stallions and hooting and celebrating murder. They weren't conscripted soldiers like the ones in Anga.

They were monsters.

They were the Rakshasas.

Shanaya was pushed towards the treasury, which was a large marbled building, carved out of a hill. It was designed specifically to not have an entrance at the other end, for you can't dig into a hill, as it was physically impossible to do so.

She walked with her soldiers, for her father's men had now dressed themselves up as the soldiers of Anga, wearing all the purples, blues and golds. Shanaya saw her father, Captain Archimedes, acting all normal, as if he was born to play the role.

"I hate you," she said.

"Every daughter hates her father," he said. "They just don't know it yet."

They reached the gates where the guards were. The entire treasury was heavily protected.

"I would like to enter," she said with authority.

"Yes, your majesty."

They didn't even flinch or say anything. They began to move past the moneymen, the bankers, the ministers of coins and finance who worked on the collection of the taxes, and keep track of the income from the various kinds of businesses the state indulged in. Until she entered the huge vault, made of gold, which too was protected by the guards. But she asked them to leave, and they immediately followed her command.

There was a wheel on the front.

"What's your plan?" She asked. "I open it and you steal everything?"

"Oh yes, and then we will go to the dockyard, and steal the ships. From there, we leave, and you have no worry of me or you."

"Where will you keep the gold? What use would it be of in Greece?"

"Gold is useful in any part of the country, my lady." Her father mocked her. "But no, after I have the gold, I shall go to another country and buy an army. Then with that army, I would spike every traitor's heart who has ever troubled or ostracised me."

"Fine."

She began to turn the wheel, but she wasn't sure whether it was the right combination. Was it left to right, and then right to left to open the vault? Or was it the other way round?

"Come on, don't act like a fool."

"Tell me."

"I am trying to remember, give me time. I don't loot my state every day, right?"

And then she remembered. She recalled the combination which she had installed as a queen, not sure whether Karna had changed it or not. Soon she realised he hadn't. The vault opened.

And when it did, she saw someone sitting amidst all the gold coins, playing with a crown made of jewels, his eyes shimmering.

"So nice to meet you, mother," Satyasena said. "It's been a while."

Vrishaketu was in the prison, along with Tripti, who was on the other side of the lane. They looked at each other, while she lay there in a corner. Her face was now visible, she wasn't hiding it anymore.

"So you were a Naga?" He asked. "Great."

"I never told you to trust me," Tripti said.

"But I did. And I was a fool. And now we both are in this," he said, cursing under his breath.

She didn't say anything.

"If I knew, I was working with a Naga, I would have..."

"What would you have done?" Tripti asked.

Vrishaketu went quiet.

"I was abandoned and stolen as a child by slavers. Lived a long time as a wench for rich merchants. When I got to know of my true heritage, I returned only to find them mutilated, burnt and destroyed by the very men whose prison now I am in," she said. "My kind were killed, for a kingdom to flourish. Do not say they didn't know. If it was a mistake, then be apologetic about it, instead of hiding your true selves." She pursed her lips. "All these bloody things were done so I could be here, and witness what had actually happened, who was behind it. And now I know, now I shall exact my vengeance. I will bring forth the wrath of the Maharogas, the ones who protect the Nagas, the ones who fight for the Nagas."

Vrishaketu stood there, frozen and surprised, and remained quiet for he had no justification to provide. He stayed there against the wall, until they both saw a hooded figure enter, flustering with the keys in his hand.

"All right, come out, guys, it's time to leave."

Vrishaketu recognised the voice, and immediately pushed the hooded figure against the wall, as other prisoners woke up and began to make loud noises.

"You...you did this."

And the hood fell back, to show who he was.

Babhru.

45

Vrikodara rode on his bull, obliterating anyone who came in his way with the bull's horns.

Those who didn't get trampled by the beast, were struck by his mace and smashed. He had entered the war in full glory. Along the way, on a stallion was his wife, Hidambi, who moved along fighting with her spear, her muscled body shining under the sun.

"How does it feel?" Vrikodara said.

"Oh well, this is what I was missing!" She yelled.

Vrikodara smiled. The Rakshas were paid as mercenaries to fight in armies, or as personal guards. But Vrikodara knew that they didn't need a reason to get paid, they needed a reason to fight. They loved war.

"Why are you taking over this city by the way?" She asked, as she threw her spear across the sky into to a horseman's chest, who fell from his horse.

"Childhood trauma." He smiled.

"What did the king do?"

"He showed the poison mark on his body. But more than that, it was the shame. I was retching, shitting and doing what not, while everyone laughed at me, and so did Karna."

"You know why I loved you? When I realised that you had been saved from the poison. You were so just majestic that even the poison couldn't kill you." She licked her lips in anticipation. "I want to make love to you over the corpses of our enemies." And she hurrayed in the loudest way. More Rakshasas appeared, attacking the men.

Vrikodara grinned. As he rode through the other side defeating his enemies, he saw an element of fire appear out of nowhere. Even though the catapults were broken and disarmed by javelins thrown by the Rakshasas, he saw a broken wheel, fiery, just rolling in the middle of the battlefield and he stopped, afraid of what he had just witnessed beyond that wheel.

The image of a woman and her child appeared in front of him.

No.

And the moment he saw them, he fell from the bull, and his eyes strained, while he held on to his mace. A soldier from the opposing army appeared, stabbing him in the back. He yelled, turning around, grabbing the throat of the person, throwing him on the ground, before smashing his head like a watermelon with his mace.

"I am done with people."

And in all this chaos, he noticed something else. An arrow, coming towards him and stabbing him in the chest. He began to bleed as he pulled it out, before noticing it was Karna, in his broken armour and his bloody bow.

Moving for him.

Ready to take him head on.

Satya had never seen the men his mother was with. But he was, after all, excited about the entire thing. By the time they had arrived, he had already been informed step by step about the entire thing by Ashtar's people. They were coming for the gold. Satya placed himself there, and he had the rest of his soldiers behind them.

As the old man and his group appeared in the vault, they were stunned, along with his mother.

His arm still hurt, and instead of a hand of flesh and blood he had a wooden hand, carved by Lord Surya's followers.

"Take them away but leave the queen here. I would like to speak to my mother."

Satya saw his mother, and he knew to be in the good books of Lord Surya, he had to kill her. She was the filthy version of his bloodline and ending her would mean ending this mediocrity. He could revel and live like his father.

But the soldiers didn't listen, as they began to fight back the soldiers of Satya. Satya brought out his sword to enter the fight, while Shanaya came to a corner.

Satya attacked the old man as they both began to duel, when Shanaya screamed and asked him to stop.

"HE'S YOUR GRANDSON!" Shanaya yelled to Archimedes, but he didn't care.

He slashed Satya's face, who fell on the ground. Shanaya came close to him, bashing him on the forehead, killing him instantly.

Satya looked at his mother while he bled, holding his cheek.

"What happened to your arm?" She knelt, concerned.

Satya watched her and her motherly concerns, immediately realising that even though she was Greek…

She was his mother.

And she had loved him, taken care of him, and would do anything for him.

"He was my grandfather."

"Yes. And a madman."

Another Greek soldier appeared to attack, but Satya used his wooden hand, to deflect it, realising it could be used for this purpose too. He punched the soldier who fell on the ground, while both mother and son hugged.

"I will tell you everything, once we have left this dreadful, dreary place," said Babhru, as they made their way out of the prison cells.

Everyone was yelling slurs and calling out to them, which had woken up the guards and the bells had begun to ring. They were running as fast as possible, on the opposite side of the prison cell, as the watchtowers rose the fire brazens and numerous guards began to be dispersed on the field.

"Oh dear, this is not good," Babhru said. "Around the stable, there's a way out. It's a small hole, dug by one of my smuggler friends."

"Why did you get us into this?"

Babhru rasped at Vrishaketu. "All in time, my dear friend."

They crouched, as they made their way towards the other side of the prison fields, moving with furiousness, as darkness had engulfed the place, and the guards were all in frenzy, holding the torches in one hand while their other hand were holding the weapons.

"RELEASE THE HOUNDS!" Someone called.

And the hounds came out.

The coyotes were let out led by the guards to smell and track. They howled and hooted, while making their way towards them.

They reached the stables close by.

"You could have just told me about the plan!" Vrishaketu cursed.

"You would have never listened to me."

"Of course, I wouldn't have. I should have never trusted you."

"I am saving your and your girlfriend's ass, okay? You can trust me. I don't have to, but I am."

"And why this sudden change of heart?"

"Because I am not the bad guy here."

"Then who is?"

"The ones above us. The ones who treat us like pawns. The ones who treat us like insects. They think they have the gold and the crown, and they wouldn't rise up. No. I am a revolutionary baby. I am the destroyer of kingdoms."

And immediately the coyote howled, growling at them, having found them.

"Oops, off we go!" He immediately ran towards the stables, and both of them followed.

They entered with the guards behind them and made their way to the hole that he had dug, which opened to a cascading field. Tripti went first, sliding in, meanwhile the coyote had launched itself at Vrishaketu. But Babhru managed to come in between and used his knife to stab it mid-air.

"Yeah, that's going to be good."

"Why should I trust you?" Vrishaketu asked again, before entering the rabbit hole.

Babhru looked at him. "Because my father is Arjun, and I have made it my life's mission to hurt him."

46

Karna shot more arrows at Bhima, which he kept deflecting with his mace, and then launched himself at Karna.

He smacked his mace, Karna rolled over, his body felt the thunder of the weapon, the might of it, but still remained steady. He was shaken up for a moment, but by then Bhima had appeared close to him, grabbing him by the breastplate, and head-butting him.

Karna fell back, looking like any other small, diminutive person around him, his forehead bleeding. He began to scamper off, as he went for his quiver and shot an arrow at Bhima. It stung his arm, but he removed it as if it was a prickly needle.

"You have been nothing but a nuisance for me," Bhima said. "All my life you and Suyodhan have tormented me."

"You were bullies."

"I WAS A CHILD!" He yelled. "I would have grown up and realised I was wrong. You don't understand, that poison, it made me who I am today."

Karna was pulling himself up.

"What do you mean?" He asked, amidst the war cries.

"I grew so big, I ate so much, I became obese, and I am what I am today because of that poison. I would have grown normally otherwise, but my stomach couldn't handle it. And I can't live without excess food anymore. You robbed me of a regular life. You robbed me from becoming a warrior. I became a brute, and I became nothing but a giant, when I could have been a man, and a happy one."

"I don't see you complaining though."

Bhima had tears in his eyes. "You were not laughed at, not mocked, not belittled for your height, for your size, for your appetite. As a kid I was, and I would never forget the decades of humiliation. I will break your spine."

He went for Karna and held him up, groping him by his feet and his head. And immediately tried to hit him with his knees but Karna pushed him aside, twisting his arms and legs, fighting back.

Both fell on the ground, and Karna came forward and hurt him with a bow, hitting him on the head.

"We did it because you used to trouble us too much. Bully us too much. You say we robbed you of your life, you robbed us of our childhood."

Bhima looked up, scars all over his body, as he stared into Karna's eyes. "First you, then your best friend. I will kill both of you, while looking into your eyes."

"Then don't look."

Saying that, he pulled the quiver string and shot an arrow.

The arrow stung Bhima in the eye, making him bleed and confusing him. He began to fall back, messed up and broken.

"You piece of shit! YOU!" He yelled and scowled.

Karna jumped on him throwing him on the ground, and got ready to plunge him in the throat with his knife, when Bhima grabbed Karna's hands, being much stronger than he was...

He twisted Karna's arms.

"I WILL BREAK YOUR PRIZED POSSESSIONS!"

Karna felt an instant jerk and heard the sound of breaking bones, making his arms feel wobbly, but more than pain what he felt was numbness.

Bhima escaped, holding his eye, as Karna lay on the ground, defeated. The Rakshas and the Brute Company had won, and they were now breaking through the barracks, attacking the kingdom, breaking down the gates.

Karna sighed, his eyes weak and he felt a strong desire for the sweet release of death.

Shanaya and Satyasena were racing towards the sewers.

They knew the kingdom had been infiltrated, and instead of the civilians they would be the first ones to be hunted. The palace would be taken over. Shanaya held her son's hands, while they navigated as ordinary people—the rest of the city, including the soldiers and the royal guards chasing after brutes and the Rakshasas, fighting them.

They had the Royal Guard along with them, in silver armour.

Shanaya couldn't believe the war they had been fighting for so long was now coming to an end. They had lost.

They began to run to the sewers, entering through the rabbit hole. Along the way, they met the followers of Surya, who saw what was happening—two members of the royalty escaping.

Shanaya had to though, because if she was caught with Satya, Bhima wouldn't spare her. He would kill her to make a point.

As they entered the sewers, and were finally close to the exit, they heard a voice coming towards them: "COWARDS!"

Both of them turned around, along with the Royal Guard. And they saw Ashtar, the hunchback, moving towards them, along with two of his followers, holding torches in their hands.

"You leave the state in this manner. You are cowards and you are traitors. For that, I will execute you and I have every right to do so."

Shanaya came forward. "You must escape too. He will not be too kind to you either."

"I do not betray the state that has helped me for so long. I will stick by them, no matter what, even if I have to kill you for it."

"You are looking for reasons to," Satyasena said. "You want nothing else but to kill mother and me. You're bringing your personal reasons into the picture, because you are, after all…angry. Angry at us."

The hunchback looked at Satyasena. "You don't dare speak to me. You have no right. I am your birth-giver. I am your saviour. I am your god. And you've done nothing but hurt me and for that, I shall strike my fury against you."

The followers appeared and attacked them, while the Royal Guard came in between fighting for them.

"GO! GO!" Satya said. "I will join."

Shanaya looked at her son, worried. "Are you sure?"

"Yes, I am sure. I will join. GO!" He scowled.

Shanaya nodded, and she went for the ladder, climbing up, still able to hear the cries and pleas behind her. She closed her ears, for she didn't want the pleas to be of her son's. She stayed there, confused, waiting.

She waited for Satyasena. She had got away from the carnage, outside the kingdom...

But...

Who else will come out of the hole?

And she saw a figure exit...

Satyasena.

He was drenched in blood, with a haggard face and his eyes were dead. He wasn't the same boy who was used to doing stupid things.

He was different.

He was a warrior.

Vrishaketu remained stoic, as they were again in the forest, all of them, escaping the kingdom, and they had the mares waiting for them.

"Where are we going now?"

Babhru answered, "Away from here."

"You are Arjun's son."

"Yes."

Vrishaketu shook his head.

"How...how?" He was so confused.

"I am an illegitimate child of his. My full name is Babruvahana. He fell in love with my mother, Chitragandha, a long time back, and he forgot about her. I was born without a father, and she had asked him multiple times to make me legible for the throne, but he never did," Babhru said, shaking his head. "I have done what I did to piss my father off."

What a sorry tale, though now Vrishaketu realised that's what he had been doing as well.

"How did you piss him off?"

He showed Tripti. "She did stab him. It was to gain their trust. I wanted them to fall apart, and it did. They were unaware that a Naga had been escorting them."

"And why hadn't you told me he was Arjun?"

"You would have killed him," Babhru said.

Tripti flared her nostrils. "That is true, but that's not the point."

"It does make a valid point, my dear girl. I am a liar, but killing Arjun is not the solution. You wanted vengeance for your people, the entire Kuru clan has to be demolished and it is a carefully laid out plan which includes the inclusion of the other colonies of Nagas, especially the Maharogas."

Vrishaketu arched his brows.

"The Maharogas," Babhru continued, "want nothing but rights for their people. Blood for blood, right? Well, now we tell them what you heard, Tripti. They will trust you and they will wage a war against the Kuru clan, and we will finally do what is good for us, and good for me. We both win."

"That is why you helped them," Vrishaketu said. "To gain their trust. While we as evidence collectors would get you what you want. You let them enter Anga, and they killed my grandfather. Now, you have the trust of the Maharogas, you have the evidence, and you want to use that to attack."

"We don't know that, lad."

Vrishaketu and Tripti began to corner Babhru.

"Come on both of you, you need a shrewd guy like me."

"You are a liar. You lied to both of us," Vrishaketu said.

"But I have a grander vision, just listen to me."

"I am done with you," Vrishaketu said. "You are out."

"Me too," Tripti said. "I wouldn't kill you because you have helped me before, but I cannot trust you anymore."

And saying that, they grabbed their mares, while Vrishaketu looked behind.

"And I wouldn't kill you because you saved my life," he said. "Goodbye, you be with your games and your plans."

They disappeared in the shadows and the mist, not knowing where the path would take them.

Probably somewhere.

Probably nowhere.

PART TWO

47

Sahasra watched the lake which killed.

His bulky arms were folded, his eyes looked straight ahead, watching the large lake. The lake had been a part of him and his kind for a while now. Ever since he was a child. It was the lake he had prayed to. It was the lake that he had loved. It was the lake, where he first fell in love. It was the lake where he learnt how to fish. The lake meant a lot to him…

And yet it meant nothing.

Sahasra arched his brows, as he saw one of his chief commanders, Takshaka, appear from the tropical forest behind, and he said, "Chief, they all are here."

He had been a loyal servant. Sahasra had been a part of his colony—the king, the chief, the provider, and many more things, and there was a huge responsibility on him.

"What are you thinking, chief?" His commander-in-chief asked again.

"I wonder if what gives us freedom, also cages us," Sahasra replied to the bald commander.

"Why do you think so?"

"Images of the past haunt me."

"Are you remembering Vatapi?"

Sahasra nodded, closing his eyes, controlling his tears. He had not heard his son's name in a while.

"I have always believed in family. When our people had shifted here, we were the pioneers of finding such a fruitful land, after all, where there was no corruption of any kind. The humans hadn't destroyed this place yet. And we lived close to nature, like our kind should." Sahasra sighed, recalling his childhood. "When Vatapi and his mother passed away, I held Vatapi close. I never thought I would end up loving someone as much as my wife, to be honest."

"I am sorry about what happened to him."

"I don't know what happened, and when the water around us got corrupt. I don't know what went wrong."

In front of him, he saw a swan. It was on the lake, but unfortunately its skin was torn apart, and his bones were visible, and it couldn't fly off or swim anymore. It remained the way it was, still and frozen like the water beneath. And it looked like a stone statue under the harsh sunlight.

It was dead, of course.

Everything on the lake was dead.

"I brought him here, and he played the way I used to play as a child, close to the lake. He ran in, to get some fish for himself. He ran into the water, and I clapped as I was happy." He shook his head. "And that was the last time I saw him. He swam in but he never came out. Lord Varuna took him away from me. For my karma. For all those horrible deeds I might have performed in my earlier life. I was a forager, a hunter, and now I was a father to a dead son." He looked at Takshaka. "Little did I know the lake had been poisoned, and it had been that way for quite a while. And my son died in it. You know how it feels, right? That you can't even do the last rites for your blood. His soul will never be free from this world. He became a part of the world, and his flesh and bones dissolved. The poisoned water engulfed him. What we had come for, became our damnation."

Takshaka nodded. "It's because of humans, I tell you. The corpses they threw into the water must have corrupted it. The war has led to many deaths, but it has killed nature too. Chief, they destroyed everything of ours. Our home is taken, our men are ill-informed, and most of all our children are unsafe."

"I know. It could be Lord Varuna punishing us, for we allowed his water to get ruined, while we watched and did not fight back."

"And now we help the humans, help them in the war."

"We have to do what's necessary."

"Hopefully, the stranger keeps our bidding. Keeps our side of the bargain. We did our job, as was told."

Sahasra nodded, touching the many bones of his victims that he wore as a garland around his neck. He was bare-chested, dark-skinned, and had tattoos of snakes made all over him. "We will get justice. We will get what we deserve. We will get our home, so our children wouldn't have to live the way we live." He paused. "The Maharogas, a myth, became a reality. It was told to me as a child that the Maharogas would come at the time of peril for the Nagas. They were our gods, our warriors sent by Lord Shiva, to protect us. Because after all, we were nature-loving people, harmless by attitude. But I got it all wrong. They would be unafraid of the poison and the corruption. They would be stronger than anyone. But it was all wrong."

"How?"

"The Maharogas are nothing but a story. But we have the power to make those stories turn into reality."

And he began to walk further towards the lake, where his feet touched the sand, and he felt the same current his son would have felt. Takshaka hadn't stopped him, but Sahasra did what was needed, and what could have been considered as suicide.

He entered the lake of death.

And he felt the current. He felt the foul smell of the dead marine life. And yet, his body didn't burn from the poison, instead he felt liberated.

He had learnt when he had gone to be one with his son in the lake that he couldn't die. He was immune to the poison the men had concocted.

The Maharogas are us. We are the warriors of Lord Shiva, who protect nature. They never came to help us because they were all along—us.

When he had done so, all the people had begun to worship Sahasra. He was their saviour.

"Bring them." He ordered.

Takshaka brought out the warrior Nagas who were afraid to enter the water, but one by one they came.

When one entered, he immediately felt his legs get paralysed and fell in the lake, dying on the spot. Another one entered, afraid, but nothing happened to him.

He reached close to Sahasra, who helped him take a dip in the water and feel the poison and become one of them.

"You are the chosen one," he told the Naga warrior, smiling. "Like many in our tribe. And now you will fight for us for you are stronger than death itself, you will be indestructible, you will have powers greater than anyone else, you have passed the trial of Varuna and have been reborn." He paused, holding the face of the Naga warrior, who was wet, shocked by the revelation of what was happening to him.

"You are a Maharoga."

48

Satyasena washed his face in the river and looked at his own reflection.

Blood dripped from his face, and it fell on the water, turning it into a gory sight. He was surprised by how much he had changed, looking at his shimmering reflection on the ravine. He had chapped lips, greasy hair, scars and bruises all over, a half-grown beard, and tattered, scorched clothes.

"Are you all right?" His mother cried out from behind.

She was leaning against a tree, holding on to her stomach, where his brother or sister would be. He couldn't believe, to appease a guru like Ashtar, he was going to kill his future sibling, his own blood. He was feeling disgusted by that idea.

Ashtar deserved what I did to him.

Satyasena came back and helped his mother, he had collected some berries from around to feed her. They had been out of the kingdom with no money, no guards, no possessions. They were ordinary civilians, stripped off their royal status by the usurpers.

"Thank you, son." She smiled warmly. "You are a good boy, you know that."

"I feel embarrassed every time you say it."

"Why?"

"Because you never said it before."

Her smile vanished. "I know I should have. I...uh..." she paused. "We had great expectations from you."

"And I never fulfilled them, I know."

"I don't care. You are my son. That matters the most, my child." She played with his hair, ruffling it, something she used to do when he was a child.

"Whatever happened to your father, I wonder?" She asked.

"I don't know, but I know, we have to walk to the local village. Get ourselves treated and move along. We can go to Hastinapur. Lord Suyodhan will keep us."

Shanaya nodded. "Yes, he will."

"I will send a raven when we reach the village. The problem is, I have no idea where we are."

"Close to the battlefield," she said. "It's right towards the east."

"It must be empty, no?"

"No, son. A battlefield is never empty. You have the corpses and souls of the dead, always lingering around. Cost of a war. Thus, I used to appease everyone around me. I would never fight, but ally and subdue myself."

"Yeah well, we are too late for that. Come on, I'll help you."

Satyasena and Shanaya began to walk, by the edges of the war fields, passing the foliage through the woods, to the deserts, hoping they were moving in the right direction, until they came along an interesting sight. Satyasena made his mother lie down again, so she won't feel strained, while he saw with his spyglass what was happening.

There were naked men, charred with the ashes of the dead, carrying corpses from the field, and whispering to each other in a language he had never heard before. Satyasena had heard of them. They were the Chandalas, the ones who would bury the dead or do their last rites. That was their job, and that was what they were paid for. To clean the fields and keep them tidy for the next war to dirty it again. They had bullocks with them, and crates too, for the bodies that were all chopped up they had large wooden carriers, and broken chariots.

But that was not what intrigued him the most. It was the bodies they carried.

Satyasena asked his mother to wait, while he walked towards the Chandalas, who he knew were harmless by nature. He approached them carefully, and with a smile.

"I don't mean any harm, my friends. I am just looking for one corpse, of someone I used to know."

But the Chandalas didn't understand him, and they began to ask what he wanted and what he could give for a corpse.

"Money? Gold?"

Satyasena pursed his lips. He had nothing of value to be honest, when he realised he was wearing a gold ring that could work. He pulled it out from his finger, and when the Chandalas saw it they began to jump and hoot. Shanaya was noticing everything from behind.

"Take care of this. Someone very close to me gave it to me."

"Which one?" The Chandalas didn't care, and they asked. "Which one?"

"That corpse. I require that one."

The Chandalas pulled it out from the carrier, and kept it near Satyasena's feet. Soon after they departed, elated that they had earned gold for a dead body.

But it wasn't just any other dead body. And his corpse was far more valuable to him than any gold on earth.

He knelt on the ground, and checked the man's heart, it was still pumping.

Unconscious.

A smile swept through his face.

"Mother," he called out, asking her to come forward, and she rushed to see what he was up to.

"What happened?"

"I suppose," he looked at the kundalams and the dirty hair, the thick, crusted, white beard, "I suppose, I found my father."

49

Vrikodara had dressed up for the royal day.

He wore a tunic up to his neck, along with purple gloves a lopsided crown. His dhoti was tight against his waist, along his sandals zigzagged up to his knees. He walked up the stairs of the palace, which had been cleaned of the blood of the soldiers. Many died here when he took over the kingdom. Alongside him was Hidambi, who had a dress on her, even though she didn't like it.

"I don't like being a queen," she said. "I hate it. Want to rip this dress apart."

"Well, let me do that for you, after this." Vrikodara chuckled. "But we need to do this, to instil faith in the people, otherwise, they might get a little anxious."

It was Pukkasati's idea. It was okay to usurp the royalty, but it was not all right to upset the people. They would revolt, rebel and that army was far bigger than the ones that the royalty ruled with.

"What are you thinking?"

Vrikodara looked at her, with his one good eye while the other was bruised, over which he wore an eye-patch. His hair had been trimmed, and his beard had been shaved, with the long, handlebar moustache greased and oiled.

"I have been thinking about only one thing for a few years now."

"What is it? What troubles you?"

He clenched his jaw. "You know, I am not afraid of violence, and I love to be in the thick of it."

"I know. I love that about you. It is definitely very attractive." She grinned, and her teeth reminded him of the times she would bite his skin off.

"But I had done a horrible thing a long time back, and it continues to haunt me," Vrikodara said.

"What is it?"

Vrikodara closed his eye, while he circled the top of the palace, and his mind took him back to those days. "We had begun to be quite popular with the people back in Hastinapur, and that made my cousin Duryodhan very jealous. To the extent that he had convinced his conniving father, the blind man, that he should do something about it. So he sent us to the local town to attend the festivities as royalties do. We stayed at a house for quite some time, almost a few months, as we gracefully saw the festivities over. But my brother, the Dharmaraja, he could sense something was off. Why was Duryodhan being so insistent? Eventually he understood that the house we were living in had flammable contents stored inside—made of hemp, resin and what not."

"Oh?"

"Yeah, some architect called Purochana did it. And instead of leaving that place, Dharmaraja played along because he had a plan. To fake his death. To show he had been burnt and killed." Vrikodara shook his head. "On the last day of the festivities, we decided we would escape from the tunnel that we had created. And that was the day Duryodhan had asked Purochana to burn the bloody house, so we die with it. But to delay the unforeseen incident, we invited the townsfolk to our palace, and they all drank and got inebriated. Purochana had to wait. I still remember, one of the families also had come with their five children, who were very excited to be invited to such a big palace. I told her there's madeira and it's not meant for children, but she insisted that she smelled food. I allowed it, thinking it might be all right. They said they'll be in a corner, and they will not partake in any kind of activities. When Dharmaraja saw this, he planned our exit. I was responsible for getting all the drunkards out of the house, so they don't die, and as Purochana decided to burn the place, we escaped.

Until I remembered…

"What?"

"I missed a room." He clenched his jaw. "I returned to the burnt palace, and I found five corpses of children along with a woman's corpse. Due to my stupid mistake, I ended up killing an innocent family who had simply come to feel close to the royalty."

They had reached the rooftop, from where they could see all of Anga, built of tall flat structures, made of bricks and mortar.

The people had gathered downstairs, and they all were looking at him.

"I had begun to fear one thing in life which I never had imagined. I had begun to fear fire." He told his wife. "I don't want to have any fears, but I also had no one to share this with."

"It is not your fault. Their death perhaps was meant to be."

Vrikodara smiled a little, and kissed her on the cheek, before moving to the front where a pedestal had been placed. He had a flag in his hand, which waved and thundered with the winds, bearing the symbol of an elephant, the symbol of Indraprastha, the crown that belonged to Dharmaraja.

"Say," Pukkasati said, "that this kingdom belongs to Lord Yudhistr of Indraprastha."

Vrikodara looked at the dwarf and yelled: "I will protect you and I will give you what you need. I will fight for you. I will not be feeble like your last king. I won't be absent."

And then he said.

"I will be your king. And this kingdom now belongs to Lord Bhima of Anga."

50

Karna woke up to realise it was better if he had died, than live like this.

He blinked and found his wife Shanaya and Satyasena looking at him, looming above his head like owls. He couldn't believe they had survived, and that he was with them.

"How...how..."

"Calm down."

They made him drink some water, and they gave him some fruits to eat, feeding him with their hands, while he lay in one corner of the field. He figured he was in a deep, dense forest, somewhere in the empire of Anga, or close to Magadha probably.

"How are you?" Shanaya asked.

"Terrible." He chuckled to himself, realising he had lost the kingdom to a brute. He couldn't believe that, and he wanted to hate himself for it. "Really terrible."

"Rest for some time. We are living in a farmer's house, and he has been kind enough to help us, in exchange of a toe ring, that I offered him," Shanaya said.

Karna knew that after the royalty had fallen, the only thing of value to them was the gold that they were adorned with. The one thing he knew he would never give away was his breastplate and his earrings. They held great value to him.

"What happened to Anga?" He thought about his kingdom, his people, his flag. All of it had been now obliterated. "Did you witness its fall?"

They both shook their heads.

"You should have protected it." He cursed at Satyasena, who remained quiet and stoic. "But rather, I don't know where you were."

"I was being manipulated by your religious order, that you had set up."

"They were good people."

Shanaya entered. "They wanted to kill me and your future child. I don't think you would characterise them as good."

Karna sighed, clenching his jaw. He had bangles in his arm, made of gold too, that could be sold as a last resort for their survival. He was cranky, and in a lot of pain. And his tough words had led Satyasena to leave the idyllic room along with Shanaya.

"I have to keep up with you because you are my husband, but you need to start worrying about your son too," Shanaya said. "You can't treat him like a log."

"I treat him just fine."

"The tough love might have worked for you, but it won't work for him. He hasn't been born in the same conditions as you had. And I even learnt you made him cut his fighting hand, so he can't even battle now. And yet while you have been lying down here, he practices with his left hand, hoping to be of help. He's the one who found you from the corpse rubble, and he gave away his ring for it. The least you can do is appreciate what your son has done for you."

Karna sighed, remembering the times he had been appreciated by anyone around him. His parents were absent for most of his life. He had a guru who taught him enough, but became a drunkard down the road. He had another guru who wanted to kill him. In every instance of his life, he had been cornered.

And every time, he had fought back against the tyranny of circumstances.

"You leave too. I don't want anyone here. I don't care about anyone. I am all alone. I am fine with being all alone."

Shanaya shot him a look of anger and frustration before she exited the room, quietly, not uttering a single syllable. He was somewhat glad that he had been saved, and he was still able to see the forest, the leaves and the birds. But he had lost everything. His kingdom, his crown, the love he got from the people and, of course...

He looked at his fingers. They were shaking. They were numb.

Possibly, he had lost his ability to be an archer as well.

But the exhaustion had sunk in, and he slept off, the way he had been sleeping off for so long. In his dreams, he had begun to see a utopian life which he lived with his family, his friends, and his crown. He saw he was the greatest archer of all time, and yet the blurriness of his dream continued to turn into a nightmare, and he had lost himself in the mirage of his illusions...

When he woke up.

Something was off. Something around him had shaken, and he looked around to understand what it was. There had been situations in which his ears had picked up more than his eyes or his body did.

He came on his feet and made his way out, and he found Satyasena and Shanaya fast asleep near the fire logs, while a young man, a shadow of a kind, had appeared close to them, stealing one of the other toe rings from Shanaya without her knowledge.

Karna shouted, to alarm Shanaya, who woke up and kicked the thief, as he fell on his back. Karna brought out his quiver and bow that were strung on him. He aimed an arrow at the thief who was running away. Karna aimed it at him carefully, taking a deep breath…

But his hands continued to shake. They were not able to concentrate, even though his mind was focused, and the thief continued to run as fast as he could, the distance between them getting larger, and it was becoming difficult for Karna, to aim at him.

"HIT HIM! HIT HIM!" Shanaya shouted.

And he did hit, but the arrow went in totally another direction. He hit another, and the arrow fell five feet away from him. He continued to hit, and yet there were no results and the thief had escaped.

Karna couldn't believe his aim had gone for such a toss, even his ability to hold a bow properly had become a problem and now the weapon he so loved, so dear to him…

His fingers no longer supported it.

"What went wrong?" Shanaya asked, along with Satyasena who followed her.

"I...Bhima...he broke my fingers, but I never thought... it would lead to this." Karna continued to stare at his ordinary, simple looking fingers, and he made a decision.

He decided there was no point to live anymore.

He decided, it was better to kill himself.

51

Vrishaketu couldn't sleep at night.

It was late, and the moon had appeared with its shiny sliver of hope, glimmering at them. He was sleeping on the floor on a sheet of cloth, while Tripti slept on the bed. But something told him that she wasn't comfortable on a thick cushion like that.

"What are you thinking?" Vrishaketu asked.

"How did we get into a situation that we have no idea how to escape from?"

"We got manipulated from every end," Vrishaketu said. "Now it's our job to not let that happen to us again."

They were at the town of Dandakappa, which fell in the territory of Kosala. After the entire shenanigan at Indraprastha, and basically moving like fugitives, they had no idea where to go now. They did consider Babhru's idea—that it was indeed workable, and could actually help, but they were not sure.

"We are enemies from both ends," Vrishaketu said. "At least, I am. I have no home anymore. The home that I fought for is the same home that betrayed me. I do not know what to choose anymore—who is right or who is wrong. Guru Keshava had got it all wrong, and I have been a fool, thinking I was fighting for the right side."

Tripti turned and hung her head from the bed. "You don't have to be so hard on yourself. For now, come with me to my colony, where we can stay till we figure out a plan. We have the evidence we require. The Maharogas will be very happy to join a cause that decimates the Kuru clan."

"But are they as big in number as anyone?" Vrishaketu asked.

"I don't know. For me, they are just stories. But I am determined to avenge my family, those who I was stolen from and if it means welcoming more carnage—so be it."

Vrishaketu wasn't sure that bringing such news to the Maharogas, to the other Nagas, would be the right call—it would lead to more violence, surely. He wanted to not be part of it anymore. After all, he had seen too much already.

While they lay in their bed in silence, Tripti broke it by saying: "You don't have to be a part of my journey, by the way. You can carve your own path if you don't support it."

"I don't know what I am a part of anymore. All I know is, you feel like my home."

She was quiet, and for the first time, Vrishaketu saw her smile at him. He smiled back. And she did indeed have a smile that resembled a thousand moons.

They slept for a while, letting their exhaustion get the better of them, when he heard something. Someone was screaming. Something was wrong. Vrishaketu woke up along with Tripti, and they stared down the inn they were living in. In the middle, he saw a bunch of soldiers bearing the elephant flag appearing, with one person leading them.

He was screaming, they had torches in their hands.

"VRISHAKETU! COME OUT! COME OUT!"

They looked like bullies, like people who had no boundaries and no territories. They would ride in an ally's kingdom and play the part of usurpers.

"Who's he?" She asked.

"Satyaki, one of Arjun's lieutenants and a close apprentice," Vrishaketu said. He had noticed him, at one of the many parties of the royal heritage too. He was also one of the people who when Vrishaketu was recruited, used to be his direct supervisor. "Have I trained you like that? Like a piece of shit that you do this to your masters?"

The townsfolk had shut their doors. Their windows were down too.

"We need to escape," Tripti said.

"No." Vrishaketu grabbed his sword. "I'm done running."

And he did what Tripti used to do. He jumped from the window, on to the ground, rolling over. The soldiers looked at him, and so did Satyaki, who wore a heavy metal breastplate made of iron and platinum. He dismounted from the mare.

"Oh well, you are here and my spies were right. You've been summoned back to the palace. Dharmaraja wants to talk to you."

"I am not going anymore and he's no more Dharmaraja to me." He held the sword high.

Satyaki took the sword too. He was a young lad, someone who had practiced very closely with Arjun.

"You can't fight me. I recruited you."

"I can do whatever I want to do."

Satyaki rolled his eyes, as he brought his sword forward. They began to spar at each other in the middle of the town. Vrishaketu used all his energies as he noticed Tripti slowly approaching from behind with her knife, to cut the throats of Satyaki's soldiers.

Vrishaketu felt the sword stab him in the thigh, he turned and stabbed Satyaki on his arm. He fell down and slammed himself against Vrishaketu who fell on the ground too. He brought the sword over Vrishaketu's head, which he somehow dodged when it came inches away from his face. Vrishaketu punched him and threw him aside.

"I would have never joined this bloody cause of yours if it wasn't for Guru Keshava," said Vrishaketu. "But he told me, you are the person to talk to, to help dismantle my father. I was wrong siding with you."

"You think your father is so good. He has been dismantled from the throne by Bhima. Your reign is over."

And he reached closer, ready to annihilate Vrishaketu. He pushed him away and brought the sword close to Satyaki, who jumped away from his attack, kicking him in the groin. Vrishaketu was taken aback by the pain, and tried to come to his senses, when Satyaki thrust his blade deep into Vrishaketu's back.

He felt excruciating pain.

"You don't know half the things that has happened to you, right? You don't know anything."

The pain began to subside, but with the blade inside his flesh Vrishaketu kneed him and then elbowed on his face, breaking his nose. He began to hold back, when Vrishaketu slashed the blade still inside him against

Satyaki's chest, making a dent on his breastplate, and then went for his face, slashing it, making him bleed.

He saw that the rest of his soldiers had also fallen since Tripti had assassinated him.

Vrishaketu watched Tripti who was bleeding and so was he, as he fell on the ground, feeling the adrenaline die down.

"I need...I need..." he went pale.

"We had been training you," Satyaki said, from afar, before leaving, "we had been prepping you to go against your father, you idiot. You are done now. You are no more needed to my cause."

"What do you mean prepping?" He asked, still in pain.

Satyaki moved back, confused, ready to escape, as a mare appeared at his whistle and he jumped on it. Before leaving, he said, "You were always our key member in the preparation of the guerrilla warfare against Anga. You were always a weapon. Even Guru Keshava believed so."

"How...how was he involved?"

"Oh, you idiot!" Satyaki smiled. "He had been working for Dharmaraja. And not just you, he was everywhere, in all those kingdoms where Dharmaraja felt the children had to go against their fathers. Dharmaraja believed that to kill an empire, you have to find the killer of the king's blood. And that was it. Guru Keshava agreed. It fitted his plans." He smiled, before leaving. "After all, Guru Keshava is Lord Krishna."

52

She had never felt so responsible.

Shanaya had been burning the midnight oil when she saw the farmer in front of her. She had lit a fire, Satyasena had gone to sleep along with Karna.

Out in the open, a storm brewed. It was raging like a madman, as the groves were crashing on each other, and thunder was crackling. The shack they lived in would also collapse if it would go on for longer. The farmer sat next to the fire and said, "I can't sleep too."

"How can anyone?" Shanaya said. "Thank you for being hospitable towards us."

"Father taught me that," the farmer said. "I heard about what happened."

Shanaya was quiet.

"Unfortunate yes, but I deal with bandits and thieves often. I close my doors, for that matter, and don't go out when they are around. There's so much of this world that is corrupt, I can't understand when all of this will end," the farmer said, sighing. "Father told me about a lot of stuff in life, and he said stay away from fights, no one comes out winning from it."

"Yeah, well tell that to my husband."

The grizzly man chuckled. "I've seen him before, I suppose."

Shanaya felt a cold streak, and then she paused, clenching her fist. She didn't want to be called out for being royalty, otherwise he could report it to the authorities, and they could be taken away.

"I suppose, I remember it from the stories my father told me." The farmer sighed, wondering.

"Whatever do you mean?"

"Oh no, he said, he was a Bhisak, after all. And he had treated this couple that was escaping the wrath of Jarasandha. The king Bhima had torn apart into two? Yep. That one." He sighed, trying to reminiscence. "And he remembered every second of it, because he got close to death for protecting that couple. The woman was pregnant, like yourself. And he gave them refuge. Jarasandha found them and attacked. He was in the crossfire, but he got saved. It was a tumultuous time for him, and for us, but he was able to recover, and he told me about the child, the kundalams and the kavach. He had them, you know. That's all he remembered. When I saw your husband, he had the same things." He was scratching his beard. "Probably a coincidence."

Shanaya arched her brows, wondering whether she had chanced upon the son of the person who had saved Radha and Adhirath.

"Your husband, he suffers from this thing, right? Paralysis? Or whatever. I think there's a solution," he said.

"What is it?"

"My father, being a Bhisak, had managed to learn about medicine from across the country. But one thing he never understood was the medicine of the Nagas. They know magic of some kind, and they could cure something like this," he said. "If you want to help your husband, you can give that a try. One of the colonies of the Nagas can help you out. They often help the homeless. He said this specific medicine was from the Valley of Forgotten Dreams."

But we are royalty. We are the ones who destroy their livelihoods, their natural surroundings. Shanaya bit her lips. Plus, it was the Maharogas who had murdered Karna's father. There was just too much of tension.

"Thank you for giving me company, but I should check on my husband."

"Right, madam. It was nice talking to you. An old man like me can always do with some good company. That's the only thing you have at the end of the day."

Shanaya smiled out of courtesy, and began to leave for her quarters, when she noticed from the window that someone was moving out of the shack and towards the storm. She went near the door and check who it was, and it looked like the figure of her husband.

She began to follow him, but he moved quickly like a shadow and reached a cliff. She continued to chase him, before she saw her husband, standing at the cliff, ready to jump.

He was about to make a leap, when Shanaya got hold of his hand, and pulled him close, while the rain sputtered on their faces, and she saw the pale, reflection of her once-crowned king husband. He was broken, he was defeated, and there was so much of pain and anguish in his eyes.

"You are not leaving us so easily!" She held him tightly.

But he was frozen.

"What happened?"

"I can't use the bow...my hands..." He was in shock.

Shanaya held him close to her chest and cried, knowing very well what she had to do.

She knew she had to make the trip. She had to help her husband reclaim himself.

She had to be the pillar of the house.

Vrishaketu woke up to find himself in a hut, and a large bandage wound around his body. He also saw the head of Tripti next to him, lying on her stomach, having fallen asleep. He had no idea where he was, but he knew it felt magical.

Tripti, knowing he had woken up, smiled at him and said, "Are you fine? Are you all right?"

"Yes."

He could smell the herbs and the Ayurvedic.

"Where are we?"

"At the colony where I was saved."

"Oh!" Vrishaketu said. "We are in the land of the Nagas."

"Yes. The Valley of the Forgotten Forest. They were my rescuers. They were my champions when they saved me from the slavers," Tripti said.

"Oh god! I let my anger take hold of me."

"Very surprising. Does it hurt even now?"

Vrishaketu tried to come up, and smelled the Ayurvedic even more as he did. And it still hurt badly, but he was trying to be all right, and the weakness had subsided with the numbness. "I'll be fine."

"I talked to Mother."

"You have a mother?"

"No. The Mother. The sacred aunt who takes care of the community with her medicine," she said. "She does all the work. And she told me, the Maharogas had come here after their supposed battle with the Pisach. And they were hurt, but they had managed to wipe out an entire Pisach community with their strength."

"What are you trying to say?" He was confused.

"The Maharogas are powerful. She said, they are born from a poisoned lake and they have powers greater than a human. I don't know how that is possible, or what is the secret," Tripti said. "But if they are the way they are, they can help us out. They should know about what we want, and then we should plan the downfall of the humans."

Vrishaketu and Tripti walked towards the door, and it opened to a large valley of pure greenery, a waterfall where the children of Nagas were playing, and there were huts, fireflies, butterflies, all sorts of insects and what not.

"How is this so beautiful?"

"Untouched by men and their development projects that's destroying nature," Tripti said.

For a moment Vrishaketu paused, wondering what she had just proposed.

"It sounds insane," Vrishaketu said. "Poisoned lake? Superhumans? This is straight out of myths."

"I do not know how real it is," she said. "But it is something. A hope. Something to thrive for. That's all we have right now, Vrishaketu."

And she had said his name for the first time. He licked his lips, nodding. “All right. Let’s go.” He wanted to avoid the carnage that would follow, and he couldn’t do it without being with her. It would give him time to convince her.

Tripti hugged him, and he felt a wave of anxiety rush down his body.

“Where is this place?”

“Apparently it’s called,” she said, “the Valley of the Forgotten Dreams.”

53

Vrikodara hated being the self-crowned king.

Because aside from the glory that it brought him, it was also the administration work that he had to look over. In the war room, that had been specifically created according to his needs, Vrikodara was bombarded with questions from Pukkasati. Ranging from what to do with the grains, to the farmers, to agriculture, how to levy taxes on the merchants, the export, the import…

"Argh!" He slammed his fist on the table. "Don't we have people to for all this stuff? Ministers, nobles?"

"Half of them you have already killed, commander," Pukkasati said snidely. "And the other half awaits your decision. They will execute it, but it has to be the king's decision. You, after all, wanted to be the king."

Vrikodara flared his nostrils. "My friend, someday I might cut your throat for the words you use against me, but for now I might just laugh at my fate."

"What makes you think you want to rule the kingdom?"

Vrikodara hadn't thought through that. "I have no idea. I just know I'm done being Yudhistr's arm, and I need to be my own man."

"Yeah, well that comes with taxes!" Pukkasati displayed

the scrolls. "Also, you took debt from the Rakshasas. You know how it works. A debt paid in blood, must be given in blood."

"She's my wife. I own half her army too."

"That doesn't work among the Rakshasas. After all, they are savages." He rolled his eyes. "Now, I thought, we should hunt for the best boars across the kingdom and present them and their people with gifts. A debt would be paid then, because that will be in blood."

"Yes," he said. "Whatever, whatever, I don't care."

"But I happened to talk to Hidambi, and she said the colony or whatever that cage nonsense was, was a part of a greater collective of colonies, ruled by her brother."

"Hidamba, I know."

"No, the other brother. So we need to just renegotiate the new terms, and we will be good to go. Then we need to face your brother." He chuckled. "God! So many brothers and sisters to deal with. I am glad sometimes that I am an orphan, otherwise I would have a knife on my throat."

Vrikodara thought that Pukkasati should know that he would not be able to make these jokes anywhere else, but it was good to have a dwarf friend, harmless by nature and the brain behind most of the operations. He laughed at his joke, while he touched his wounded eye. The black eye-patch hid the monstrosity of the bruise behind.

"I sometimes wonder if Karna died," Pukkasati said.

"He did. I rechecked with the Chandalas and his lifeless body was thrown around with the other corpses," Vrikodara said. "We won, dwarf."

The door opened and the royal guard, appointed from the Brute Company itself, appeared.

"Commander, there's an envoy from Indraprastha here."

Vrikodara rolled his eyes, and sat up on the chair, with his legs up on the table, where the wooden figurines were kept. They all fell by his heavy feet.

The envoy appeared, holding the sigil of the elephant.

"Lord Bhima, I come with you from the court of Lord Yudhistr of Indraprastha..." and he was about to rant, the full title and name, when Vrikodara ordered him to skip forward.

"Go on, move on, what is it?"

"Lord Yudhistr was not happy with the treatment of the soldier that you had sent back to him."

"The spy you mean?" Vrikodara shook his head. "Tell him to not poke his bloody nose in other people's businesses, all right?"

The envoy got nervous. "Lord Yudhistr would also like to congratulate you on your win over Anga. He presumes that after the stay at Anga, you plan to conquer more territories for him in the east, and he was asking what your next plan would be."

Vrikodara smugly looked at the envoy and then walked towards him, with the madiera in his hand that slipped and splashed on the ground. In front of the envoy, Vrikodara looked like a giant amongst men.

In response, he burped at the envoy.

"I am going to stay here for some time now. He can send any of his other people to conquer more territories. I am done listening to him and taking orders from him," Vrikodara said, as he pushed the envoy out of the room.

Pukkasati was standing at the back looking at Vrikodara

with a sigh of frustration. “You know, commander, you will eventually lead us all into a heap of trouble.”

“Why should we listen to that old fart?”

“Because he’s trying to do right by his father, who had given him his throne, but vultures like Suyodhan circle around it. He’s fighting for the right that your bloodline deserves.”

“Gah!” He waved the thought out, as he looked out of the window. “Yudhistr had always been someone who wanted too much attention for his own good.”

He saw his wife was duelling with someone outside, while training them. He gladly laughed at the sight. Things were going quite well when there was a knock on the door again. Instead of Pukkasati, he went and opened the damn door, to witness not the envoy, but a soldier of his standing outside.

“Commander, we have a problem. You might want to come to the rooftop.”

“Rooftop?”

Vrikodara followed him, along with the dwarf, who kept muttering to himself.

“What is going on?” He asked the little man.

“I had a feeling things might not go our way, just had a strong feeling.”

“Keep that feeling and shove it up your tiny ass, midget.” He angrily spat, as he moved towards the top floor.

As soon as they reached, he noticed the palace was so large that he was able to see the entire outskirts of the gated kingdom, that stretched for yards, and yards, where the forest and the desert met. It almost looked unreal how big Anga was, while it seemed quite tiny in comparison, and he was in awe that Karna and Shanaya had built this splendid place. He noticed a swarm of tiny ants at a distance, circling the gates, all the major ones, standing still but buzzing like mosquitoes.

"What are they?"

They handed Vrikodara the spyglass.

"A problem, my lord." One of the soldiers, who used to work with Karna said.

Vrikodara looked at the ants, only to notice the half-shaven heads, furry coats, long, abnormal weapons, with incisive teeth, roaring and growling. "Rakshasas...but why are the Rakshasas here? We already have Rakshasas inside, and we have given them enough."

Pukkasati slapped his head. "Oh dear, that's not good."

By this time, even Hidambi had appeared . "My love!" She called out to him.

Vrikodara looked back.

"What is going on?"

"It's nothing really. But I used to report to him. And he's here. It's going to be fine."

And she looked nervous. Vrikodara had never seen her ferocious wife so nervous.

"I thought he won't. We were a small colony, hardly not a big thing for him, but...but I don't know why he's here, or probably I do know why he's here, and that's not a good thing."

Vrikodara knew she was talking about the debt that had to be cleared. "It's Kirmira, right?"

Pukkasati and Hidambi nodded.

"We will deal with him." Vrikodara growled. "Let's go."

"Just want to let you know one thing..." Hidambi said.

"What?"

She blinked. "He's Hidamba's older brother."

54

Vrishaketu, for the first time, travelled comfortably.

After leaving the Valley of the Forgotten Forest with enough food and a horse and the supplies they'd need to survive, they knew they had a comfortable journey ahead of them. Though, as they travelled through the mountains, the forests, and the arid regions, moving as silently as possible, Vrishaketu got to know a lot about Tripti, and about himself too along the way.

They created camps, ate together, sometimes they would stare at the sky, and the stars, sometimes they would just sleep peacefully. Vrishaketu understood Tripti's aggressive, violent behaviour, for everything she had gone through herself since her childhood. And Tripti understood why he was always on the side of dharma, because he had only seen the wrong things. He wasn't sure who was right and who was wrong.

On one of their journeys, Vrishaketu happened to talk about his insecurities.

"I have been manipulated since childhood," he said. "If only I had known that Guru Keshava was Lord Krishna, I would have been careful. And it was done so discreetly, he had hidden himself so well, that it would make a wise man feel foolish. He also told me to go against my family. I am not sure what is dharma—to be with your family or to be on the side of the good. But then, what is good even? It haunts me to think."

"There's no good," Tripti said. "These are our own perceptions of ourselves. We believe and we think that we are good, but we aren't. We think we are bad, but we aren't. It's a perception, and we can't help it. The Pandavas believe themselves to be good, but to many they might not be. Not to my kind at least. They have done horrible things, and they have to pay for it." She had a sternness in her voice.

During one of their journeys when they had stopped, and it was raining heavily, and the cold had set in, they realised that they needed blankets but there was only one, so they shared it hugging each other. Vrishaketu had never felt that kind of warmth and that kind of love before, and he kept his chin on her shoulder, and they remained like that for hours.

"It's a journey," he said. "Everything is a journey. And in that journey, we meet heroes and we meet villains, and sometimes, we meet both within ourselves."

They met all kinds of people along the way. They met cowherders and soldiers, who didn't pay heed to them, for they were on the outskirts, probably in the north-east direction, moving up colder regions, passing the mountains, and finally reaching the tropical lands of the east. Islands. For the bridges were broken and boats were allowed there. Tripti had a map shared by her mother, who had showed her the right direction where she should go.

They even had met a beggar along the way, and they gave some money and some food to him atoo. Vrishaketu had done it against the wishes of Tripti, for she thought they had very little even then, and they wouldn't be able to survive if he continued to distribute like that.

The beggar, a lady, had gone through some bad times. She had beautiful eyes, and curly hair, and olive skin. She asked, "Where do you plan to go, my children?"

"None of your concern," Tripti replied.

Vrishaketu arched his brows. "Why do you ask?"

"So I can pray for you, so I can say that the gods would be kind on your journey." She gave a weak smile.

"We are going to a settlement known as the Valley of the Forgotten Dreams."

The beggar smiled. "And you shall be blessed for helping a young lady, and for taking care of her. My prayers will be with you."

And they continued on their journey. He had learnt from his father to be as charitable as possible, to help the needy, no matter how big a problem it might cause.

"The journey we take," she said once, "is it the right journey? Or is it not?"

"The journey we take probably is the only journey that is right, because it's ours and no one can take that away from us. We are doing what is best for us."

They had reached a cliff with their mares, and they looked over the tropical lands ahead, the broken islands, and the interspersed lake around those islands.

"We are close," she said. "It has taken time, but we are close."

"How do you plan to introduce yourself?" He asked.

"They might be hostile in the beginning. My mother said, they are quite indifferent towards outsiders, even the Nagas, for they are a closed community. Possibly. They might act in whatever way, but we need to be calm, and we need to meet the Chief of the tribe, to explain what we know."

"I have often wondered about the history of Nagas."

"We are the children of Shesh Naag."

"And we are the children of Vishnu. So why are we separate?"

She paused. "Because anything that you don't understand, you keep them out. We have different cultures, we have different histories and myths. We do not conform to the kind of living that you all do. The Nagas, the Rakshas, the Pisach...these are names that were given to us, or we created ourselves, because we wanted to have a separate identity from humans...from you. There was so much injustice caused by the human race that we grew tired of it." Tripti spoke, and she spoke so much that it left him quite surprised.

"Why do you think they haven't attacked till now?"

"Because they didn't have a reason," she said. "The Nagas are peace-loving, but the Maharogas...they will do the bidding if convinced otherwise. They might act in state of anger as well."

"The lake ahead, that is poisonous, no?" He asked.

"It could be, we have to be careful."

Vrishaketu and Tripti traversed ahead towards the hills, and he could sense that there were eyes following them. They had to stop for a break, but he suggested they go inside the hills and find refuge in the caves. As they moved up and the air got chillier, it also began to rain and thunder. They parked themselves in one of the leaky caves and began to make fire. The cave was long, and it had been dug up in a manner that it led to the other side. But they stayed right there.

When all of a sudden, an arrow appeared out of nowhere, it was on fire and it landed on the ground in front of them.

They both got shocked by the sudden movement, and Vrishaketu got up to check the ornate arrow made of obsidian blade. A letter was attached to it. Vrishaketu plucked it out, and the fire had begun to dissipate too after touching the wet, cold surface. When he read what was written in the letter, it sent chills down his spine.

Vrishaketu came to the edge of the cave, to see downwards from the cliff, towards the forest that they had left behind. Tripti asked, "What is going on? What is in that letter? Who has sent it?"

Far below, with a little army behind him, it was none other than Arjun on his stallion. He waved at them, a gleeful smile appeared on his face at the thought that he had found them. And they were now cornered.

Behind him was a woman—kissing him on the ear, touching him on the chest, with a sly smile on her face.

But she was recognisable, even with all the dirt covering her body, her beauty radiated even from so far away.

She was the beggar they had helped couple of days back.

But he also knew who she was at that moment.

The most beautiful woman in the world.

Draupadi.

55

Karna had done a lot of things in life, but one thing he had never done is given up.

And when of course, life gives up on you, there's family which takes care of you.

And that's what had happened, when Shanaya saved him from himself. He was about to commit such a horrendous act of violence on himself, but she stopped him.

She told him that there was a doctor far from where they were but he could solve Karna's problems. And that they should make the trip for the same.

Karna agreed grudgingly, letting his mood dissipate and actually listening to his wife again. They had travelled for a long time, before they had happened to reach a Gurukul, where they requested to be stationed and rest. They were told by the farmer where they would have to go, and it would be to the heart of the greenery, where nature began and the development of humans had stopped. But Karna had no idea where it was, but he listened, and only listened.

He looked at the Gurukul, and the young kids, meditating, training, studying martial arts and other forms of warfare. They were being trained in batches, some were practicing sword fighting.

Shanaya, Satyasena and Karna had given each other duty at the Gurukul while they stayed there, in return for alms and shelter. The Guru had been kind to them, and Karna concentrated most on the archery lessons.

He saw the children practicing over a tree, towards an apple that they were trying to hit.

Karna, though, was given the job to wash clothes, actually taught the children.

"You need to square your shoulders, take a deep breath, hold your chest high, and look in the direction of your target. That should be it," he told the children, with a smile. "There should be nothing else in front you, but the fact that your target is your goal, and it is the only thing that matters. You know how to become the greatest archer in the world, right? It is by knowing your enemy and where it stings him the most."

As he was teaching, he noticed Satyasena had been looking at him, from afar. Karna walked towards him, knowing very well that he had no idea about his suicide attempt.

"What are you thinking?" He asked.

"That when was the last time you taught us like this. Me and Vrishaketu." He was leaning against the thick trunk of a tree.

"I have done plenty when you were young."

"And why don't you remember?" He asked.

"You always have to complain, don't you?" His eyes struck fear then he remembered what Shanaya had told him, and his face turned bitter. "All right, you know what?

I will teach you. Come now."

Satyasena was confused. "I don't have a hand. Thanks to you."

"Come on. You don't need your hand to shoot a bow."

"That's the stupidest thing I've ever heard."

"Take an arrow using your feet and hold the string using your teeth, while your left hand holds the other part of the bow."

And he did exactly what he was told.

"String it and breathe. Look ahead carefully, at the apple tree, what do you see?"

"I see the tree."

"No. You should see the apple. Focus is the key to success, no?" He chuckled, as he told Satyasena to shoot, but he missed terribly.

"That's all right." He patted his back. "You'll learn soon."

Satyasena smiled. "You seem cheerful."

"I like the place. You know, I was the king of Anga because of my mother. She made me promise, but that was never my dream. All my life, I always wanted to have a Gurukul of my own," he said. "Somewhere I could train, a place for kids to get actual opportunities. And never the royalty. No. It would always be the outsiders, those like me."

Satyasena was quiet.

"You don't know what it feels to be an outsider," Karna said. "Probably that's why, you and your brother…I began to notice as you grew up, you were becoming exactly the kind of men I hated—partial, spoilt, and privileged. So I stole that privilege from you and what do you do in return? Exactly what a spoilt brat does. Whine. Cry. Rebel. Your brother went on to betray me, while you just tried to disappoint." He looked at him, and Satyasena was about to retort, when he said, "But in the process, I forgot I was also a father, and I shouldn't have." He patted his son on the back. "I should have been there for you. Probably us being here, out in the open, will allow us to know each other better."

Satyasena raised his brows. "Why do you continue to be a king? Why don't you leave the palace?"

"Probably I will. Probably. But I know, the kingdom doesn't belong to the likes of Bhima and his subjugates. If it was, it would be a free kingdom, welcoming outsiders, welcoming the outcast. If I don't do that, probably I have not done a good enough job myself," Karṇa said, remembering the opportunity Suyodhan had given him. He wondered about his friend, and what he might be up to. He was sure, he would get furious about the usurping of Anga.

"Mother is taking you to the Nagas, by the way. She has got news that they can heal your hands." He revealed.

Karna, instead of anger, held the bow and the arrow, and shot it, missing the target. His hands were shivering. "You know, son, I learnt a long time back—you should listen to your wife. They know more than you do. I should have been kinder to her too. I was too busy. At the end of the day, the only thing you are left with is your family." He paused, though he wondered if it was the Nagas who had murdered his father? But seeing that cliff, life flashing in front of his eyes and him witnessing all the events, he realised he had to be kind.

Circling his arm around his son's hand, Karna began to move towards Shanaya who was feeding the children outside, under the peepul tree. Seeing the father and son this way, a beaming smile on her face appeared instantly.

"What's with both of you?" Shanaya asked. "Is everything all right?"

"Everything is grand," Satyasena said, "though father is being a bit too nice for a change."

"I have to make up for the years I have lost, no?" He chuckled.

And the three members of the family laughed, feeding the children together.

Karna knew, before the kingdom, before the crown, before the friendships—he had his kindness and his never-giving-up attitude. And for that alone, he decided to continue living.

56

It wasn't long before the sun had hit hard, and Vrishaketu and Tripti had escaped the caves and made their way to the other end.

They were moving in breakneck speed from the intruders. They knew this would be a big problem, when Tripti scolded Vrishaketu, and said, "I told you to not be charitable."

"Father has always told me to be one."

"Well, that's an attribute one should let go of, especially during these times of moral crisis."

Vrishaketu was a tad bit surprised, that Arjun had led him into the situation. They wanted to stop him. And they possibly wanted to kill him too. For they held vital information against Indraprastha. And Indraprastha, unfortunately wasn't at the peak of their military support. They were gaining, by acquiring kingdoms all around, but they could be easily attacked and taken over by the Nagas or even the Maharogas for that matter.

"They want us to chase," Vrishaketu said, riding his stallion through the innumerable large trees that covered the hefty clouds above, letting in little to no sunshine. The ravines followed, but even when their throats were parched they couldn't drink the water, afraid it could be poisonous. "They want us to be worried, to act as prey."

"They are hunters," Tripti said. "I know. And I don't like them."

They slid their way towards the clearing, and they looked in the direction where the Valley of the Forgotten Dreams could be. But he didn't see any waterfall around, nor any settlement in the distance.

"The map shows a few miles from here, but we should have noticed something by now. Surprising."

And then they saw—the rain of arrows appearing in the sky, blazing in red, dropping close to them, hitting Vrishaketu's horse as it neighed and immediately jumped throwing him off. Tripti tried to help him with her hand, while the other hand held a shield above their heads to prevent the arrows from hitting them.

"Come on, get up!" She said.

He went for her hand, and an arrow went past between them. Vrishaketu fell back, to defend himself, and he saw arrows appearing from everywhere. And there was a figure that had entered on a large chariot, pulled by thick, muscled hyenas.

And it was none other than Draupadi, in her dazzling red sari, with a vicious look on her face.

"Come on, both of you. Don't make it easy for us. Come on!"

"Run!" Vrishaketu said to Tripti, and she moved in another direction, while he went the other way.

Vrishaketu sprinted like he never before, with his rucksack hanging on his back and his boots going through the mud and the dirt. The hyenas followed him with incredible speed, while she flogged them to control them.

Vrishaketu was moving quick, to stay ahead of the ferociously speeding chariot, jumping over branches, until he reached a dead end, almost close to a cliff.

Draupadi was grinning, her skin dark as charcoal, with lotus-coloured eyes, blue locks and fair brows, and a deep bosom. "You resemble your father a lot, except your skin disease," she said, with the lash in her hand. "I miss him, sometimes. He's a good memory, but a distraction from my cause."

"And what is your cause?" Vrishaketu asked.

"To destroy whoever tries to harm my family, and to stand by my husband, Arjun," she said and flogged the hyenas, who roared loudly. "Whatever I do, and whatever I have done, it is to make my family proud of me, and I will protect them with whatever I have."

Vrishaketu arched his brows. He pulled out his sword from the sheath, which Draupadi saw and laughed.

"Oh please, do not trouble yourself with that tiny weapon, it wouldn't help."

The hyenas looked at Vrishaketu with vicious eyes. She let go of them, unbuckling them, and they instantly moved for him, he was their food. Vrishaketu deflected one of the hyenas and threw him off the cliff. The other two began to chew his feet, when he stabbed them on their neck. Another grabbed him by the tunic, and he flipped his sword back to kill the hyena. He was bleeding profusely, but he had defeated the hyenas.

Draupadi got off her chariot, and pointed her crossbow towards him.

"Me and my husband, we often take the challenge

ourselves, when we like to hunt a rabbit. We go out in the wild, we make love, and we have the best kind of hunting experience. It excites us too, for some reason. The world is a filthy place, and we like to be filthy in it. That's how you survive, no?"

"Damn you, woman," Vrishaketu said, with pure hatred in his voice.

"Oh, and I thought you would be able to work for us again. We came to kill the girl, but you, you had shown promise with whatever little you had done. Yudhistr calls the little brainwashed soldiers of his—his acolytes. I prefer to call you all servants, but so be it. I'll just say I found you like this, rotting..."

At that moment a dart hit her neck, she fell on the ground instantly. Vrishaketu was shocked to see what had transpired, and wondered whether it was Tripti. Instead, he noticed men with bones around their necks, tattoos of pythons, larger than most people with matted hair, all woven and interspersed with each other, signet rings and different kinds of jewellery around their body, half-naked, smelling her and staring at Vrishaketu.

He threw the sword away to surrender.

"Me...friend..." He said.

Meanwhile, a man with a thick tuft of beard arrived.

"Me friend...he said...Naga friend," Vrishaketu said.

The bearded man with a bamboo spear in his hand said, "You don't need to speak to us like that. We are civilised people too. My name is Takshaka and I would like to inquire..." he held the crossbow in his hand, "what in the seven snakes are you doing here, in our bloody territory?"

57

Vrikodara rode his bison out of the gates, trampling the entire Rakshas army, scattered away by his might.

He was alone, just like every time, but he had made sure that the archers on the top, were all aiming at them. The arrows were dipped in poison, and they would end up wrecking the entire place and poison those who tried to hurt their king.

Vrikodara had his wife Hidambi with him, along with Pukkasati. He was moving along, prepared for any fight. In fact, looking for one, since several weeks had passed by since he had taken over the kingdom from Karna.

He looked at the Rakshas, and they seemed similar to how he had seen them earlier, but they seemed rowdier than Hidambi's lot, certainly were more aggressive, hissing and roaring at him, like beasts from the forest.

"Who's Kirmira?" He asked his wife.

She tried to look for him.

"He doesn't seem to be here. Very unlike him."

"I'm not going to entertain your people, if their leader is not here," Vrikodara said.

"You are married to me. They are your people too."

Vrikodara growled under his breath. "Identify

yourself!" He shouted at the Rakshasas, who were also barking back at him. "Identify your purpose of this visit. If it is friendly, you're most welcome to feast and dine with us, but if it is hostile, we shall be very unkind to you."

There was no response, no one said a word. He had learnt a few things about the Rakshasas, being married to one. He had learnt how they worked with a hive mindset. They didn't have a thousand different opinions like humans, but follow whatever their leader commanded, even to death. They were savages, and of course, cannibalistic, but they had a debt system. Now, Rakshasas were often foot soldiers and personal butlers and such kinds. Primarily because of their strength and their savagery. In a nutshell, they were very difficult to beat. But they were also friendly, especially after years of fighting against humans, they had made a pact—they would do their bidding from time to time, but for something in return. It could be of anything of significant value. That would be based on the debtor, who will ask the debtee. And if you didn't complete, they showered their wrath over you like a hundred comets. If you listened, they abided and gave you more debts. Now, mostly the debts would be in blood, and in return you had to give them hunted food, and hunted people too, from time to time. This was done because there was a time when the Rakshasas would attack in multiples, but now they have stopped doing that, ever since the debt system had come into place. The humans couldn't be killed by the Rakshasas and the Rakshasas would be forbidden to do so. A rule was created. The Rakshasas were happy hunting the criminals, or being fed by the humans they helped, and it was a nice supply-demand system that was established.

When Vrikodara had killed Hidamba, he had something great in the eyes of the Rakshasas, for a human capable of killing a Rakshas in modern times was unheard of. But Vrikodara displayed such immense strength that even Rakshasas would shy away from him.

Vrikodara decided to wait another second, when he saw a horse appear from between the crowd, people making way for it, and a man was on it, with hair like thorns deep red in colour and blazing like a fireball, wearing rings across his lips, nose and ears with a cheeky smile on top of it.

"Oh well, well, well, my brother's killer here," he said. "I would like to introduce myself. Kirmira it is." He looked at Hidambi. "Hello, sister."

"What are you doing here?" She asked.

"Oh well, nothing, just came here to pick off a debt from your husband. He did happen to use our army for his purpose, right?" He asked. "So I just thought it'll be a good thing to do so. When I learnt that you finally took the bidding, I was quite excited. We usually don't get to have the royalty at our disposal."

"These rules were created by my bloodline, and I have no qualms in breaking them."

"Oh, but you won't, because your people would start to say that you are worse than the savages out there, that you don't keep your word. So you kind of...have to now."

Vrikodara grudgingly nodded. "What do you want? What debt do I have to repay you for?"

"Unlike my sister who was pretty okay with you killing my brother, I wasn't. I had a hard time losing someone like him. He was a good old man, may his soul rest in peace, now he's a servant of Lord Raavan in the skies." He bowed gently. "In return for such injustice, all I want is one thing."

Vrikodara asked, clenching his jaw, knowing fully well, what was coming. "Your life."

58

Vrishaketu wanted to die by then.

He had been bound by reed strings and pushed around, just like a long time back in his kingdom. He felt that history was repeating itself, and his life would continue to be an ordeal. Vrishaketu remained stoic, as he was pushed around by the Maharogas. He noticed the difference between them and the usual Nagas. They weren't so decorated or majestic in their approach, and they didn't have the python tattoos on them. While the Maharogas did. The Maharogas were larger in size, bulkier, as if they had been working since birth. The ordinary Nagas were lighter in skin too, while the Maharogas were darker, something akin to Draupadi's skin colour.

He was thrown into the centre of a large circle, dozens of Nagas and Maharogas watching him keenly, as a human had entered their territory. The place wasn't beautiful as the last Naga territory he had seen. In fact, this one reeked of death for some reason, and everyone was glum. He hardly saw children here, as if there were only adults in this land.

There was hooting and chanting going on. Drums were playing, and horns were bleating. He noticed they all had houses built on trees, as if to escape the dirty ravine that flowed in between. They had horses too but they looked stolen, yet well fed, fatter than usual. He couldn't see Tripti anywhere, and he wondered if she had got lost somewhere. That thought scared him.

The night felt young, and they all were beating their chests, howling, as if it was some kind of a ritual, while he remained in the middle, a little skewed. He noticed a cushion had been set up for someone to come and sit down.

He saw the bearded fellow who had greeted their chief.

The chief though was bald, while everyone had some kind of hair on their heads, and his eyes painted with deep kohl, multiple bones around his neck, the highest number of them all, and he carried a javelin with himself. But what struck Vrishaketu the most was his nose ring. It was a stick jutted across his entire nose, he wondered how the man was even breathing.

"Chief Sahasra is here!" Takshaka announced.

They knelt down and began to worship him. Seeing this, Vrishaketu did the same, wondering if it was the appropriate thing to do.

"Sahasra..." Vrishaketu mumbled under his breath. "Never heard of him."

"You enter our lands without our permission. No human has ever set foot here, in years," he said. "Not because we have fences or barricades, but because they are afraid to do so. And you stepped inside like it is not a big deal."

"I come with one of your kind."

Sahasra gleefully stared. "I know. We found her too.

She was bruised, but she had escaped an invader, who we fought."

A relief washed on his face.

"She's resting." He continued. "Though we do not trust her completely as well."

"I come in peace."

Sahasra nodded. "No human ever comes in peace."

"I helped your kind to enter Anga. I am Karna's son," he said. "I work with Babhru."

Sahasra narrowed his gaze. "The bloody smuggler?" He raised his brows. "Interesting, that you know him."

"He suggested I should come and say what must be said." Vrishaketu said.

"Then where is he now?"

"He betrayed us, so we came ourselves," he said.

Sahasra paused, while Takshaka said: "He looks like a liar, chief! Kill him! Roast him! And throw him in the lake."

"Calm down," Sahasra said, "you do not mess with our guest, since we are the host."

He came on his feet, bringing himself close to Vrishaketu, and he seemed quite the man. His body was perfect, and he smelled of lavender too.

"Tell me everything, and I will judge whether it is true or not."

Vrishaketu had wanted Tripti to do it, but then he continued, relating whatever had happened between the Pandavas and the Nagas. How they had hidden everything. How Arjun is behind it, and how they should be wronged for it. After hearing all of this, Sahasra looked at Vrishaketu briefly. All the Nagas and Maharogas stared at Vrishaketu and listened to his confession in silence, and in horror, hearing what human beings were capable of.

"So you have come here to tell us this?" Sahasra said. "Made all this effort to help us know our enemies."

Vrishaketu nodded. "I want to do right by the people."

"Interesting," Sahasra said. "Though I already knew this. You wasted your time."

He made him kneel.

"I have known the Pandavas were behind the murder, but we choose not to do anything, because we must be in the good books of the powerful. We have to support them, and then once we are in, we enter their territory and snap their checks." He chuckled. "That is what a snake does, and that is what we do."

"Aren't you angry?"

"We have been angry for long. But we move with strategy, not with aggression."

Takshaka, on the other hand, Vrishaketu noticed, was not happy with the way Sahasra was going. He was calm about it, his demeanour after hearing all about his people's genocide was surprisingly sombre.

"But you have entered this territory and you have encroached our lands. You have brought the invaders, and for that, you shall pay," he said, bringing his long nails close to his neck where his veins were. "I sharpen my nails every day so I could use them against my enemies, slit their blood vessels and make them bleed and I shall do that honour even for you."

"No...no..."

He felt the sharp nails digging inside him.

"We are the good guys, we are on your side."

"There's no good side, my friend. There's only politics, and the efficient wins," Sahasra said, and he was about to dig his nails further in, when he heard...

Tripti entering the scene, breathing, panting and sweating. "Don't! Don't hurt him, please let him go."

"And why is that, my child? We don't harm you because you are one of us." Sahasra raised his brows. "What good is this human is to you?"

"He..." Tripti glanced at Vrishaketu. "He's on our side."

"No, he's not. For all I know, he could be an assassin sent by his father to avenge his grandfather's death, no?" Sahasra said and Vrishaketu realised he was talking to the person who knew about it. "Yes." He looked into Vrishaketu's eyes."

"He's not!" Tripti answered for him. "He's...he's...you cannot kill him."

"Why?" Sahasra said.

"Because he's the father of my unborn child."

Sahasra stopped, and so did the others. "Interesting. A hybrid of sorts. A star-crossed romance. What a pathetic tragedy." And he threw him down.

Vrishaketu was himself surprised, wondering when he had the opportunity to impregnate Tripti, but then he realised, it was a ploy to save his life. And Sahasra didn't do anything more.

"Unfortunately boy, you are allowed to live till the child is born, and you name the child. After that, I will decide your fate, but you live like a prisoner, till we figure out your place here."

"Aren't you going to attack the Pandavas?"

"Don't be a fool girl," he told Tripti. "Have you seen their army? Even though we are mutated by the poisoned lake, we are barely a few hundred in number, while they come in thousands. We have to be smart about it. Not idiots."

He looked at Vrishaketu, and he spoke with a smile.

"You know something?"

He asked before leaving.

"What?" Vrishaketu shivered under the deathly gaze of Sahasra.

"It was me who gave the instructions to assassinate your grandfather."

59

Karna believed he had reached where they were supposed to reach.

The Guru at the Gurukul had even managed to mention about the Valley of the Forgotten Dreams, and he had said—it was a dangerous place, full of venom and deceit. But Karna still decided to venture deep into it. Unfortunately, he didn't take the route through the mountains, but through the forest. He rode on his mare, along with Satyasena and Shanaya. Shanaya had gotten exhausted multiple times in between, and they had to take rest at intervals. During one of those intervals, when he tended to her, she asked, "Aren't you angry, I am taking you back to the Nagas? The same people who killed your father."

"I should be, yes, but if this is the way, then this is the way. They might have knowledge about medicine that even we don't, and if they can help me, so be it. And what are the odds that the ones who are going to help me, are the same ones who killed my father? Every Naga is different, and we need to see that." He paused. "But I have moved on. I don't know…when I was on that cliff, several realisations came to me and I knew I was going down the wrong way."

"You seem at peace."

"Probably. I had a dream."

"Yeah? About what?"

"That I am going to have a daughter." He smiled, touching her cheeks, placing it next to his palms. "And also, most of my anger was incited towards you by a person who disguised as Lord Surya's servant. The more I think about it, the more I realise that I was a fool to believe that Lord Surya would make me his son if I commit these violent acts. He has always guided me to be a good person, and that's what I should focus on, rather than anything else."

They continued to move further, and travel towards their destination, when they suddenly realised they were at a crossroads. On one route, a broken boat had been abandoned, but it could take them ahead. While the other route would take them through the hills.

"We should separate." Karna suggested. "You see that boathouse?" He signalled to a quaint cottage at the edge of the shore. "I assume that is a human house, and the Nagas, they live in the trees, as far as I know. Meet them, understand the situation, while I will scan the area, and I'll meet you back at the boathouse again, and then we can discuss further. As for the boathouse owners, make sure you are just a bunch of travellers, looking around to understand and appreciate nature. Remove whatever gold you're wearing and hide them somewhere. We cannot just enter a Naga territory without being prepared. They are a careful lot, for sure."

Satyasena and Shanaya both nodded in unison.

"Take care of your mother, son," he said to Satyasena,

who hugged him, and off they went on the boat.

Karna carried his quiver, and his bow and the arrows inside the quiver, but he was unprepared and slightly afraid too. He didn't want no fight that he would not be able to win. He was at his lowest, as far as physical strength was concerned. His hands shook, and his mind was a bit torn apart. He had tried to set things right with his family, as much as possible. He didn't tell them one thing though. At the cliff, when he was about to fall to his death, he had seen the effulgent light of Lord Surya who told him that he was going wrong, and there was still scope for readjustment and redemption.

He moved further and for the next couple of hours he scanned, looked around, being careful. He knew that yards away there were houses on top of the woods, and there were people walking around with javelins. He crouched, and lay still on the ground. Rather than entering, he tried to notice each thing very carefully, when he suddenly his eyes fell on…

There was a cage, and a long-haired man was inside dangling from it. A group of Naga kids were playing around it, poking him from below with their spears, and were trying to push and shove the poor man in the cage. For a moment, Karna felt funny about it, the way the entire scene played out, but he knew he had to intervene. He brought his bow and arrow and shot at the cage, but it didn't hit properly. He shot again, this time making the cage fall. The moment the kids realised it was going to fall on them, they instantly rushed in different directions. They were excited about the entire thing, but also afraid.

The cage fell down, and it shattered.

Karna noticed the prisoner who was in the cage, a human, and he began to walk towards him.

"Are you all right? You can thank me later but what are you doing here, out of all places?"

The man held his hand, "I am grateful..."

And he paused.

They both did. They were staring at each other, squaring off, when instantly the man punched Karna on the chest, and he rolled over, while shooting an arrow towards him but missing again.

"Not you again," the man said.

Karna rolled his eyes too.

For it was his old rival.

"Arjun."

60

Vrikodara prepared for the worst.

The little he got to know from everyone around him—Kirmira was not someone you could mess with. He was frenetic and mad. Vrikodara though had bruteness in him, wasn't crazy. Kirmira's weapon of choice was two tiny daggers, but he held them backwards, like he was meant to stab with them. Vrikodara, on the other hand, was twice his size, and was absolutely in the moment of retribution. His eyes saw red, and he was ready to give it all.

"You are going to kill my other brother," Hidambi said, cupping her hands on his cheeks.

"Yes. Regretfully." He shook his head, while his squire was getting him to wear his armour. "I don't want this on me. I want to go naked in the battlefield and murder him bad." He turned to Hidambi. "I am sorry for this, by the way. I didn't bring the fight to him, he did."

"I don't care. When a Rakshas marries the other side of the race, their only home is the one of the husband's. I do not care about my brother. He's an idiot, after all. But you, my prince, you are my future and you have great things planned for yourself. Protect the great, and fight well. You deserve the most honourable duel, and if at all, regretfully, an honourable death." And she kissed him hard on the lips, he could taste metallic taste of her tongue, realising what a wild woman Hidambi was, and how much he loved her.

He lifted the fifty-kilo weight of the mace and exited his tent, walking towards the duelling zone. The crowd had gathered around. Vrikodara's focus was only on Kirmira, his chest heaving but a smile on his face. He had killed a lot of Rakshasas in his heyday, but today he was more than just nervous. He had heard how Kirmira was unpredictable and capable of a kind of craziness which could be lethal.

The sun was shining bright over him, its rays striking his body like thunderbolts. He hated the heat. He had always been a creature of the cold. He remembered the trips he would make to the hills during winter months to take in the chilly weather. He would be naked and out in the snow, chop logs and feed his pups, wolves and bears. He would wrestle a bear, only to reward it with fish later. This was his idea and definition of a holiday gone right.

He waited for Kirmira and shouted, "ARE WE GOING TO WAIT LONGER OR ARE YOU SCARED, YOU PANTSY LITTLE SHIT?"

There was no response among the Rakshas, other than the occasional growls and snarls. Beating his chest, Vrikodara announced again, but this time the crowd dispersed, letting Kirmira enter, with his fuming eyes, and his armour, two daggers in his hands, and a fiery orange grin on his face, his red, wavy hair all striking and bloody. But his hair was tied up, for he was wearing a helmet of sorts, that had two large horns, making him look like a giant goat, all twisted and bent and dipped in something shiny.

"You seem excited," Kirmira said. "Yes, I am."

"Good. Then I would like to *burn* your excitement right away."

A Rakshas appeared with a fire torch and lit his horns up, turning his helmet into a flaming inferno.

Vrikodara's heart leapt in horror, as he exchanged a glance with his wife, Hidambi. He was confused about how to react, when Kirmira launched himself at him, attaching him to his own chest like a baboon. The fire was so close to his face that Kirmira didn't try to stab him, but rather just made him to stare at the fire.

"I had heard grand stories of Bhima the Great, but he seems to be afraid of mere flames. What sort of greatness is it then, when you have fears that gag you so bad?"

He closed his eyes, but he could still feel the heat on his face, and pushed back with all his might, throwing Kirmira on the ground. He wanted to escape the battlefield, when Kirmira threw a knife which pierced his back.

He scowled under his breath, pulling it out.

"I can't…I can't…"

He looked at Hidambi who shouted at him. "DO IT! DO IT! DON'T BE AFRAID. FACE THE FIRE, MY PRINCE! FACE IT!"

Vrikodara nodded.

"If not face it, go around it."

Vrikodara didn't understand for a moment what she meant, but he pressed his feet on the dagger and it broke into pieces. He looked at Kirmira, who held his other dagger and was moving in circles.

I need to move on.

I need to fight my fears.

I need to push myself out.

He closed his eyes, and with a quick swish of his hand beat his mace on the ground, as Kirmira tried to escape it. He opened his eyes again to see where he was, and this time he avoided looking at the flames, instead just stared at the face of Kirmira.

He hurled the mace towards Kirmira, striking him on the chest, as he fell down. Instantly, he jumped over him, and the first thing he did, was...

Burn his hands.

He pulled the helmet out of his head and his fingers begin to burn, but with a quick tussle of his arms he broke the helmet, letting the fire exhaust itself. He was breathing heavily, his anxiety had reached its peak, and he was still in fear.

But he had done it. He had broken the helmet, and it made him feel free.

He had faced his fear and it definitely made him feel more assured, more snide too, for that matter.

Kirmira, on the other hand, was surprised by his strength, but more shocked to witness his mental stability.

Vrikodara remained on top, and tried to push and prod, hurting him while he struggled. Vrikodara turned his gaze towards all the Rakshasas and said, "Anyone who dares to challenge me, will meet the same fate that you are about to witness now."

Then he brought his thighs next to the face of Kirmira, and pressed it hard, squeezing his head, squishing his eyes, turning his face into pulp in moments.

Soon he came on his feet, wiping the blood from his clothes, as he looked around.

Hidambi was smiling from ear to ear. Another brother died, but she knew it was an honour to be killed by someone as great as Vrikodara.

Her husband walked towards her and kept his tired head on her, kissing her on the forehead.

"I have no fear."

"You have no fear."

"I HAVE NO FEAR!" He announced.

And everyone rejoiced.

61

The boathouse felt like a dream that turned into a nightmare.

Shanaya had reached the shoreline, while Satyasena hooked the boat next to the shore, helping her pregnant mother deboard it. They began to walk towards the house.

"I wonder who lives here," he said.

"Anyone who lives so close to a Naga settlement, and has an architecture resembling human residences, will surely have some stories to tell," she said. "Though one wonders, why a human settlement is here at all."

"You know a lot about our land now."

"I am from this land, son," she said sternly. "I don't know what you've filled your mind with, but I was born here."

"Really?"

"Yes. This has always been my home. Probably my roots are from elsewhere, but I was born and brought up here, living the life of a Bharatvarshi. I know a lot of alienation, racism, prejudices, ancient customs that continue to haunt and destroy the fabric of the community—I know about all of them." She paused. "Though I don't blame the priest completely. Little did I know that he was tortured by my people, and he has a certain prejudice towards us because of that. He was against foreigners. But isn't this land all about giving equal opportunities to everyone? We have to evolve with time, and we have to allow people to work with us, to share the burden with us, because that's how a country can progress, no?"

"You've thought quite a lot about this."

"I have got my reasons to do so. That is why always remember, my son, it doesn't matter where you're from, what matters is where you go." She patted him on the back.

"I hate to say this, but this is the longest we have talked to each other." Satyasena chuckled.

"I am sorry about Roma, by the way. My heart grieves for her. She was an unhappy woman, and she died an unhappy woman. I know you loved her, though for the longest time your father thought it was an act of subtle rebellion towards him."

Satyasena smiled. "Oh, I wish. But she was a nice woman, and hope she found her peace in the skies."

They reached the top of the boathouse and knocked on the door. It had a heavy shed with open windows, along with bricked walls. It was like any other house, but a little bit bigger, but it also bore a strange haunted look as if ghosts from its past still roamed on its premises.

No one opened the door.

"Try the back if you can." Shanaya told Satyasena.

He nodded, going around the cottage, reaching a ledge which was narrow, and if one fell one would land straight into a lake. He came around, carefully gliding through it, and opened the door from behind. He reached the front gate, and unlatched it letting Shanaya in.

"Be careful of the smell, mother. It is indeed horrible." He held a cloth to his nose and tore another piece for her to grab. "Someone died here."

They began to move around, checking the old supplies, checking the rooms and the empty shelves. There was no light, just darkness, and the place reeked of something horrible. Death was permeating from all corners, the food they found had gone stale. No one had surely come in here for quite some time.

"Check here, there are corpses," he said.

Shanaya entered the room and found a dead woman in a corner, her body completely decomposed, sunken bones, no hair. She had been here for quite a while. She noticed there were a series of parchments as well as figures drawn around them.

"What does it say?" Satyasena asked.

"This one shows there were two people. A husband and a wife. They couldn't have children, but they found a basket floating in the lake. They realised the child was special for them, a gift from the gods. As the child grew older, he developed sociopathic tendencies. He used to kill, he hurt others. They tried to stop him but he continued to live his life, travelling out of this place, towards the snowy lands..." she saw pictures of gray mountains, "where he learnt of a strange gift that could make him really strong. He returned, only to find his adopted parents had ostracised him, and now he had to live in the local Naga settlement, and become like one of them. He was angry. Very angry. He left, went away for years, and they missed him, but they knew he was mad, he wanted to destroy everything...and then there's this mention of the local Naga tribe, whose lake had begun to get poisoned, and they had no home anymore, there was nowhere to go, and they were looking for a new land, and they could do anything for a new land. They had even talked to the human parents, and they were very nice about it."

"What happened next?" Satyasena asked.

"There are no pictures. I believe they died before they could recreate it."

"Why were they drawing?"

"The woman may have been deaf and dumb, this was the only way she could communicate, leave behind a message, I suppose."

"Who is this person?" Satyasena wondered, as he made his way to the other room.

Shanaya followed him to the main room, which was the bedroom, and a body was lying there, of a man, presumably. He had a scroll in his hand, tightly wound up. Shanaya said, "He must be the husband. He too was killed. Probably the adopted child did it."

"The story is quite similar to that of father, except the bit about murdering the parents."

"Yeah. Plenty of children get abandoned. If they get adopted, they are ascribed their status. And if they are ostracised, they are welcomed by some other race out there. All the Rakshas, Nagas, Yakshas, Pisach—you see out there, they were ostracised, spat out by a society that didn't think them as one of their own. In fact, my kind is not called humans too. We are called Yavanas. But it's not just any status, it's an abuse, a vulgar statement, that would continue to haunt us forever."

Satyasena nodded, breaking apart the bony fingers of the corpse, to grab the scroll in his hand. It was written in a strange language, probably indecipherable as it was in symbols belonging to the Naga. He put it in his pocket.

"I think we should wait outside for father to return."

"No, we should bury them, son," she said. "The right way they were supposed to go."

But something was off about the whole thing, and it was becoming puzzling for Shanaya.

Only time would tell, who their mysterious son was.

62

Karna had no idea he would end up meeting the last person that he wanted to come across.

"I suggest we don't kill each other in enemy territory," Karna said to Arjun.

"You are correct."

But the moment they met again and faced each other, they began to punch and kick one another, blaming each other for everything.

"We need to calm down. We are in the land of the Nagas, and we cannot let our emotions get the better of us. What are you doing here?" Karna asked.

"I would like to ask you the same thing."

"You tell me first."

"No, you tell me!"

Arjun growled under his breath. "I met your son here. I was here to kill him."

"Did you succeed by any chance?"

"No, that rascal got away."

"Vrishaketu is here?" Karna was surprised when his name was mentioned.

"Probably, I'm not sure," Arjun said. "My army was taken away from me, killed horribly and I was left like this, to be pecked by the vultures, until you came along. I was okay with dying in misery, by the way," Arjun said.

Karna and Arjun, they looked strangely similar, only one had a beard with shorter hair while another was clean-shaven and long-haired.

"I have so much gripe with you. And I should kill you for whatever you and your brothers have made me go through," Karna said.

"But that won't be an honourable fight, would it?" Arjun said. "That would be a coward's way to kill someone, especially when that someone has no weapon in his hand."

"Here, take my bow and arrow, then I'll kill you with my bare hands," Karna said.

"No, thank you, I don't want it."

"Take it!"

"I don't want to give you a reason to kill me. Gah! Don't think of me as a fool," Arjun said. "What are you doing here? Did my idiot of a brother finally happen to take over you?"

Karna sighed. "Unfortunately, yes. I am here to..." He paused, unwilling to reveal the true reason behind it. His rival shouldn't know his weakness. "Go on then. I have saved your life. Let me be. And don't go around showing your face or you accidentally might get killed by someone in the forest."

Arjun sighed. "I need a favour though."

"Yes?"

"Help me with Draupadi. You don't have a weapon to share, and I know she's been kept captive close by."

"She's here too?"

Karna was quite taken aback.

"I know you don't like her very much."

"Of course. She berated and humiliated me by not taking my hand during the swayamvar, even though I won fair and square. But no, she had to mention I am a suta!"

Karna shook his head. There was a time when there was fiery passion between them, but now Karna simply hated her for being such a cruel human being. The worst thing was she made it impossible to form allies with the Panchal kingdom, which would have been a great asset to his shipbuilding activities.

"She loved me."

"Sure she did! Draupadi doesn't love anyone," He said. "She only loves one thing and that is power. As long as you stick to that, you'll be fine. Now, where is she?"

They continued to walk around the forest. Karna had never thought he would be helping his bitter rival someday, they moved quietly in the land of the Nagas.

"It was a mistake to come here. I should have killed your son earlier."

Suddenly they heard a noise. Of a woman. Crying.

They moved past a broken cage and trampled grass.

They reached a clearing where he saw the Nagas had grouped around, dragging Draupadi to the forefront, ready to display their brutality on her. She was weeping, and loudly whining.

Arjun had an impulse to help her, but Karna stopped him, as the Nagas...they seemed different.

They had red eyes, and they had foam coming out from their mouths, and they had veins bulging out of their faces.

"They don't look normal. As if they are under some kind of a trance," Karna said.

And they were growling like a hound dog, left for many days without any food.

"I have to save my wife!" Arjun whispered back irritably.

"I know. Promise me one thing?"

"What?"

"If we happen to escape from here, you will not harm my son. And in return, I will help you. Promise me now!"

Arjun looked at him, visibly under pressure. "You are an ass, using my wife as a means to save your son."

"I'm doing what's right for my family."

"All right."

They shook hands.

"How do we do this?" Arjun asked.

"They seem quite powerful, and I don't think fighting them directly makes sense, when we are the weaker lot here," Karna said. "I'll distract them to follow me, and you run away with Draupadi, and we never see each other again."

Arjun nodded.

They went their separate ways as Karna made way to the eastern route, where he came in front of the hungry Nagas, who he felt resembled the Maharogas. It was a possibility.

He shot an arrow at them, to divert their attention, and they all turned to look at him, a distraught Draupadi behind them who had been fighting for her life.

"Come on, come on!"

The Maharogas punched their chests, as the three of

them left Draupadi, and like manic fools began to chase Karna. He saw that Arjun by then had grabbed hold of Draupadi and was taking her away.

But one of the Maharogas happened to see it.

Karna had to act quickly. He instantly jumped at him, hitting him with his bow, the Maharoga showed no sign of pain, but fell down.

Another Maharoga appeared next to him, and snatched his bow and his quiver. While another hit him on his feet. He fell on the ground, and the one who tried to chase Arjun…

Karna grabbed his feet, stopping him from chasing the couple who slowly disappeared in the distance. The Maharogas circled him, then they broke his bow, and grabbed him by the chest and threw him against the trunk of a tree. By the time he noticed the couple had gone out of sight, Karna felt relieved, thinking he did right by someone—something good, with some selfish motives yet meaningful. His thinking didn't last long as the Maharoga punched him on the face, and broke a tooth. Karna stabbed one of them, but it didn't seem to hurt him at all.

He decided to skid, and run quickly. But they ran even faster than him, at an impossible speed, threw him off course, before dragging him to a side.

Grabbing him by his legs.

Towards his probable death.

63

Vrishaketu was in love.

And he knew it for sure.

Tripti was lying on the bed, and that day when she had come to save him, she had managed to put all her efforts to help him out of the situation. Now, she had been resting, and she had a large wound around her feet, which made her weak. But she was alive, and she was laughing and chuckling with him.

"That was a good one," Vrishaketu said. "Pregnancy. I like that lie."

"Naga culture doesn't allow the husband to die, before they name the child, otherwise the child remains nameless for the rest of their lives, and it is considered worse than death. Imagine yourself..." she paused, and she looked pale, and she was weak.

"Don't speak much," he said. "So it's okay to have children out of wedlock?"

"There's no concept of marriage, but only union. You are married to nature, and we all are products of that nature, so you are married since childhood."

"Oh dear, sometimes it is good to have knowledge like this to protect yourself." Vrishaketu smiled, holding her hand. "I want to tell you something."

"Don't tell me you like me!"

"No. I am going to tell you, I love you."

"What a horrible thing to say. Why do you love me?" She smiled, feeling a tad bit happy, more talkative than usual.

"Because you are one of the few reasons I like to wake up in the morning and I want you to know, I'm there for you and our fake baby." He chuckled.

"The fake baby definitely needs you."

They both had a good laugh.

"Our plan failed, by the way," he said.

"I know. I don't know what to do anymore."

"To leave is one of them. We are alive, for now, but once they know you faked your pregnancy, it might lead to more troubles for us. So I believe we should scoot, before it happens."

Tripti nodded. "My feet seem better than before and I think we can definitely make that leap at midnight, when everyone is fast asleep. But what after that? What then?"

Vrishaketu thought about it. "Have I told you about my dream?"

"No."

"Uh, my goal. I knew I had to protect dharma, but I also knew I wanted to travel to the icy lands of the north. And I wanted to fish for eels and live in an igloo."

Tripti raised her brows. "Do you plan to keep me in a bloody igloo?"

"I don't know what I want. But I do know that our lives are intertwined and we can go anywhere we want to. When we have the opportunity to fight for the rights of the ones who have hurt your people, we will use that opportunity. But let's not squander the better part of our lives on this, no? Don't you think so?"

She was determined. Her eyes were tired. "I don't know what I'm going to do. I don't know whether I have a personality beyond my goals of fighting for my people's rights. But it is true, that if my people don't care and want to remain afraid, then so be it."

Vrishaketu kissed her on the cheeks and asked her to sleep for a while. He left the treehouse, and looked around the other houses underneath which the ravine flew. There were bridges too, all lopsided, which helped people to travel, it reminded him a lot about the Vanaras. He hadn't seen many, but then he hadn't travelled much in his life either.

He also thought about Sahasra, and how he had a role in his grandfather's death. That bothered him. Harming them indirectly was one thing, but being responsible for their demise is another, and that was a guilt he knew he could never get rid of.

As he mulled over his thoughts, he heard the beats of drums from afar, it sounded familiar, and it reminded him of his trial.

There was another intruder, an invader from the outskirts, put to trial by Sahasra.

And he wondered whether it was Arjun.

Karna was bound and displayed like a puppet in front of the bamboo throne of the Maharoga chief.

His hands were tied, the little he had picked up from conversations around him, he had happened to understand who is who in the entire scheme of things. There was, of course, the Takshaka, who had been the right-hand person of the chief. And then there was Sahasra, who had taken up this settlement and made it his own.

Karna was quiet as a bat, because he knew the more he spoke, the worse it would make his case.

"What is with intruders entering our territory this time? So many of them. You being the second one." The chief Sahasra said, while the drum kept beating around them. He walked over to Karna and touched his earrings. "I love the kundalams, reminds me of a warrior who wears them in battle. Could it be true that you are that warrior?"

"I do not know what you speak of," Karna said, not revealing his identity.

Sahasra paused. He was taller than Karna, and broader too, though not as big as Bhima. He had a faint smile on his face, and papery thin lips, with dark skin, and deep, auburn eyes. "Why are you here? Identify yourself then."

Karna was quiet. "I do not wish any harm."

"No human ever does, but they still do it, don't they?"

"I have come for the medicinal advantages you have over others. I have come to heal my hands."

"Ah, interesting. And in return, what would you give? Something of value, perhaps? Perhaps the kundalams that you wear?" Sahasra asked.

Karna clenched his jaw. "Never my earrings."

"But that's the only way to do this exchange, otherwise I would rather kill you and be done with you."

"Then do so. We can barter something else, but my living body will never give the kavach I wear, and the kundalams I adorn," he said loudly and impassively.

Sahasra's snake-like eyes, blinked. "Indeed, then." He hissed. "And I only want that. Unfortunately, negotiation cannot be done, and I have decided that you die."

The Maharogas, with their foaming mouths, approached him, ready with their claws, and weapons to attack him.

Karna closed his eyes, awaiting his death, hoping his family would be fine, when instantly he saw someone skidding and entering the circle of the court.

"He's my father. Leave him."

Karna looked at the familiar figure, and for a moment, he couldn't believe it was his son. He had changed, matured so much.

Vrishaketu.

"Of course, he is," Sahasra boringly said. "Why did this reveal need to be so dramatic? You know, boy, your father coming here, convinces me that you have come to us to seek vengeance for what we did to your grandfather."

Karna felt a chill run through his body.

He killed him.

"And you are both assassins and that makes you threats, which would nullify our arrangement," he told Vrishaketu. "I believe it is time then we do the needful."

Vrishaketu was pushed to the spot beside Karna, and they both stood adjacent, with spears placed close to their hearts and faces.

"Don't kill us. Please, don't. Don't kill him," Vrishaketu said, but Karna remained unafraid. "Kill me."

"Oh no," Sahasra told his men to put the weapons down. "Kill you? I don't want to kill you. Na. Na. I would rather see something else."

Karna narrowed his gaze. *What?* Was his reaction.

"I would rather..." Sahasra smiled. "See you both kill each other."

64

Vrikodara was lying still, when he thought he had a dream. And in that dream, he was killed brutally.

But then he wasn't sure.

It was just a dream.

Because the killer was none other than his brother. Yudhistr. He had always had a strange relationship with his brother, in which he was asked to do something and he did it without questioning. And this was the first time he had gone against his brother's wishes, thrown his envoy out, thrown his spy out. He almost couldn't believe himself, such were the horrifying state of affairs.

But when he opened his eyes, healing in the process by the thick smell of the Ayurvedic pasture on him, he saw the very man sitting on a chair next to his bed.

"How are you, brother?" He asked.

He was sitting idly, with his short hair, handsome face and angelic smile on it. Vrikodara wasn't as good looking as him, and that envy always haunted him, because he had a bulbous nose, and big, fat lips.

"How did you enter?"

"It is my vassalage that you hold to it so dearly."

Vrikodara sat on his bed, a tad bit afraid. "Who let you in? Am I dreaming? Is it the medicines?"

"It's nothing, to be honest. I am really here. Let me pinch you." He brought out a dagger and poked him.

Vrikodara felt it.

"See. It's all fine. I am here."

Vrikodara watched him carefully. "Are you angry with me?"

"Why would I be?"

"I didn't listen to you."

"And rather played around with the Rakshas? Wasting your time? Entertaining your Rakshasi wife?" He rolled his eyes. "Why would I be frustrated with you, big boy? You are, after all a free man, so to speak, do what you please."

There was sarcasm all over his statements. He knew that Yudhistr would not be pleased by this.

"I have to be my own man. I have to come out of your shadows, someday. This is the kingdom I deserve."

"You are a brute."

"I am tired of listening to that."

"Don't indulge in politics. You are a warrior, the best one at that and I have full confidence in your abilities, but I also know that you can't run a bloody kingdom," he said. "Do you remember mother used to make you do all the heavy lifting in the house, while I decided what has to be put where in the palace? Because I know stuff. I have not been given the strength that you have, but I have this." He touched his head. "One should know their limitations and you have many. One being, you should not cross me, the one who has given you everything."

Vrikodara paused, clenching his jaw.

"I won Anga myself and I deserve it."

"Do you know what politics entails? Do you know what all I had to do to make things possible?" He asked. "I had to convince Karna's wife's father to return and steal the ships, creating ruckus amongst husband and wife. I had to pay the Nagas, especially the ones who claim to be Maharogas, to assassinate Karna's father, to create mental trauma for the ruler. You might have the brawn, my friend," Yudhistr said, raising above him, like a towering giant, and patting him on the head. "But I have won the kingdom. And you are just my muscle, someone who did the dirty deed. A lot of planning goes into taking over a kingdom, and swords alone unfortunately don't cut it. No pun intended."

Vrikodara was horrified by the revelations his brother was dropping on him, one after another. "You killed his father?"

"Well, it was kind of a message from me, you know. Be careful what is coming for you."

"But why did you stop me in the middle then? If you wanted Anga all this while, why did you make it so hard for me?"

"There were some complications with Arjun involved, but I sorted it out before you could approach him. That also has complicated matters further, and I'm trying to sort that out too, but you, my big brute, you need to learn to listen, otherwise it'll be a bigger problem."

Vrikodara felt Yudhistr's hand over his forehead and his chin, as he was calmly patting him, brushing it.

"And now I have heard that Karna has reached the Nagas. I am worried, he might be preparing a defence strategy, or worse, an offence plan."

"He's alive?"

Yudhistr slapped him on the face. Hard.

"Of course, he is, you idiot. I told you. Complete your bloody job, and you didn't do it," Yudhistr said. "And now look at where we are. You rule like a fool on a kingdom whose king is displaced not dead, and he can come back anytime to take it over. And the Nagas, they would be on it, as well. So I am here to warn you, to prepare you, for defence. I am leaving a portion of my army here, and I am leaving for Indraprastha. Once you are done with him, please for the love of Vayu, who you worship dearly, complete the bloody job."

Vrikodara was paralysed, almost emasculated by Yudhistr's actions. He had never been abusive like this.

As he left the room, he couldn't believe what all goes into protecting the crown, and the lengths one goes to, to achieve the throne.

But seeing all of this, he knew very well he didn't want to participate in it.

Not anymore.

Not after what he had heard.

65

Karna had seen his son after a long time.

And he had never expected, it would be on a wooden log, in the middle of a poisonous lake, with their swords next to each other, while the Maharogas, had circled them to watch the spectacle. He didn't want to do this, but apparently, the duel stated clearly that one had to come out alive from it, and the one alive would be given amnesty.

"Instead of doing this," Vrishaketu shouted, "you should do what is needed. Attack the bloody usurpers of Indraprastha, kill the Pandavas, and do right by your people."

But Sahasra just yawned when he heard that statement.

"Should we begin?" He asked, and then he clapped.

The horn bleated.

And the log shifted.

Karna and Vrishaketu stood still on their spots. They were locking eyes.

"We need to have a plan," Karna said. "We need to escape from here." His sword was shaking in his hands, it was difficult holding a blunt instrument.

"How do I know that you won't attack me?" Vrishaketu asked. "All you ever wanted was my death. Ever since the beginning."

"I was wrong. I shouldn't have."

"Isn't it too late now? Look at us. Fate has brought us where we are supposed to be. You against me."

"I was wrong. I was too hard. I want to do right to you."

Vrishaketu stood there, as Sahasra yelled, "HIT HIM!" And he clapped.

Vrishaketu struck Karna's sword lightly, and then did it again, out of formality. There was no passion in it. Karna watched the lake around him, it was green and it smelled of something dark and sinister.

"We are like the lake. We have become spoilt because of other people in our lives, but we should remain pure in our actions."

"You don't treat yourself as a victim of the times. You have orchestrated many."

"I want to solve things with you."

And Vrishaketu hit his sword again, this time harder. They continued to spar lightly to continue the show, when accidentally, Vrishaketu got a cut on his arm. Thinking it was done deliberately, Vrishaketu attacked back, kicking him on the chest.

Karna fell back.

Vrishaketu came over him, trying to stab him, his eyes bloody red, almost teary when he was about to kill him...

Vrikodara watched the kingdom of Anga from his window, probably wondering what it would become under the watchful gaze of Indra.

He had been called the son of Vayu, for how powerful he was. Like a storm, he would destroy the world around him. He had the strength of ten elephants, they also said. He stood there, naked against the window.

Vrikodara saw Hidambi, walking towards him.

"What happened?" She asked.

She was holding a mug, sipping from it.

"What are you drinking?" He asked.

"The little man gave me some milk to drink, for my health and recovery. So tell me, what is it? And don't avoid the topic."

"I'm wondering if there is a reason for me to continue here."

"Why are you thinking that way?"

"My journey has made a son lose his father," he said. "I remember how it was to live without a father for so long." He clenched his jaw. "What kind of a monster have I become under the horrible regime of my brother? He is callous."

Hidambi hugged him tightly. "Then I believe it's not the right time to tell you."

"What happened?" He asked.

"I am pregnant," she said. "And you are the father, Bhima. You are definitely the father."

Vrishaketu was feeling a surge of emotions going through his mind and body.

But with a quick flick, he made his father fall on the log. The log shifted a bit, and his hand almost got dipped in the lake, but Karna kicked it away, so it doesn't touch the lake water.

Vrishaketu deflected the attacks and slid between Karna's leg and hit him on the head with the hilt. Karna fell and turned and said, "You have learnt well. You have learnt like a true king. You know what you have to be."

"Mother wanted to kill me, in your absence. You were afraid enough to not even be there during my death penalty organised by you."

"She didn't do it, did she?"

"No, I was saved by my people."

"It wasn't your people. It was her," he said. "I checked later, and I learnt. They found the hooded person, and my spies had seen her wearing that same hood. I never told her that I knew this, but I'm telling you. There is a king, and then there's a father. There's a queen and there's a mother. Unfortunately, Vrishaketu, you will understand when you'll become a king."

"I shall never," Vrishaketu said through gritted teeth, tears in his eyes, realising what his mother did for him. "I have lost all hope and meaning."

"You have us. We are always there," he said. "You have your family. We were not there in the beginning, but we are here now. Be with us again, and you will have no troubles anymore."

Vrishaketu stared at him, and his genuine eyes. He immediately threw him down, and brought his sword close to his chest, but Karna didn't put up a fight anymore. He just lay there.

"Kill me, if you don't believe me. Kill me and be done with me," he said, lying flat.

Vrishaketu held the blade close and went through multiple emotions of betrayal, of disbelief and lack of trust in his mind, before he gave in, throwing the sword aside.

Sahasra shouted, "You have been quite a disappointing affair." And he ordered the Maharogas to point their crossbows towards them. "I think now we have to complete our duty. Shoot them and throw their bodies in the lake." He ordered.

Karna and Vrishaketu raise their bows, when suddenly they heard the wailing of someone. Vrishaketu had heard that voice before, as Sahasra allowed the person to come, and it was none other than...

His mother and his brother, gagged.

"Don't kill them. Don't kill them!" She shouted.

"Oh, we have the entire family here, I see." Sahasra sighed. "Who else? Are the uncles and aunts here too? Do we need to know about anyone else?" He sounded exasperated.

"I have an offer." Shanaya announced, so that everyone could hear. Even Takshaka's ears stood up.

"You have nothing to offer to me. You have no leverage."

"I know what you want." Shanaya sternly replied.

Sahasra narrowed his gaze, out of curiosity.

"I know what you want," Shanaya said. "I know you want to change the location of your people. You have been unable to do that and you need a new land. We can help you with that."

66

Sahasra was ready to listen.

Karna's entire family was put in front of him one by one, he watched calmly. Takshaka was by his side. Sahasra had grown tired of this nuisance, and everything he was doing was out of sheer amusement. He knew his people would enjoy this kind of fun, since they had grown pretty tired of the Nagas being treated like circus animals.

"How do you know about our land?" Sahasra asked Shanaya. She was an outsider, just like them.

"It doesn't matter how I know…what matters is, I know that you are searching for a sanctuary. We are the royalty from Anga, and we can provide you that sanctuary in the kingdom. We have enough land where your people can stay peacefully."

He impassively nodded. "The same was offered by the people of Indraprastha in return for killing the head of your family," he said, looking apologetically towards Karna. "We did our job, but we did it with no enthusiasm."

Karna didn't react. He was folded on his feet, on the ground, and he was listening quietly. "You did what you had to do for the rights of your people, and I understand that more than anyone else."

"But..." Sahasra continued, "it was not fulfilled. We have done our deed, and we have not received any communication from the humans of Indraprastha about our land. We have been shortchanged, or probably the constant reminders haven't worked in our favour."

Takshaka breached the code of conduct, when he added, "I do not trust them. Not at all."

"We are unable to attack them even though we have the means, the weapons, and a power greater than anyone else," Sahasra said.

"The Maharogas, I noticed some of them looked different. More beastly, one would say."

"Yes, it brings the monster out in you," Sahasra said. "It is from the lake. While some died, some remained alive and more powerful than last time. We have to take this." He showed a vial hanging from his neck like a pendant, "Whenever we go to war, to recharge ourselves."

They all nodded.

"But this Anga...we have heard great things about it, but you say you have been ousted. How do you plan to take it back from the usurpers?" Takshaka asked. "Do you expect us to help?"

"Yes, to take back the land."

"The army you want us to fight, will be large in number," Sahasra said. "We are only a handful, and we will ask for money, more than the usual. But still, it can get out of hand, and I cannot risk the lives of so many of my people for your cause."

Shanaya, after much deliberation, was about to speak, when the young lad with a wooden arm said, "I have an idea, and it is perhaps a good one. Can save a lot of lives and can get us back on the throne."

Vrikodara had entered the war room, where he saw Pukkasati was writing a letter with his diminutive hands. He was working on a few scrolls, sending letters, while there were others too in the room, but he was dictating. He couldn't believe that the man that he knew for so long, one who had saved him from becoming a jester, could be such a strategist.

"I have to have a word with you," Vrikodara said.

"Sure." And he made everyone leave the room, while he sipped on his wine. "To what do I owe the pleasure?"

"You seem glad," Vrikodara said.

"Yes, the debt of the Rakshas have been paid off and we are quite happy about it," he said. "I was worried that'll be a stinger within us."

Vrikodara nodded, as he moved and sat on the opposite chair. "Did you hear about Hidambi?"

"Oh well, of course, congratulations commander." He took a wine goblet, bigger than his usual one, and handed it to Vrikodara, who took a sip from it. "We should celebrate. I gave her a special drink that my caregiver used to make for me. By heating up the milk and adding some honey in it."

"I see," Vrikodara said. "I have been thinking about a few things."

"All right, what is it?"

"To go back to Indraprastha."

"I believe there are few soldiers left behind by Dharmaraja, who might think otherwise. We could have an impending attack by Karna. You must have heard, he's alive."

Vrikodara nodded. "He is, of course. Can't believe it. But I don't care anymore."

Pukkasati sighed. "Why do you have to be this moody, commander? Why can't we just do what is expected of us?"

"Because I don't want to do what is expected of me."

"When I was a jester, I was supposed to make people laugh. That was my job. Your job is to make sure you listen to Dharmaraja. And our lives would be simpler."

"You sound a lot like him, wow!" He rolled his eyes. "But I don't care, little man. Prepare the bags and the carriages. We leave for our state, and I would like to get a good night's sleep on the mother's lap."

"What about Dharmaraja's wrath?" Pukkasati asked.

Vrikodara drank the entire contents of the goblet. "He could be vulgar and abusive and a lot of things, but he's not someone who's into fraticide. As long as my mother is alive, he shall not kill me, so I'm immune. He's going to be annoyed for sure, but that's also the idea behind going back. I'm kind of done, with the entire shenanigan. Let him take over the rest of the territories by himself now. I am not going to help him anymore. Not anytime soon, at least."

He came on his feet, moving towards the door.

"You know, my caregiver had also told me about a secret ingredient," Pukkasati said, as Vrikodara turned to look at the dwarf. "She said, the milk and the honey, it hides the true essence of what you want to be hidden."

"What do you mean?" He asked.

"Like the poison I have given your wife," Pukkasati said. "And the only antidote to it, I have hidden it somewhere. And if you want you and your son to live, you do what Dharmaraja says."

"He got to you, that bastard!" Vrikodara cursed under his breath.

Pukkasati shook his head. "No, my dear brute," as he sipped his wine, "I was always his. I was, after all, his spy all along."

Satyasena continued, "there's a sewer system, across the city, that would help you to enter the kingdom from within. We know where it ends, and it can lead you to an army and not be worried about the archers, or the cavalry. Once you enter, you disable all the catapults, and attack the watchtowers in secret. They'll not know what you have come with."

Sahasra watched him with impressive gusto. "You have an intelligent son."

Satyasena almost blushed.

"Their army is limited," Shanaya said. "And we still have our loyalists within the kingdom. Once they see it is us leading this insurrection, they will rise up and join you as well."

"Once this is over..." Karna continued, "a portion of the kingdom will be given to you for your support."

Sahasra glanced at Takshaka. "All right. I am interested

in this deal, and we will be smooth, we will be stealthy and we will do it our way. I am leading this battle."

Karna nodded. "Of course, and we and our allies are with you. Right now, they think we are dead, and once they know we are back in power, they will join us in our crusade."

Sahasra nodded. "And what do you want in return?"

"Our kingdom, of course," he said. "And my hands... they need to be cured. You must be in possession of some kind of medicine that could help it."

Takshaka raised his hands. "I am the doctor here too." And he looked at the arms, which were shaking. "Interesting, your nerves are damaged."

Karna asked, "Can they be healed?"

"Anything can be healed, with time." Takshaka said. "But it needs time, and our journey to Anga is more urgent. I can give you a temporary solution, of course, for now."

Karna smiled.

Sahasra smiled back.

It wasn't an ideal partnership, but it was something.

Now it was a matter of time, of course, to decide who would be the one who would betray first.

67

As the party had left for Anga, Karna had received treatment along the way.

Whenever they stopped, his arms and shoulders would be massaged with some kind of a green paste. Karna had not noticed but the journey back was quite ordinary, for they knew the ins and outs of the roadways. They knew where to go, which valley to cross, which bridges to miss. Karna, after each round of treatment, was feeling better.

Alongside, he was trying his hand in archery, and was teaching his sons too. With Vrishaketu, the conversations were less, as lot of things still had to be sorted out, but he was glad they had started somewhere.

He had even managed to meet Tripti, and he was glad his son had found someone for himself. But he was also sad that Roma, Satyasena's love interest, had died because of the extremist ideas. Along the way, he learnt a lot about his family.

Karna also learnt a bit about the Nagas and their differences with the Maharogas. When they were not in their inebriated state, they were pretty kind. They would hand them food. They would sing songs to the snakes at night. They would worship the Shesh Naag and Lord

Vishnu for protection. They would dance too, whenever they would pass a hurdle along the way. There were hundreds, moving in a pack.

Karna knew that life outside his kingdom was beautiful. He had spent a lot of time with his friend, but he never took his family along, now realising that he should have. Because in the end, what he was fighting for, was his family.

Vrikodara had managed to check out the nooks and crannies of the kingdom, fortifying it. The ones who were under Karna's regime, worked in the central part, while the archers were being disposed. He wasn't happy with this entire arrangement of Pukkasati and Dharmaraja, and he had been bested by both of them. He felt lied to and cheated, and he hadn't felt that way for a long time.

The cavalry was placed in front, and Anga as a fortress, was not that easy to decipher. There were lots of things on the table that had to be minutely checked.

When he wasn't commanding the military, Vrikodara was tending to his wife. Once a ferocious lioness, she looked tame, weak and pale. He didn't have the heart to tell her that she was unwell, that she had been poisoned. She had to be given doses of antidote to remain well, and Vrikodara was afraid for his child and his wife. He knew he was in a position to lose everything.

And he also knew if she died along with his child, he would murder Pukkasati and Dharmaraja, not giving a damn about the fact that he was his brother.

"Are you all right?" He asked his wife, placing his large hands over her.

"I am better than before, but still feeling miserable. I want to help you out."

"And you shall."

"Do you think they will come?"

"Who?"

"Karna."

"The sparrows have brought news that there's some movement from the Naga settlement. Now I'm not sure, how much of that is true, and we have sent out spies, but none have come back with an answer. We don't know when they would attack, but we are definitely prepared."

"What would you name our child?" She smiled.

He couldn't believe that she was thinking about this, and he didn't want to indulge her more. Not when there was so much at stake. "We will see, once we get out of this." He smiled at her.

"Yes, we will."

And she closed her eyes, before falling asleep again, while he held back his tears.

By the time they had reached, Satyasena had managed to get one of the children—a squire to Sahasra—to help him decipher the scroll.

He had been antsy for a while about it. One of the children had agreed to read it, in exchange for a simple basket of apple.

"What are you up to?" His brother asked.

"I have to know something."

"You are being suspicious." Vrishaketu raised his brows.

"Comes from the person who has been secretly getting it on with a Naga. What is that about?"

"Oh, wait till you hear from her. You are really trying to get into her bad books by speaking like that."

Satyasena knew he was the notorious one, while Vrishaketu was the simpler, gentler one. "I am glad for you, buddy. I want you to be happy. I want you to have a good life."

On seeing such genuine emotions, Vrishaketu handed the basket. "What is with you being nice all of a sudden? All for the apples, I presume. Quite important, they would be for you."

Whatever was in that scroll was haunting him. But Satyasena was definitely happy about his brother. He could never be half the man his brother was. He stood for his rights, even though they were wrong. But he had the courage at the very least.

"How's your hand?" Vrishaketu asked.

"Making it difficult to stroke myself to be honest."

"Ew, get lost, you creep."

And Satyasena chuckled, as he made his way to the child again, handing him the basket. "Can you do it for me now?"

The child looked at the scroll and went through it. "Yes, sir, it is of course, an ancient script, written in a familiar handwriting."

"What does it say?"

"It says—I have..." he was having difficulty to go

ahead, “I have begun to achieve what I was meant to achieve. I have brought goodwill to my people—the Nagas—and given them something which will help them fight against their oppressors.” The child continued to read. “They will be more powerful than ever, but it is not for everyone. It will free them from the poisoned lake, but it wouldn’t be for everyone. Some will die along the way, and some will live. You told me I was good for nothing all my life. Well, I have done something fabulous for my people, and they will continue to live a free life now. My mission continues to be clear, getting rid of people like you from this world, who have ostracised others like us. You will face wrath from me soon, and you will die by my hands. I have given them false stories about my past, so they would pity me and accept me. And they would hate the humans more, so when they attack them they would have a purpose. Once I have a way to enter the human lands freely, and possess their riches and resources, I will build myself an army and conquer everything. I have a new name now, something I call myself.”

Satyasena was about to hear the name, when someone entered his tent.

“What is the new name?” He asked the child.

But the child, immediately got hit by an arrow in his chest and flew back.

“You shouldn’t have heard what you have heard till now.”

Satyasena turned to face the intruder, but he was knocked out, smacked on the head, making him unconscious.

68

Vrishaketu listened to the war discussions happening between Karna and Takshaka, about how they would be infiltrating the sewer system. Even his mother Shanaya was there, and he listened to her carefully too.

Eventually, Vrishaketu came up to his mother, who had not been meeting his eye.

"Are you not planning to talk to me?" He asked.

"I do. I am just...a little embarrassed, that's all. The last time we met, I tried to kill you."

"No, the last time I met you, I was hugging you on the back of a horse." He smiled.

"You know about it?"

"Of course," he said. "Father told me, but erm..." he rubbed his neck. They were in the middle of the camp site. He could see that the Nagas were preparing to leave for the secret entrance towards Anga. "I was not aware that this would be the case. And I know I have not been a good son."

"You have been a great son," she said, holding him dearly. "Don't you ever think that way. We are all confused, and we all abandoned you. If we could have made it clearer, it would have worked well for us." She touched his cheek. "Can I give you a hug?"

"Of course."

Vrishaketu held her, and felt the warm and soft embrace. Smiling to himself, he pulled back, only to see Tripti running towards him in a frantic way. She looked at Shanaya and then at Vrishaketu, as she said, "There's something you both need to know."

Vrikodara watched with his spyglass from the top of the local watchtower, he saw the army that had arrived and was inching towards Anga, but still not attacking.

"I am wondering if they are a travelling circus or actually an army, planning to attack us," he told Pukkasati who was standing on a pedestal. "Do they want to attack us? Because they have been quiet."

"We can send emissaries to check up on them and know who they are. There's no flag, which means they are Nagas," Pukkasati said. "And they are low in number, so they could also just be an outpost gang, probably keeping an eye on us till the actual army comes."

"Something feels off," Vrikodara said, turning to one of his lieutenants. "Have all the clearances been cleared off?"

"Yes, commander."

"Is there any way in or out of the kingdom that we are not aware of?"

"No, commander."

"Interesting." He turned back, looking at Pukkasati.

"Do you know anything that I don't know, Bhima?"

He asked, without a sign of respect and suspicion in his eyes. "Are you trying to win this war or let it win over you? I am having my doubts right now."

"Don't overthink too much, little man. I am doing my duty, as per my brother's wishes."

"Yes, of course, as you said. After all, I went to great lengths to involve your wife into it. There was another Rakshas colony, more peaceful than the one that your wife led, but we still went there. I wanted her to be a part of all this, so I could use her as leverage." Pukkasati smiled, as he spoke calmly.

At that moment, Vrikodara grabbed him by the throat and lifted him up with ease. Pukkasati, instead of feeling afraid, laughed it off.

"You won't be able to learn about the antidote if you kill me and your wife would die with the child inside her. What a great tragedy that would be!"

Vrikodara clenched his jaw, and released him. He went back on the pedestal, and fixed his collars. "For a man as big as you, you can be quite a romantic. I have told you so many times, never have a weak point in your defence. It could lead to an issue like the one you are facing right now." He paused. "I suggest we attack and be done with them, so they don't come back again."

"I suggest we wait."

"You are waiting for the inevitable," he said. "But you see, I won't."

Vrikodara clenched his jaw. "REIN YOUR HORSES EVERYONE. WE ARE GOING TO SEEK AN AUDIENCE OF THE NAGAS!"

And the horns began to blow hard, while everyone

hooted, but Vrikodara remained impassive and afraid.

What more was yet to come?

"Talk. Talk. Talk. Let's see if these diplomatic talks with savages help us or not." Pukkasati said, with venom in his words.

Satyasena was pushed in the corner of the trunk and thrown on the side of the forest by a fuming, foam-inducing Maharoga.

He was punched, then kicked, and he realised they were far from the campsite, so no one from his family members would know. His eyes had swollen up, and his body was breaking.

"I kind of understood that scroll seemed familiar by the way it looked, and I was surprised when you had it," Sahasra said, holding the parchment in his hand. "I had given it to my father before sending an army to kill them. Surprisingly, it's still in great condition."

"You...you are not here for a sanctuary," Satyasena said, as Sahasra was watching him intently. "You want to rule the human kingdoms."

"Of course I do, and I want to ostracise them. Sanctuary is a boring concept, a rather trivial idea," he said. "I didn't travel to Scandinavia just so I could come back to find new lands. We have, for years, traversed all over listening to other people, and you lot appeared to be ready to give me something served on a silver platter. All this while I was afraid of attacking and now finally, I have the perfect moment to infiltrate. Well, that is something, no?" He paused. "And you had to make things complicated, but I'm glad someone knows about me, at least. Kill him." He callously said to a Maharoga, who began to choke Satyasena. He kicked between the Maharoga's legs, and the Maharoga fell back.

Sahasra held him up, choking him against the trunk of the tree, when he felt a stab in the back. He turned to see who it was, and even Satyasena did the same, in all the haze and blurriness, to see it was none other than…

His brother Vrishaketu.

"Oh god!" Sahasra spoke with frustration.

Vrishaketu had a sword that he had plunged into Sahasra, but he didn't seem miffed at all. More Maharogas appeared, and they grabbed a frenetic Shanaya as well as Tripti, as they tried to attack.

"Well, if everyone knows about it, so be it." He pulled the sword from his back. "What's mine is yours."

And he stabbed Vrishaketu back with it.

Tripti let out a scream, so did Shanaya, horrified by what had just transpired.

Karna had appeared by then too, while Sahasra said, "I didn't want this to happen, but your son had to be a rat about it."

And he left. "Goodbye and thank you for presenting such a grand opportunity."

Vrishaketu was lying there with a large, gaping wound. The Maharogas had circled them and holding all of them hostage.

"Someone give him medical attention! Someone please!" Shanaya cried.

But Vrishaketu remained still, until he couldn't speak,

until he couldn't breathe, and the light in his eyes were slowly dimming, as he lay dying.

While his entire family watched him perish.

69

Vrikodara had arrived at the meeting point, waiting for one of the Nagas to approach as well.

He waited with Pukkasati, who was acting as a spy. He didn't trust Vrikodara, suspecting he might backstab him. The dots in front of them began to turn into flesh and bones, when one of their emissaries had gone for a meeting in the middle, with no army in sight. By the time he reached, Vrikodara saw the chief and his second-in-command next to him.

"To whom do I owe the pleasure of meeting?" Vrikodara said.

"Chief Sahasra." He nodded, smiling at him. "And he's Takshaka."

Vrikodara nodded too. "We are in the middle of the desert, under the hot, dry sun. And you have been an inconvenience."

"But we haven't even done anything," Sahasra said. "We are simple travellers."

"With stallions like those, sure!" Vrikodara replied. "What is your intention being in the Angan territory?"

"To question, and to be inquisitive," he said. "I'll be honest with you, Lord Vrikodara, if you may please. I was under the impression that this lovely kingdom of yours, was owned by a man named Karna."

"Yes, I've taken over from him."

"Lovely." Sahasra smiled. "Well then, you belong to the infamous Pandavas, correct?"

Vrikodara nodded. "More famous than infamous."

"I am not sure if you are aware that I have made a deal with your brother."

"And that deal will be honoured, Chief Sahasra," said Pukkasati at that moment, as if speaking for Dharmaraja himself. "But everything takes time."

"We have been waiting for months now. Did we ever say that we will take time when doing your dirty job?" He asked the dwarf, as if treating him as an equal. Not calling him any names. "You see, that's what I don't like about the royalty. They never stick to their words."

"I have a lot of land here," Vrikodara said. "I can give you some of it. Have a ball with it. Grow, cultivate, whatever you wish."

Sahasra smiled, and it was the kind of smile that could hurt a few. "I wish it was that easy, because we also happened to learn something interesting recently. About the genocide that happened, of our people, where Indraprastha has now been built."

"It's all bogus."

"We have reliable claims and witnesses for that matter," Sahasra said. "And now, I have dozens of messengers, waiting for my command, to share that lovely information to all the colonies of the Nagas, leading to a full scale battle with an entire community of people. We are vicious when we have to be."

Vrikodara's jaw stiffened. "What do you want?"

"To start with the kingdom of course, the entirety of it. I always wanted to live in a palace, you know. Tired of the entire treehouse gimmick, to be honest." He laughed with Takshaka, who was forced to laugh for his leader but wasn't into it completely.

"I am not going to surrender because of a flimsy threat. I can kill your people, with just one wave of attack. You aren't even that many."

Sahasra smiled. "Then we shall see. Do we consider this request to be rejected?"

"We shall see you at sundown. Be prepared for bloodshed," Vrikodara said, as he turned around, riding towards his kingdom, followed by the pony-riding Pukkasati.

"Have we been smart about this?" The dwarf asked.

"In carnage, there's nothing called smart." The giant replied.

Sahasra saw an unlikely combination of a fat man and a small man leave and become dots themselves.

"Well, that incited them," he told Takshaka.

"We should be happy with the land, chief," Takshaka said. "We should not be greedy. Our people will live a bountiful life in a lovely land like Anga."

"Let me do the thinking, my friend. And I know what I'm doing," he said. "Have our people left for the sewers and the secret entry?"

"Yes." His eyes were lowered, as if he had spoken out of turn.

"Great," Sahasra said. "I want very few at the camp, and all of them in the sewers. We are going full throttle, before they can even think of attacking us. Within minutes, we would have disappeared from their line of sight, and that'll be great, because they'll be confused."

"And I'm going as well."

Karna never knew how it would feel to lose a child.

And it did horrify him completely, making him feel numb, as he was held by the Maharogas. He wanted to fight back, but he was weak, and timid.

He screamed. "NOOOO!"

But they were being placed in one line by then—Karna, Shanaya, Satysena and Tripti, while Vrishaketu's body was dragged away by the Maharogas. The Maharogas had their crossbows aimed at them, ready to launch an attack.

"So this is it," Karna said, "this is how we die. Losing, and then losing some more."

Shanaya and Satyasena were quiet, Tripti too said nothing.

Karna closed his eyes, and for the first time in many days, he prayed to Lord Surya. If I was your son, he said to himself, protect me from this horrible fate. Protect me, so I could avenge my son's death.

The arrow was launched.

But instead of hitting him, it hit the Maharogas.

Karna opened his eyes to find more arrows attacking them. They were all confused, while horses rode out of the hills, with large banners, and a large cavalry, and archers moving behind the horsemen. All the Maharogas and Nagas had begun to disperse as a result of the surprise attack. The sun was shining bright, and the arrows continued to hit them.

Karna came on his feet and instantly went for a sword lying on the ground, cutting his ropes quickly, and then helping the others too.

The army had appeared from the hills, as if it was hiding there, waiting to pounce, waiting for Lord Surya's command. The Maharogas started leaving and the camp suddenly was almost empty.

"I am going for Vrishaketu's body." Shanaya shouted, and the three of them ran.

"Yes, yes, let me figure this out in the meanwhile."

He saw the leader of the army, wondering who it was who had come to rescue him. While the soldiers of this band had destroyed most enemies, Karna was unharmed. When he came in front of the leader, the man introduced himself and extended his hand towards him.

"Hello, my dear friend." He was grinning, asking him to sit behind him on his stallion. "I told you I would come to you when you are in peril."

Karna couldn't believe, but it was none other than his friend...

Suyodhan.

70

They rode through the thick, hefty desert, followed by none, moving towards their goal.

"Where are we going?"

"To the secret entry of the kingdom."

"Just a heads up—don't build these kind of entries from now on, can be really bad for you."

"It saved my wife and son."

"Well, *sometimes* it can be really bad for you." He chuckled.

Karna was behind him, holding the back of the horse. "How did you know that I was in trouble?"

"I had an inkling. And after hearing about the takeover by Bhima, I had to do something. I told my father about it, who was as indifferent as always, so I took a bunch of my loyalists and I told him, I'm going hunting. And I came here. I was scouting, when I happened to see you and when you were close to your death, I knew I had to attack now." He explained. "I was too late for Vrishaketu, and I'm sorry for that. I wish I could have come sooner."

"You came and that matters, brother," Karna said.

"What have you been up to?"

"We have a lot to catch up on. Right now, I have to kill a poisonous snake."

Suyodhan grimaced. "They always are a bloody headache."

"I thought you would be angry I didn't come along with you."

"It makes sense to be with your family," he said. "Now that I have a family with Bhanumati, I have realised what it means. Next time you come, I would suggest you come with them."

"Have you played the game of dice till now?"

"I await you, my friend."

They were nearing the trees when Karna noticed that there were Maharogas waiting outside, guarding the entrance. He could also hear the loud sounds that were coming from within the kingdom, and he knew the imminent attack had happened. There were explosions, and Karna had told him to use the oil and fire to scare off Bhima and his forces. He had told them about all kinds of his weaknesses, where to hide and where to attack. But he hadn't said one thing.

Karna's weakness.

"Drop me here," Karna said, and Suyodhan halted his horse, as he climbed off the stallion. "Thank you, I'll take it from here."

"I know you, my friend, and those creatures awaiting you at the entrance, not a good sight. I suggest, let me do the handiwork for you, one last time." He smiled.

Karna couldn't help but smile back. "Thank you."

"Also, you require this." From the rucksack behind him, he pulled out a bow and a quiver, along with arrows in it. "You seem unarmed, and we need to change that."

He hadn't used the bow properly for some time now, and he was a tad bit afraid to do so.

"Yes."

"Use it and meet me soon. We have a lot of work to do."

Saying that, he rode forward with his mace in his hands, as he launched a singular attack on the Maharogas, hammering them with the mace.

As he dealt with them, Karna found the secret entry unguarded, and he made the leap towards it.

Vrikodara was on the long staircase of the palace, where he was to get rid of the Maharogas.

With one swing of his mace, he handled one of them, and with another swing he smashed another, when he heard another explosion. In another place, someone else was dying. And in some other place, someone else was falling. The sudden attack towards them was not expected, but it did happen. And now he had to deal with the consequences.

The marble staircases were drenched in blood.

What were white once, were now greasy and muddy.

The Maharogas, Vrikodara noticed, were in a frenzy and they didn't seem to bother about the pain. They continued to move and jump on them, drinking from some kind of a vial in their hands, their eyes were red, and they were bleeding from their ears. They looked undead when they attacked Vrikodara, though he could see and feel it was an adrenaline-inducing liquid that they were consuming, leading them to be this way.

Vrikodara battled them one by one, and many couldn't touch him, until he noticed the main one.

He walked on the marbled staircase alone, with his long sword in hand, tattoos swirling around his body.

He took the vial, tore it apart from his neck, and just drank every drop inside it. All of a sudden, he felt a powerful urge and instantly launched himself.

Sahasra looked like a powerful opponent. The moment Vrikodara brought his mace forward, Sahasra turned around and went behind him—stabbing him.

He tried to hit him again, but he deflected the blow speedily. He was sharp, and he was swift, moving at a breakneck speed.

Sahasra used his sword to deflect his mace attacks, and then kicked him, he fell down the stairs, crashing on the ground.

All he could then think about was Hidambi, who was locked in a room, protected by the guards.

Vrikodara found some strange strength within him, but Sahasra had kicked him on the face by then, making him bleed, as he threw him to a corner.

An explosion occurred, but Sahasra was unharmed by it. Debris starting falling, but Sahasra punched Vrikodara, and he punched him again, till his mouth began to bleed.

"The great Bhima, getting defeated by a Naga. This is going to be in our history books. We shall rule!"

And then he punched him again, when an arrow came out of nowhere, stabbing him in his hand, going through it. He immediately cried out in pain, and turned around in confusion to see who it was.

It was Karna!!!

Shooting another arrow that went through Sahasra's face, who pulled it out, and was in a lot of pain.

"YOU! YOU!" He rasped. "Why don't you just die?"

He moved for Karna and brought his sword forward, which Karna deflected with his bow, rolling over, stabbing his neck. He pulled it out again.

"These arrows mean nothing to me! I am invincible! Don't you realise?"

And he used the long sword, nearly cutting off Karna's leg, but he managed to pull it back.

Vrikodara had got up by then, and he launched himself jumping from the top of the stairs, with a mace in his hand, going for the head of the Naga chief, while Karna, from beneath, took three arrows, stringing them...

And shooting straight towards Sahasra's heart, face and groin.

The mace struck the Naga chief on the head, and the arrows pulsated and got plunged inside him. Sahasra fell on the ground, over the debris, rolling over like a stone, moving for Karna and Vrikodara.

Vrikodara came in between...Karna held on to the stone with his mighty power. He paused to look back at his enemy, who was on the ground.

"Are you all right?" He asked.

"Yes," Karna said.

He left the stone, when Karna moved aside and it fell down, hitting one of the other surviving Maharogas. Karna was pulled up by Vrikodara, who gave his hand.

"Thank you," Karna said.

"No, thank you, for saving my life."

They both looked at the crying and whining Sahasra, who was still trying to drag himself towards them, and he was reaching for his long sword, all smashed and bloody with his bones visible. Karna and Vrikodara, stood over him, and one kept his feet on his hand while another kept it on his injured back, with the arrow pointed towards him, and the mace ready to strike as well.

"After you?" Vrikodara asked.

"After you."

And they finished the long awaited dirty deed.

71

A few days later…

Karna watched the burning funeral pyre in front of him. It was of his son, the one who had been sacrificed while protecting his family.

Weirdly, he had Satyasena with him, and Shanaya and Tripti holding and hugging each other, while no one else had come in. Suyodhan had been busy giving excuses as to why he had attacked an army outside Anga.

Karna began to recount the days that passed after Sahasra's death.

Vrikodara had forfeited the kingdom peacefully but in return, his wife had to be saved. Takshaka managed to heal her, and in return, he was given a far bigger land in Anga, for him and his people. Vrikodara had happened to grab hold of the little dwarf, who had escaped when he learnt the antidote was created by Takshaka.

And as far as Karna knew, Vrikdora made sure the dwarf saw the insides of his rear part, by juxtaposing his body into a puréed mess.

Anga no more operated as a monarchy, rather it was run by ministers, and there was no king or queen. Then who did it belong to? It was a question that only a few could answer, but none cared. The Rakshas had lain for themselves, as well as the Nagas, and it was specifically instructed by Karna that all outsiders and outcasts who have been ostracised were welcome there, to this land, without any hesitation. And everyone would be given a place to live. If he could make a change like that, so could others was what he felt.

Vrikodara, before leaving, had thanked Karna and said, "When there will be a war, and I know there will be one when the two flags will fight each other, I assure you I will not be the one to kill you. What you have done for me and my family, I will always remember. Our bloodlines separate us, but our intentions should not. I will be there in the battlefield, but we will not fight each other, and that is a promise I shall keep."

Karna had shaken hands on it, realising that weirdly the wisest brother out of all was none other than the one who was called a brute. Because he understood the value of gratitude, and he realised that a war doesn't lead to heroes or villains. It just leads to deaths, and the purity of evil to live on.

As the rites were completed, Karna asked Tripti, "You are welcome to join us."

"No."

Shanaya asked, with teary eyes, "What do you plan to do then?"

"Go to the north, probably. I'll probably move on. I have realised I have sought vengeance for so long, it doesn't matter to me anymore, because it has no value for me. When you lose people close to you, for the vengeance you desired, you start questioning what was the point of it all?" She smiled. "I'm sure our paths will cross again."

She looked at the burning pyre of the man she loved, and grabbed the horse, leaving for a better future.

Karna's chariot was behind them, and they all begin to walk, closely and calmly.

"What's the plan, father?" Asked Satyasena.

"I have to go to Hastinapur. Suyodhan needs me now more than ever. The damage Yudhistr has done to our lives, we need to reclaim it, and I need to help him with that," he said.

Shanaya and Sataysena nodded glumly.

"But you both are coming too."

"What do you mean?" They asked in unison.

"We have to defeat the Pandavas. How do you think we can do that without the help of you both? I need you on my side when I put the nails in everyone's head." Karna smiled. He saw his hand still shaking, but Takshaka had given him some medicine to be applied regularly.

"Hastinapur…I don't know what will happen," Shanaya said with uncertainty.

They sat on the chariot, as Karna began to ride. He was sitting on the front, like a charioteer, remembering his father, who had been a charioteer to the king of Hastinapur for the longest time. And now he was the one for his family.

It was worth it, he felt it in his bones.

"There's more that will happen. And I know that not everything will be in our favour, and not everything has to be. But we have to continue with the memory of Vrishaketu in our hearts and decide what he would have wanted. He fought for dharma till his last breath, and I believe very strongly that dharma is about the family you choose, and we have chosen each other at every level. And for what's about to transpire, I believe we have to meet this fellow called Shakuni of the Gandhar Kingdom. Seems like an interesting fellow."

And they began to ride, towards the rising sun meeting the horizon and expecting the unexpected, that reminded him a lot about Lord Surya, and how much he had gambled in his life, one way or the other.

He didn't have to do all that he did for Ashtar, to be the son of Surya.

He was one.

He was born as one.

Because it is not who you worship, but your deeds that define the person you are.

THE END

To be continued...

Book 3

KARNA
AFTER DEATH

Acknowledgements

A book is not made by one person's efforts, but a culmination of many people working towards the same goal.

I would likc to thank the divine power that has allowed me to write for so many years, and letting the world recognise these stories as their own.

I would like to thank my parents too, who have always supported me in my writing endeavours.

My wife, Kiran Malik, who has been a pillar of support in my life, in every decision I have taken, however crazy or stupid.

I would like to thank my agent, Anuj Bahri, for being a guiding light while taking some major career decisions, and for being more than just an agent but a mentor too.

Also, to the Simon & Schuster India team, for always being awesome—Sunny, Rahul Sir, Abhay, Mahesh Sir, Richie Sir, Uday Sir, Indranil Sir, and the rest.

And last but not the least, my readers who have been after my life for this sequel! I know it's been two years. But I hope it was worth the wait.